P9-CCS-412

Books by Peter Matthiessen

Sal Si Puedes

Random House  *New York*

Peter Matthiessen

Sal Si Puedes

CESAR CHAVEZ
and the New American Revolution

Revised Edition

Copyright © 1969, 1973 by Peter Matthiessen

All rights reserved under International and Pan-American Copyright Conventions. Published in the United States by Random House, Inc., New York, and simultaneously in Canada by Random House of Canada Limited, Toronto.

Library of Congress Cataloging in Publication Data

Matthiessen, Peter.
  Sal si puedes.

  1. Chavez, Cesar Estrada. I. Title.
F866.2.C5M3 1972   331.5′44′0924 [B]   72-10675
ISBN 0-394-48492-4

A portion of the contents of this book appeared originally in *The New Yorker,* in somewhat different form.

Lines on pp. 228–29 from "If I Had a Hammer" (The Hammer Song) are used by permission. Words and Music by Lee Hays and Pete Seeger. TRO © Copyright 1958 and 1962 Ludlow Music, Inc.   New York, N.Y.

Lines on page 226 from "Pastures of Plenty" are used by permission. Words and Music by Woody Guthrie. TRO © Copyright 1960 and 1963 Ludlow Music, Inc.   New York, N.Y.

An excerpt by Rev. Wayne C. Hartmire, Jr., from an article in the June, 1966, issue of *St. Joseph Magazine* is reprinted by permission. Copyright © 1966 by Mount Angel Abbey, Inc. All rights reserved.

An excerpt by Reverend Drake from the October, 1968, issue of *Presbyterian Life* is used by permission. Copyright © 1968 by Presbyterian Life.

The Editors of *Ramparts* Magazine have granted permission to quote from "The Tale of the Raza," by Luis Valdez, July, 1966. Copyright © 1966 by Ramparts Magazine, Inc.

Manufactured in the United States of America by The Book Press, Brattleboro, Vermont

9 8 7 6 5 4 3 2

FIRST REVISED EDITION

To the farm workers and the American future

The 1967 Report of the President's National Advisory Commission on Rural Poverty begins as follows:

1. The United States today has the economic and technical means to guarantee adequate food, clothing, shelter, health services, and education to every citizen of the Nation.

2. Involuntary tragedy is a tragedy under any circumstances and poverty in the midst of plenty is both a tragedy and a social evil.

3. The rural poor are not a faceless mass. They are individual human beings. All programs designed to eliminate poverty must therefore give paramount consideration to the rights and the dignity of the individual.

4. Every citizen of the United States must have equal access to opportunities for economic and social advancement without discrimination because of race, religion, national origin, or place of residence.

5. Because rural Americans have been denied a fair share of America's opportunities and benefits they have migrated by millions to the cities in search of jobs and places to live. This migration is continuing. It is therefore impossible to obliterate urban poverty without removing its rural causes. Accordingly, both reason and justice compel the allotment of a more equitable share of our national resources to improving the conditions of rural life.

Sal Si Puedes

I

ONE Sunday of August 1968, I knocked on the door of a small frame house on Kensington Street in Delano, California. It was just before seven in the morning, and the response to the knock was the tense, suspenseful silence of a household which, in recent months, had installed an unlisted telephone, not as a convenience, but to call the outside world in case of trouble. After a moment the house breathed again, as if I had been identified through the drawn shutters, but no one came to the door, and so I sat down on the stoop and tuned in to a mockingbird. The stoop is shaded by squat trees, which distinguish Kensington Street from the other straight lines of one-story bungalows that comprise residential Delano, but at seven, the air was already hot and still, as it is almost every day of summer in the San Joaquin Valley.

Cesar Chavez's house—or rather, the house inhabited by Cesar Chavez, whose worldly possessions, scraped together, would scarcely be worth the $50 that his farm workers union pays for him in monthly rent—has been threatened so often by his enemies that it would be foolish to set down its street number. But on Kensington Street, a quiet stronghold of the American Way of Life, the house draws attention to itself by its very lack of material aspiration. On such a street the worn brown paint, the forgotten yard (relict plantings by a former tenant die off one by one, and a patch of lawn between stoop and sidewalk had been turned to mud by a leaky hose trailing away into the weeds), the uncompetitive car which, lacking an engine, is not so much parked as abandoned, are far more subversive than the strike signs (DON'T BUY CALIFORNIA GRAPES) that are plastered on the car, or the Kennedy stickers, fading now, that are still stuck to the old posts of the stoop, or the STOP REAGAN sign that decorates the shuttered windows.

Behind those drawn shutters, the house—two bedrooms, bath, kitchen and an L-shaped living room where some of the Chavez children sleep—is neat and cheerful, brought to life by a white cabinet of bright flowers and religious objects, a stuffed bookcase, and over the sofa bed, a painting in Mexican mural style of surging strikers, but from the outside it might seem that this drab place has been abandoned, like an old store rented temporarily for some fleeting campaign and then gutted again of everything but tattered signs. The signs suggest that the dwelling is utilitarian, not domestic, that the Chavez family live here because when they came, in 1962, this house on the middle-class east side was the cheapest then available in Delano, and that their commitment is somewhere else.

Chavez's simple commitment is to win for farm workers the right to organize in their own behalf that is enjoyed by all other large labor groups in the United States; if it survives, his United Farm Workers Organizing Committee will be the first effective farm workers union in American history. Until Chavez appeared, union leaders had considered it impossible to organize seasonal farm labor, which is in large part illiterate and indigent, and for which even mild protest may mean virtual starvation. The migrant labor force rarely remains in one place long enough to form an effective unit and is mostly composed of minority groups which invite more hostility than support, since the local communities fear an extra municipal burden with no significant increase in the tax base. In consequence, strikes, protests and abortive unions organized ever since 1903 have been broken with monotonous efficiency by the growers, a task made easier since the Depression years by the specific exclusion of farm workers from the protection of the National Labor Relations Act of 1935 (the Wagner Act), which authorizes and regulates collective bargaining between management and labor, and protects new unionists from reprisal. In a state where cheap labor, since Indian days, has been taken for granted, like the sun, the reprisals have been swift and sometimes fatal, as the history of farm labor movements attests.

The provision of the NLRA which excludes farm workers was excused by the bloody farm strikes of 1934, when the Communist label was firmly attached to "agrarian reformers"; its continued existence three decades later is a reflection of the power of the growers, whose might and right have been dutifully affirmed by church and state. But since 1965, America's last bastion of uninhibited free enterprise has been shaken so hard by national publicity that both church and state are searching for safer positions. And this new hope for the farm workers has been brought not by the Communist agent that his enemies have conjured up, nor even by a demagogue, but by a small, soft-spoken Mexican-American migrant laborer who could never leave the fields long enough to get past the seventh grade.

.   .   .

In no more time than it would take to pull his pants on and splash water on his face, the back door creaked and Cesar Chavez appeared around the corner of the house. "Good morning." He smiled, raising his eyebrows, as if surprised to see me there. "How are you?" He had not had much sleep—it was already morning when I dropped him off the night before—but in that early light he looked as rested as a child. Though he shook my hand, he did not stop moving; we walked south down Kensington Street and turned west at the corner.

The man who has threatened California has an Indian's bow nose and lank black hair, with sad eyes and an open smile that is shy and friendly; at moments he is beautiful, like a dark seraph. He is five feet six inches tall, and since his twenty-five-day fast the previous winter, has weighed no more than one hundred and fifty pounds. Yet the word "slight" does not properly describe him. There is an effect of being centered in himself so that no energy is wasted, an effect of *density*; at the same time, he walks as lightly as a fox. One feels immediately that this man does not stumble, and that to get where he is going he will walk all day.

In Delano (pronounced "De-*lay*-no"), the north–south streets are named alphabetically, from Albany Street on the far west side to Xenia on the east; the cross streets are called avenues and are numbered. On Eleventh Avenue, between Kensington and Jefferson, a police car moved out of an empty lot and settled heavily on its springs across the sidewalk. There it idled while its occupant enjoyed the view. Small-town policemen are apt to be as fat and sedentary as the status quo they are hired to defend, and this one was no exception; he appeared to be part of his machine, overflowing out of his front window like a growth. Having feasted his eyes on the public library and the National Bank of Agriculture, he permitted his gaze to come to rest on the only two citizens in sight. His cap, shading his eyes from the early sun, was much too small for him, and in the middle of his mouth, pointed straight at us, was a dead cigar.

At seven on a Sunday morning in Delano, a long-haired stranger wearing sunglasses and sneakers, in the company of a Mexican, would qualify automatically as a trouble-maker; consorting with a *known* troublemaker like Chavez, I became a mere undesirable. The cop looked me over long enough to let me know he had his eye on me, then eased his wheels into gear again and humped on his soft springs onto the street. Chavez raised his eyebrows in a characteris-tic gesture of mock wonderment, but in answer to my un-spoken question—for in this tense town it could not be assumed that this confrontation was an accident—he pointed at the back of a crud-colored building fronting on Jefferson Street. "That's our station house," he said, in the manner of a man who is pointing out, with pardonable pride, the main sights of his city.

A walk across town on Eleventh Avenue, from the vine-yards in the east to the cotton fields in the west, will teach one a good deal about Delano, which lies in Kern County, just south of the Tulare County line. Opposite the National Bank of Agriculture is a snack stand, La Cocina—PEPSI, BURGERS, TACOS, BURRITOS—as well as the Angelos Dry Goods shop and the Sierra Theatre, which features Mexican films; from here to Main Street and beyond, Eleventh Ave-nue is lined with jewelry shops and department stores. Main Street, interrupting the alphabetical sequence be-tween Jefferson and High, is a naked treeless stretch of

: 7

BRIDWELL LIBRARY
SOUTHERN METHODIST UNIVERSITY
DALLAS, TEXAS 75275

signs and commercial enterprises, mostly one-story; today it was empty of all life, like an open city.

Toward High Street, Empire Ford Sales rules both sides of Eleventh, and the far corners of High Street are the properties of OK Used Trucks and Kern County Equipment: Trucks and Tractors. The farm-equipment warehouses and garages continue west across High Street to the tracks of the Southern Pacific Railroad; the loading platforms of the farm-produce packing sheds and cold-storage houses front the far side of the tracks, with their offices facing west on Glenwood Street. Opposite these buildings are some small cafés and poker parlors frequented by the workers—Monte Carlo Card Room, Divina's Four Deuces, Lindo Michoacan—and beyond Glenwood, the workers' neighborhoods begin. Fremont Street, relatively undeveloped, overlooks U.S. Highway 99, which bores through the town below ground level like an abandoned subway trench. An overpass across the freeway links Fremont with Ellington Street, which is littered with small cafés and markets. The wrong side of the tracks, a community of small houses, mostly Mexican-American, spreads west to Albany Street and the cotton, food and flower factories of the San Joaquin Valley.

Toward Dover Street, a car coming up behind us slowed too suddenly. Chavez, like a feeding deer, gave sign of awareness with a sidelong flick of his brown eyes, but he did not turn or stop talking. When a voice called out in Spanish, asking him if he would like a lift, he smiled and waved, then pointed at the church two streets away. "*¡No, gracias! Yo voy a la misa.*"

Irregularly, Chavez attends this pretty stucco church at the corner of Eleventh Avenue and Clinton Street. The

BRIDWELL LIBRARY
SOUTHERN METHODIST UNIVERSITY
DALLAS, TEXAS 75275

church sign, OUR LADY OF GUADALUPE, is garish and utilitarian, in the spirit of Delano, and the churchyard is a parking lot enclosed by a chain-link fence. But the place has been planted with cypress, pines and yew, which, in this early light, threw cool fresh shadows on the white stucco. In the flat angularities of their surroundings, the evergreens and red tile roof give the building a graceful Old World air that is pointed up by twin white crosses, outlined against the hot blue of the sky.

Chavez hurried on the concrete path, in the bare sun. He was wearing his invariable costume—plaid shirt, work pants, dark suede shoes—but he was clean and neatly pressed, and though he had said nothing about church, it appeared that he had been bound here all along. "Let's just go in for a little while," he murmured. He was hurrying now as if a little late, though in fact the mass was near its end. From the church door came the soft drone of liturgy, of late footsteps and a baby's cry, the hollow ring of heels on church stone, and cavernous mumbling. A cough resounded.

Slipping through the door, he moved into the shadows on the left, where he crossed himself with water dipped from a font in the rear wall. At the same time he subsided onto his knees behind the rearmost pew. In the church hush, the people had begun to sing "Bendito." All were standing, but Chavez remained there on his knees behind them until the hymn was finished. Alone in the shadows of the pew, the small Indian head bent on his chest and the toes of the small shoes tucked inward, he looked from behind like a boy of another time, at his prayers beside his bed.

When the hymn ended, Chavez rose and followed the people forward to receive the blessing. A Franciscan priest in green cassock and white surplice loomed above him under the glowing windows. Then he turned left, passing an American flag that stood furled in the far corner, and returned down the outside aisle. Touching the water, he crossed himself again and followed the people out the door into the growing day. To the side of the door, under the evergreens, he waited to talk to friends; meanwhile others in the congregation came forward to greet him.

"*¡Cesar, cómo está?*"

"*¡Estoy bien!*"

"*¡Bueno—día—!*"

"*¡Buenos días!*"

"*¿Cómo está?*" another man said.

"*¡Oh,*" Chavez answered, "*batallando con la vida!*"—"I am still struggling with life." He grinned.

A Filipino in his sixties came up with a fine wordless smile and pumped Chavez's hand in both his own. "That's one of the brothers," Chavez explained when the old man had gone; the term "brother" or "sister" is used to describe a Union member, but it also has the connotation of "soul brother," and is so used by Chavez when addressing strangers.

Father Mark Day, a young Franciscan priest who was assigned to the farm workers in 1967, came up and greeted Chavez heartily. The following Sunday, he said, the Catholic churches of Delano would speak out in favor of the workers' right to form a union; hearing this, Chavez merely nodded. Since 1891, papal encyclicals have affirmed the workers' right to organize—Pope John XXIII had even spoken of their right to strike—but in Chavez's opinion Catholic help has too often taken the form of food baskets for the needy rather than programs that might encourage independence: a union and a decent wage would enable the worker to escape from demeaning and demoralizing dependence on welfare and charity. Although individuals in the clergy around the country had lent sympathy to the farm workers very early, and many outside church groups, particularly the Migrant Ministry, had long ago come to his support, with personnel as well as money, the clergy, Catholic as well as Protestant, had denounced the grape strike or dodged the issue for fear of offending the growers, most of whom are Catholics of Italian or Yugoslav origin and contribute heavily to the Church. In fact, when Chavez's organization, the National Farm Workers Association, began the strike in 1965, the growers were able to pressure the Church into forbidding NFWA to use the parish hall of Our Lady of Guadalupe. ("I find it frankly quite embarrassing," Father Day has said, "to see liberals and agnostics fighting vehemently for social justice among agricultural workers while Catholic priests sit by and sell them religious trinkets.") Though more and more embarrassed by the example of outside clergy of all faiths, many of whom had marched in the Union picket lines, it was only recently that the Delano clergy abandoned its passive stance and joined in attempts to reconcile the growers to the Union. Now Father Day spoke of the large Zaninovich clan, some of whom came to mass here at Our Lady of Guadalupe. "If they would just get together with their workers," he said, "we wouldn't have any problems."

Chavez looked doubtful, but he nodded politely. "Yes," he said after a moment, "this church is really coming to life." With Chavez, it is sometimes hard to tell when he is joking and when he is serious, because he is so often both at the same time.

More people greeted him, "*¿Va bien?*" "*¡Está bien!*" Most of the people are jocular with Chavez, who has a warm, humorous smile that makes them laugh, but after the joking, a few stood apart and stared at him with honest joy.

A worker in a soiled white shirt with a fighting cock in bright colors on the pocket stood waiting for a hearing. Though Chavez is available to his people day and night, it is on Sunday that they usually come to see him, and his Sundays are all devoted to this purpose. ". . . *buscando trabajo*," I heard the worker say when he had Chavez's ear: he was looking for work. He had just come in from Mexico, and the visa, or "green card," that he carried in his pocket is the symbol of the most serious obstacle that Chavez's strike effort must face: the century-old effort of California farmers to depress wages and undercut resistance by pitting one group of poor people against another.

By the 1860's the local Indians used as near-slaves in Spanish California had been decimated; they were largely replaced, after the Gold Rush, by Chinese labor made available by the completion of the Southern Pacific railroad. But the thrifty Chinese were resented and persecuted by the crowds of jobless whites for whom the Gold Rush had not panned out, and also by small farmers, who could not compete with the cheap labor force, and when their immigration was ended by the Exclusion Act of 1882, the big farmers hired other immigrants, notably Japanese. The Japanese undercut all other labor, but soon they too were bitterly resented for attempting to defend their interests. Even worse, they were better farmers than the Americans, and they bought and cultivated poor ground that nobody else had bothered with; this impertinence was dealt with by the Alien Land Law of 1913, which permitted simple confiscation of their land. (The land was subsequently restored, then confiscated again after Pearl Harbor.)

The next wave of farm laborers in California contained Hindus (Sikhs), Armenians and Europeans; they slowly replaced the Japanese, who by 1917 were referred to as the "yellow peril," and after the war, for patriotic reasons, were kicked out of their jobs to make room for red-blooded Americans. Meanwhile, the European and Armenian immigrants, less beset than the Asiatics by the race hatred that has advanced the economy of California from the start, were gaining a strong foothold; many were the parents of the Valley farmers of today.

Throughout the nineteenth century, Mexican peasants had crossed the border more or less at will. After the Mexican Revolution of 1910, the starving refugees presented the growers with a new source of cheap labor which, because it was there illegally, had the additional advantage of being defenseless. Cheap Mexican labor was pitted against cheap Filipino labor; the Filipinos were brought in numbers in the twenties. Many of the Mexicans were deported after 1931, when the Okies, Arkies and up-country Texans swarmed into California from the dust bowls; the Depression had caused a labor surplus beyond the wildest dreams of the employers, and an effort was made to keep the border closed.

Still, Mexicans were predominant in the farm labor force from 1914 until 1934. In these years, because of their illegal status, they tended to be more tractable than other groups; the famous farm strikes of the thirties occurred more often among Anglos and Filipinos. Despite their quiet nature, the Filipinos refused to scab on other workers or underbid them. "The Filipino is a real fighter," Carey McWilliams wrote in *Factories in the Fields,* "and his strikes have been dangerous." Few Filipino women had immigrated, and the ratio of men to women was 14 to 1; predictably, the growers dismissed the Filipinos as "homosexuals." McWilliams quotes the *Pacific Rural Press* for May 9, 1936, which called the Filipino "the most worthless, unscrupulous, shiftless, diseased semi-barbarian that has ever come to our shores." After the Philippine independence act of 1934, further importation of the spirited Filipinos came to an end, and their numbers have been dwindling ever since.

By 1942 the Chinese were long since in the cities, the Japanese-Americans had been shut up in concentration camps, the Europeans had graduated from the labor force and become farmers, and the Anglos had mostly drifted into the booming war economy of factories and shipyards; the minority groups that remained were not numerous enough to harvest the enormous produce that the war demanded.

The farm labor emergency was met by a series of agreements with the Mexican government known collectively as the *bracero* program, under the terms of which large numbers of day laborers, or *braceros,* were brought into California and the Southwest at harvest time and trucked out again when the harvest was over. The *bracero* program was so popular with the growers that it was extended when the war was over. In Washington the lobbyists for the growers argued successfully that Americans would not do the hard stoop labor required in harvesting cotton, sugar beets, and other crops; hence the need for the extension of the *bracero* program. Everyone conveniently forgot that the white fruit tramps of the thirties had done plenty of stoop labor and that domestic workers of all colors would be available to the farms if working conditions were improved. But the Mexicans, whose poverty was desperate, worked hard long days for pay as low as 60 cents an hour, and were used to undermine all efforts by domestic workers to hold out for better treatment; by 1959 an estimated four hundred thousand foreign workers (including small numbers of Canadians in the potato fields of Maine, and British West Indians in the Florida citrus groves) were obtaining work in an America where millions were unemployed.

Already the churches and citizens' groups were protesting the lot of the farm workers, and the domestic migrant laborers especially, and at the end of 1964 Public Law 78, the last and most notorious of the *bracero* programs, was allowed to lapse. (This was the year in which a long-accumulating sense of national guilt had permitted the passage of significant poverty and civil rights legislation, and it would be pleasant to assume that P.L. 78 was a casualty of the new humanism, but congressional concern about the outflow of gold was probably more important.)

The death of P.L. 78 was the birth of serious hope for a farm union, but by 1965, when the grape strike began, the growers had found another means to obtain the same cheap labor. Under Public Law 414 (the Immigration and Nationality Act of 1952, also called the McCarran-Walter Act), large numbers of foreigners were permitted to enter the United States as "permanent resident aliens" on a special green visa card. "Green-carders" could become citizens after five years' residence (and hold social security, pay taxes, and be drafted while they waited), but since the Mexican may earn fifteen times as much for a day's work in the United States ($30 versus 25 pesos, or about $2), most have declined this opportunity in favor of "commuting," i.e., they cluster around the border towns and take their high harvest wages—an estimated $15 million worth in 1967—back to Mexico.

Today almost half the membership of Chavez's union hold green cards; they are welcome so long as they do not work as scabs. The law specifies that no green-carders may work in a field where a labor dispute has been certified, or where a minimum wage (now $1.40 an hour) has not been offered first to domestic workers, but enforcement of this law has been desultory, to say the least. Many Mexicans, with the active encouragement of the growers and the passive encouragement of the Border Patrol of the U.S. Immigration Service, have joined the numerous "wetbacks" (that is, the illegal immigrants) as strikebreakers. As long as they are excluded from legislation that guarantees collective bargaining, the farm workers have no formal means to force employers to negotiate. When their strike against the grape growers was subverted by imported scabs and antipicketing injunctions, they were driven to what the growers call an "illegal and immoral" boycott. Originally this boycott was directed against one company, the Joseph Giumarra Vineyards, Inc., but Giumarra began selling its products under the labels of other companies, and in January 1968 the present consumer's boycott against all growers of California table grapes was begun.

In the autumn of 1968, according to the Fresno *Bee* of November 3, an estimated twenty to thirty thousand wetbacks were working in the Valley; though their presence is illegal, there is no penalty for hiring them, and since they are both economical and defenseless, the growers replace their domestic force with *alambristas* (fence jumpers) at every opportunity. "When the *alambrista* comes into a job," one of them is quoted as saying, "the regular workers are out, just like that." The Immigration Service picked up five hundred and ten wetbacks in the Delano area in August alone—about one fortieth of the lowest estimated number.

Loosely enforced, P.L. 414 is no improvement over P.L. 78, and it poses a moral problem as well as an economic one: Mexican-Americans, most of whom have parents or grandparents south of the border, have deep sympathy with Mexican poverty and do not wish to get Mexicans into trouble by reporting them to *la Migra,* as the Border Patrol is known. Besides, many green-carders are innocent, having been hired without being told, as P.L. 414 requires, that their employer was the object of a strike; some of these people, poor though they are, have walked off the job in a strange country when they learned the truth, but most are in debt for transport and lodging before they ever reach the fields, and their need—and that of their families at home— is too great to permit so brave a gesture.

The man with the fighting cock on his shirt was a Union green-carder who did not wish to cross the picket lines. But at that time there were more Union workers than Union jobs—only three growers in the Delano area had signed contracts with the United Farm Workers Organizing Committee—and Chavez encouraged the man to take a job wherever he could find it. He did not have to encourage the green-carder to help the Union on the job by organizing work slowdowns; the man was already complaining that social security payments had been deducted from his last pay checks, even though no one had asked for his social security number.

Workers who cannot read, like this man, feel that they are chronic victims of petty pay-check chiseling on the part of both labor contractors and growers, not only on illusory social security but on unpaid overtime and promised bonuses. (In the first six months of 1967, the Department of Labor discovered that nearly two hundred thousand American laborers were being cheated by their employers, mostly on unpaid overtime and evasion of the minimum wage; this figure is probably only a fraction of the actual number of victims.) Chavez feels that the labor contractor, who sells his own people in job lots to the growers, is the worst evil in an evil system that is very close to peonage; the contractor would be eliminated if the growers agreed to get their labor through a union hiring hall.

"Those people make a lot of money that way," Chavez said. "A *lot*." At this moment, he looked ugly. "In the Union, the workers get an honest day's pay, because both sides understand the arrangement and accept it. Without a union, the people are always cheated, and they are so innocent." In silence, we walked on up Eleventh Avenue to Albany and turned south along the cotton fields. It was eight o'clock now, and the morning was hot. The flat farmland stretched away unbroken into dull mists of agricultural dust, nitrates and insecticides, still unsettled from the day before, that hid the round brown mountains of the Coast Range.

Chavez said that many of the green-carders—and especially those who would return to Mexico—felt they could beat the Union wage scale by working furiously on a piecerate basis; others did not join the Union out of ignorance —they had never heard of a union—or fear of reprisal. "It's the whole system of fear, you know. The ones we've converted—well, out at Schenley we have a contract, and P. L. Vargas, on his ranch committee—there was a guy named

Danny. Danny was so anti-Union that he went to the management at Schenley and said, 'Give me a gun; I'll go out and kill some of those strikers.' He just hated us, and he didn't know why. Today he's a real good Unionist; he has a lot of guts and does a lot of work, but he still doesn't know why. He was working inside when we came with the picket line, and he wouldn't walk out, and I guess he felt guilty so he went too far the other way. And also, he told me later, 'I didn't know what a union was, I never heard of a union; I had no idea what it was or how it worked. I came from a small village down in Mexico!' You see? It's the old story. He was making more money than he had ever seen in Mexico, and the Union was a threat.

"Anyway, we won there, and got a union shop, and all the guys who went out on strike got their jobs back. And, man, they wanted to clean house, they wanted to get Danny, and I said no. 'Well, he doesn't want to join the Union! And the contract says if he doesn't join the Union, he can't work there!' So I challenged them. I said, 'One man threatens you? And you've got a contract? Do you know what the real challenge is? Not to get him out, but to get him *in*. If you were good organizers you'd get him, but you're not—you're lazy!' So they went after Danny, and the pressure began to build against him. He was mad as hell, he held out for three months, and he was encouraged by the Anglos, the white guys—they had the best jobs, mechanics and all, and they didn't want to join the Union either. But finally Danny saw the light, and they did too. That contract took about six months to negotiate, so by the time we got around to setting up a negotiating committee, Danny had not only been converted but had been elected to the committee. So when the committee walked in there,

P. L. was one of them and Danny was another, and the employers stared at him: 'What are you doing here, Danny?'"
Chavez laughed. "And now he's a real St. Paul; he'll never turn against the Union because he knows both sides. People who don't know, and come on so enthusiastic and all at first, they may be turncoats one day, but not the ones like Danny. That's why the converted ones are our best men.

"You know how we make enemies? A guy gets out of high school, and his parents have been farm workers, so he gets a job, say, as a clerk at the Bank of America. This way, you know, he gets into the climate, into the atmosphere"—Chavez shook his head in bafflement—"and I'll be damned if in two years they haven't done a terrific job on him, not by telling him, but just by . . . by *immersion*, and before you know it the guy is actually saying there's no discrimination! 'Hell, there's no poverty!' See? He knows his place. Or he gets a job at a retail store and then feels threatened because our people are making more than he does. 'Look,' he says, 'I went to high school for four years, so how come these farm workers are making more than I do?' That *really* hurts. Either way he is threatened by the Union."

On the left as we walked south on Albany were the small houses of large families, mostly Mexican. Though these houses are simple, their neatness reflects a dignity that was not possible in the labor camps, which have always been the ugliest symbol of the migrant workers' plight. "Besides being so bad, they divide the families," Chavez said. "We don't want people living out there, we want them in their own houses. As long as they're living in the camps, they're under the thumb of the employer." He nodded toward the small houses. "In Delano the need for housing is being met, even for the migrants. I mean, if we won the whole thing tomorrow, signed contracts with all the growers, we'd have to use some of the camps for a little while, but right now the people in the camps are strikebreakers." I kicked a stone, and he watched it skid into the field. "We're going to get rid of those camps," he said, as if making himself a promise.

A car passed us, bursting with cries, and rattled to a halt a short way beyond. Two workers were driving a third to the Forty Acres, the site of the proposed new Union headquarters, and to my surprise—we had been headed for the Union offices at the corner of Albany and Asti streets— Chavez suggested that we ride out there. The car turned west at Garces Highway and rolled two miles through the cotton and alfalfa to a barren area of mud, shacks and unfinished construction on the north side of the road. Here the car left us and went back to town, and the third man, a solitary Anglo tramp, a renegade from the thirties who helps the farm workers whenever he comes to town, shouted cheerily at Chavez and marched off to water some scattered saplings that shriveled slowly in the August heat.

"We've planted a lot of trees. Elms, mostly, and Modesto ash—only the cheapest kinds." Chavez stood with his back to the road, hands in hip pockets, gazing with pleasure at the desolation. The Forty Acres lies between the state road and the city dump. Useless for farming in its present condition, the property was obtained in 1966 from a widow who could not afford to pay the taxes on it. "Don't get me started on my plans," he said. To Chavez, who envisions the first migrant workers center, the place is already beautiful; he comes here regularly to walk around and let his plans take shape. "There's alkali in this land," he said. "We're trying to get something growing here, to cut down the dust."

At the Forty Acres, near the highway, an adobe building which will house gas pumps, auto repair shop and a cooperative store had recently been completed, though it was not yet in use: the shop was heaped high with food stores for the strikers, donated by individuals and agencies all over the United States. Just across from it is the windowless small room in which Chavez lived during the twenty-five-day fast that he undertook in February and March 1968. Behind this building was a temporary aggregation of shacks and trailers which included the workers clinic and the Union newspaper, *El Malcriado* (the "rebellious child," the "nonconformist," the "protester"—there is no simple translation), which issues both English and Spanish editions every fortnight. Originally *El Malcriado* was a propaganda organ, shrill and simplistic: it saw Lyndon Johnson as a "Texas grower" careless of the lives of the Vietnamese "farm workers." Today it is slanted but not irresponsible, and it is well-edited.

One green trailer at the Forty Acres, bearing the legend MOBILE HEALTH CENTER, was the contribution of the International Ladies' Garment Workers Union; its medical staff, like that of *El Malcriado* and most of the rest of the UFWOC operation, is made up entirely of volunteers. So is the intermittent labor being done on the headquarters building, a gray shell in the northwest corner of the property. The work was supervised by Chavez's brother Richard, who had been sent off a few days before to help out with the boycott in New York. "The strike is the important thing," Chavez said, moving toward this building. "We work on the Forty Acres when we get a little money, or some volunteers." The day before, six carpenters from a local in Bakersfield had given their Saturday to putting up gray fiberboard interior walls, and Chavez, entering the building, was delighted with the progress. "Look at that!" he kept saying. "Those guys really went to town!" The plumbing had been done by a teacher at Berkeley, and two weeks before, forty-seven electricians from Los Angeles, donating materials as well as labor, had wired the whole building in six hours. "I've never seen forty-seven electricians," I admitted, trying not to laugh, and Chavez grinned. "You should have seen it," he assured me. "I could hardly get into the building. Everywhere I went, I was in somebody's way, so I just went out through the window."

The building will combine Union offices and a service center, where workers can obtain advice on legal problems, immigration, driver's licenses, tax returns, and other matters. We inspected the credit union, legal offices, the hiring hall-and-auditorium, the dining hall, kitchen and rest rooms.

In the northeast corner were small cubicles for the Union officers. "Everybody was out here claiming his office." Chavez smiled, shaking his head. "We've outgrown this building even before we move into it, and I guess they thought that somebody was going to get left out." He grunted. "They were right." We had come to the cubicle in the corner. "This is mine, I guess," he said, "but now they don't want me here." I asked why. He was silent for a little while, looking restlessly about him. "I don't know." He shrugged and took a breath, as if on the point of saying something painful. "They're very worried about security or something.

I don't know." Stupidly, I failed to drop the subject. "I guess the corner is more exposed," I said. "They want you somewhere inside."

Chavez walked away from me. "This is the conference room," he called, from around a corner. "This will save a lot of time. People are constantly coming in, you know . . . " His voice trailed off, resumed again. "The way things are going, we don't have enough office space for the newspaper or the ranch committees . . . Oh! Look at that!" He was turning a complete circle. "Those guys *really* went to town! It's entirely changed!" He finished his circle, beaming. "The first center for farm workers in history!" (A year later Richard Chavez took me out to see the progress at the Forty Acres, which was negligible. "We're so damn busy," Richard said, "and there's always something that needs the money more.")

Outside again, we walked around the grounds, in the hot emptiness of Sunday. "Over there"—he pointed—"will be another building, a little training center there, kind of a . . . a study center for nonviolence, mostly for people in the Union, the organizers and ranch committees. Nonviolent tactics, you know—to be nonviolent in a monastery is one thing, but being nonviolent in a struggle for justice is another. And we'll stress honesty. Some of these guys will be getting a lot of power as the Union develops, and some will be very good and some won't know how to handle it. If someone in the hiring hall is willing to take a bribe to put one guy ahead of another on a job, he may also be willing to steal a hundred dollars from the Union, or accept a hundred dollars for an act of violence. There's all kinds of chances for corruption, and things can go to hell fast—

we've seen that in other unions. So the best way to teach them is by example."

His glance asked that I take what he was about to say as nothing boastful. Chavez is a plain-spoken man who does not waste his own time or his listener's with false humility, yet he is uncomfortable when the necessity arises to speak about himself, and may even emit a gentle groan. "I mean, you can write a million pamphlets on honesty, you can write books on it, and manuals, and it doesn't work—it only works by example. I have to give up a lot of things, because I can't ask people to sacrifice if I won't sacrifice myself." He was glad to change the subject. "We have some great guys in this Union, some really great guys. We've put together farm workers and volunteers, people who just wanted to do something for the cause. We have so many volunteers that we save only the best; they come and go, but the good ones never go. You don't say 'Stay!' They stay of their own accord!

"In a way we're all volunteers; even the ones—the lawyers and everybody—whose salaries are paid by outside people; they're not making money. You start paying the strikers for what they should do for themselves, then everything is done for money, and you'll never be able to build anything. It's not just a question of spending money, and anyway, we haven't got it. But the farm workers stand to benefit directly from the Union; it's their union, and we've been able to get that across to them—really, you know, it's working beautifully. Most of us work for five dollars a week. Outside people, the Teamsters and everybody, thought we were crazy, but it's the only way we can stay in business. It's a long, long haul, and there isn't any money, and if we start paying wages, then it means that only a *few* can be hired, and a few can't do as much as many.

"It has to be done this way. I've been in this fight too long, almost twenty years, learning and learning, one defeat after another, always frustration. And then of course, raising a family—you have to get your family to suffer along with you, otherwise you can't do it. But finally we're beginning to see daylight, and that's a great reward. And then, you see, these farm workers will never be the same. If they destroyed our union today, these people would never go back to where they were. They'd get up and fight. That's the *real* change."

Under the eaves of the garage, in the shade of the north wall, a blue wooden bench stood against the adobe. We sat there for an hour or more, cut off by the cool clay walls from the howl of the highway. To the west was a marginal dark farm—all dying farms look dark—with a lone black-and-white cow in the barnyard, and a sign, itself in need of repair, that advertised the repair of auto radiators. Across the property to the north, dead cars glittered on the crown of the city dump; heaped high like a bright monument to progress, the cars form the only rise in the depressed landscape of Delano.

The adobe walls and red tile roofs of the Forty Acres were Chavez's own wish, to be repeated in the other buildings as they take shape: the idea comes from the old Franciscan missions, and from an adobe farmhouse of his childhood. "The people wanted something more modern—you know, kind of flashy—to show that they had a terrific union going here, but I wanted something that would not go out of fashion, something that would last." Eventually the entire Forty Acres will be surrounded by a high adobe wall, which will mercifully shut out its grim surroundings. The flat hard sky will be broken by trees, and he dreams of a fountain in a sunken garden, and a central plaza where no cars will be permitted.

Chavez drew his hopes in the old dust with a dead stick. Inside the walls, paths will lead everywhere, and "places for the workers to rest. There will be little hollows in the walls—you know, niches—where people can put little statues if they want, or birds and things. We'll have frescoes. Siqueiros is interested in doing that, I think. This place is for the people, it has to grow naturally out of their needs." He smiled. "It will be kind of a religious place, very restful, quiet. It's going to be nice here." He gazed about him. "I love doing this—just letting it grow by itself. Trees. We'll have a little woods." Arizona cypress had already been planted along the property lines, but in the August heat many of Chavez's seedling trees had yellowed and died.

Car tires whined to a halt on the highway and crunched onto the flats of the Forty Acres. Chavez became silent; he sat stone-still against the wall, gazing straight out toward the glistening dump. When the car came past the corner of the building into his line of sight, he smiled. The driver was Ann Israel of the Spectemur Agendo Foundation of New York, who had introduced us originally. We all waved. "I heard you were out here," she called. "Do you want a lift back into town?"

Chavez shook his head. "That's all right, thanks," he said. "We can walk." For a moment Mrs. Israel looked as astonished as I felt—not so much that the walk back was a long one on the hot August highway but that Chavez felt relaxed enough to take the time away. But the day before, in Bakersfield, he had won a crucial skirmish with the growers; though he gives an almost invariable impression of great calm, he was more relaxed this morning than I had ever seen him. After a week's immersion in injunctions, boycotts, restraining orders, suits and strikes, he seemed glad to talk about trees and red-tiled missions, and to remain seated peacefully in the shade of his adobe wall, on a blue wooden bench.

Mrs. Israel perceived this instantly and made no effort to persuade him to accept a ride. Chavez smiled fondly after her as she waved and drove away. A pretty girl in her thirties, Mrs. Israel is both tough-minded and kind, and she has been a good friend to the farm workers, finding support for them in other foundations besides her own. In June she had got me to edit an outline of insecticide abuses for possible use in a farm workers' ad, thus transforming my vague endorsement of the California grape strike into active participation. At that time she also told me that she was going to Delano in midsummer, to see at first hand what her foundation was considering supporting; if I cared to come along, she said, she would introduce me to Cesar Chavez.

Because he is such an unpublic man, Chavez is one of the few public figures that I would go ten steps out of my way to meet. Besides, I feel that the farm workers' plight is related to all of America's most serious afflictions: racism, poverty, environmental pollution, and urban crowding and decay—all of these compounded by the waste of war.

In a damaged human habitat, all problems merge. For example, noise, crowding and smog poisoning are notorious causes of human irritability; that crowded ghettos explode first in the worst smog areas of America is no coincidence at all. And although no connection has been established between overcrowding and the atmosphere of assassination, rat experiments leave little doubt that a connection could exist: even when ample food and shelter are provided, rats (which exhibit behavioral patterns disconcertingly similar to those of man) respond to crowding in strange and morbid ways, including neuter behavior, increased incidence of homosexuality, gang rape, killing, and consumption by the mothers of their young. But because the symptoms of a damaged habitat are social, a very serious problem of ecology (it seems fatuous to say "the most serious problem the world has ever known," not because it is untrue but because it is so obvious) will be dealt with by politicians, the compromisers and consensus men who do not lead but merely exploit the status quo. The apparatus of the status quo—the System is a partisan term but must do here for want of a better—not to speak of System ethics, is not going to be good enough when food, oxygen and water become scarce. Although it seems likely, in purely material needs, that the optimisms of the new technologies will be borne out, most men in 1985 will have to live by bread alone, and not very good bread, either. Famine is already as close as Kentucky and the Mississippi Delta, and apart from that, there is hard evidence of environmental stress—noise, traffic, waiting lines, sick cities, crime, lost countrysides, psychosis. Meanwhile, the waste of resources continues, and the contamination of the biosphere by bomb and blight.

Before this century is done, there will be an evolution in our values and the values of human society, not because man has become more civilized but because, on a blighted earth, he will have no choice. This evolution—actually a revolution whose violence will depend on the violence with which it is met—must aim at an order of things that treats man and his habitat with respect; the new order, grounded in human ecology, will have humanity as its purpose and the economy as its tool, thus reversing the present order of the System. Such hope as there is of orderly change depends on men like Cesar Chavez, who, of all leaders now in sight, best represents the rising generations. He is an idealist unhampered by ideology, an activist with a near-mystic vision, a militant with a dedication to nonviolence, and he stands free of the political machinery that the election year 1968 made not only disreputable but irrelevant.

In the heavy Sunday silence of the Valley we rose from the bench, stretched, grinned and went back out into the sun. Ten o'clock had come and gone, and the blue sky had paled to a blue-white. We walked toward town in silence. In the corner of Forty Acres, just off the highway, was a heavy wooden cross with ten-foot arms, made of old telephone poles, which had been consecrated at the time of the February fast; after Senator Kennedy's assassination it had been covered with a shroud. In late June, following two attempts to burn it, local vigilantes sawed it down. The charred remnants were left there in the mesquite desert dust so that no one on either side would forget the event. Chavez glanced at the despoiled cross but made no comment.

Our shoes scuffed along the highway shoulder, over the slag of broken stone, tar bits, glass and flattened beer cans —Hamm's, Olympia, Coors. In the still heat, tar stink and exhaust fumes hung heavy in the air. Exhaust filters were first required by law in California, where air pollution is so pervasive that the whole state seems threatened by a dull gray-yellow pall; it is appropriate that Chavez's fight for a new ethic should have begun in California, which free enterprise has reduced from the most majestic of the states to the most despoiled.

Of all California's blighted regions, the one that man has altered most is this great Central Valley, which extends north and south for almost four hundred miles. The Sacramento Valley, in the northern half, was once a sea of grass parted by rivers; the San Joaquin Valley, in the south, was a region of shallow lakes and tule marshes. Both parts of what is commonly known as the Valley supported innumerable animals and birds, among which the waterfowl, antelope and tule elk were only the most dominant; there were also wolves, grizzlies, cougar, deer and beaver. To the Spanish, centered in the great mission holdings along the south-central coast, the grasslands of the interior were scarcely known, and their destruction was accomplished almost entirely by the wave of Americans that followed hard upon the Gold Rush. Game slaughter became an industry, and the carnivores were poisoned; by 1875 the myriad elk and antelope were almost gone. Meanwhile, unrestricted grazing by huge livestock herds destroyed the perennial grasses. Oat grass, June grass and wild rye gave way to tarweed, cheat grass and thistle, which in turn were crowded by rank annual weeds escaped from imported food crops of the settlers. In landscape after landscape, the poppies, lupines, larkspurs and mariposa lilies were no more.

From the start, California land monopolies were so enormous that the big "farms" were not farms at all, but industrial plantations. (To this day, the Kern County Land

Company owns 350,000 acres in Kern County alone.) In the latter part of the nineteenth century, the huge corporate ranches were challenged for the dying range by huge corporate farms; the first big factory crop was wheat, the second sugar beets. One by one the tule marshes were burned over and drained; by the end of the century, the lakes and creeks, like the wild creatures, had subsided without a trace. As the whole Valley dried, the water table that once had lain just below the surface sank away; in places, the competitive search for water made it necessary to resort to oil-drilling equipment, tapping Ice Age aquifers hundreds of feet down. To replace the once plentiful water, the rivers were dammed and rechanneled in the Bureau of Reclamation's Central Valley Project, begun in the thirties: Shasta Dam destroyed the Sacramento, and Friant Dam choked off the San Joaquin. Today there are no wild rivers in the Valley, and very few in all of California; the streams of the Coast Range and the Sierra Nevada have been turned to irrigation, seeping across the Valley floor in concrete ditches.

Hard-edged and monotonous as parking lots, the green fields are without life. The road we walked across the Valley floor was straight and rigid as a gun barrel, without rise or curve. Passing cars buffeted with hot wind the cornflowers that had gained a foothold between the asphalt and the dull man-poisoned crop, and pressed toads as dry as leaves gave evidence in death that a few wild things still clung to life in this realm of organophosphates and chlorinated hydrocarbons.

As the sun rose the sky turned white; the white merged with the atmospheric dust. The dry heat is tolerable, yet the soul shrivels; this world without horizons is surreal. Out here on the flat Valley floor there is nothing left of nature; even the mountains have retreated, east and west. On all sides looms the wilderness of wires and weird towers of man's progress, including a skeletal installation of the Voice of America, speeding glad news of democracy and freedom to brown peoples all over the world.

Chavez crossed the highway to greet his doctor, Jerome Lackner of San Jose, who contributes many Sundays to the farm workers; Dr. Lackner was being chauffeured by Marcia Sanchez, one of a number of Anglo volunteers who has married a farm worker and stayed on in Delano. The next car blared a loud greeting on its horn, and a child's voice— "Hi, Mr. Chavez!"—was whirled upward and away in the eddy of hot dusty wind in the car's wake. Soon another Sunday car, already bulging, offered a lift, and when Chavez refused it, its occupants shouted in surprise. The car swayed on. A woman's warm laughter drifted back to us— ". . . *su penitencia?*"— and Chavez grinned shyly. "*Sí, sí,*" he murmured. "*Mi penitencia.*" We walked on.

From the crossroads at Albany and Garces, a mile ahead, a big black car came toward us; still at a distance, it eased to a halt along the roadside. Three men got out, and leaning against the car, watched our approach. As we came abreast, two of them crossed the highway to await us while the third turned the big car around and brought it up behind.

Chavez, greeting the two men, made no attempt to introduce me; I took this as a sign that I was not to join the conversation and dropped behind. In shining shoes and bright white shirts of Sunday dress, the men flanked Chavez as he walked along; they towered over him. Over the car engine, idling behind me, I could hear no voices, and Chavez, looking straight ahead, did not seem to be speaking. There were only the two water-slicked bent heads, and the starched white arms waving excitedly against the whitening sky.

At the corner of Albany the men left us. They were "submarines"—Union men who cross the picket lines at a struck vineyard and work from within by organizing slowdowns and walkouts. Submarine operations, often spontaneous, are not openly encouraged by the Union, but they are not discouraged, either. Chavez does not seem comfortable with subversive tactics, even those traditional in the labor movement; he talks tough at times, but his inspiration comes from elsewhere, and such methods are at variance with his own codes. "Certain things are all right—sloppy picking and packing, slowdowns. Or marking the boxes wrong, which fouls up the record keeping and gets people upset because they're not paid the right amount. But it doesn't stop there, that's the bad part of it. The transition to violence is rarely sudden. One man slashes a tire, then two or three do it. One thing leads to another, and another and another. Then you have real destruction and real violence."

Some of Chavez's lieutenants, respecting his personal ambivalence, omit telling him about tactics that he could only permit at the risk of insincerity in his public statements. But of course he knows that the incidents don't happen by themselves, and so, in his own conscience, he must walk a narrow line. Apparently he walks it without qualms. It is useless to speculate whether Chavez is a gentle mystic or a tough labor leader single-minded to the point of ruthlessness; he is both.

We neared the town. From the outlying fields on the west end, Delano has little character: the one-story workers' houses are often painted green, and the few trees are low, so that the town seems a mere hardening, a gall, in the soft sea of dusty foliage. The dominant structures in Delano are the billboards, which are mounted high above the buildings, like huge lifeless kites.

A farm truck came by, and the face of a blond boy stared back at us. I wondered if the occupants had recognized Chavez. "Some of the growers still get pretty nasty," Chavez remarked after a moment, "but the worst are some of these young Anglo kids. They come by and give you the finger, and you wave back at them. You don't wave back to make fun of them, you just wave back."

As he spoke Chavez stopped to pat a mangy dog, which flinched away from him; he retraced his steps a little ways to squat and talk to it. He liked dogs very much, he said, but had never owned one; he petted the dog for a long time.

" 'Hay más tiempo que vida'—that's one of our dichos. 'There is more time than life.' We don't worry about time, because time and history are on our side."

Children and a woman called to him from the shady yard near the corner, and he called back, "Hi! ¡Poquito! Hello! ¿Cómo está?" Still walking, he asked the woman whether her husband was still working en la uva ("in the grape"). Cheerily she said yes. The woman's house was adjacent to the old Union office, now the hiring hall at the corner of Asti Street which supplies workers to Union ranches in the Delano area. The present Union offices, in the Pink Building, are next door. This is the southwest corner of Delano, and across the street, to the south and west, small patches of vineyard stretch away. The hiring hall, originally a grocery, is in poor repair due to old age and cheap construction, as well as several hit-and-run assaults by local residents. "One truck backed right into it," Chavez said, bending to show me the large crack in the wall. "Practically knocked down the whole thing. See?" He straightened. "They broke all these windows. One time they threw a soaked gasoline rag through the window—that just about did it. But someone saw them throw the fire rag and called the fire department, and they put it on the radio, and my brother Richard was listening and took off and got over here quick; he had it out before the fire department got here." Chavez shook his head. "One second more and the whole thing would have gone." He laughed suddenly. "Man, they used to come here and shoot *fire* arrows into the roof with bows and arrows! We had to keep a ladder and a hose on hand for a long time."

In the late afternoon, outside the motel where I was staying, I ran into the blond boy I had seen that morning staring at Chavez from the pickup truck. He turned out to be a nephew of a local grower, and was working in the vineyards for the summer before going to college. He had stared at Chavez because one of the foremen in the truck had said that those Mexicans on Albany Street were probably some of Chavez's men, and now he was surprised to learn that he had actually seen Chavez himself: as I had already discovered, most of the growers had never laid eyes on this dangerous figure and probably would not recognize him if they did.

The nephew was handsome, pleasant and polite; he called me "sir." He said that although his generation felt less violently than their fathers, and that some sort of farm workers union seemed inevitable, the Delano growers would let their grapes rot in the fields before signing a union contract with Chavez. I asked if this was because Chavez was a Mexican. No, he said, it was because Chavez was out for himself and had no real support; even that three-day fast last winter had been nothing but a publicity stunt. When I questioned this, he did not defend his views but merely shrugged; like a seedless California fruit, bred for appearances, this boy lacked flavor.

He asked, "Do you like California?" Rightly bored by his own question, he gazed at the glaring blue-and-orange panels of the motel façade. "I think Delano is supposed to be the flower capital of the world," he said.

At dark I went to the Guadalajara restaurant, overlooking U.S. 99, where I had good beer and tortillas, and listened to such jukebox songs as "Penas a la corazón" and "Tributo a Roberto F. Kennedy." Seeking directions to this place, which is a farm workers restaurant, I earned the suspicion of the motel manager. "Guadalajara? That's a Mexican restaurant, ain't it?" In this small town of 12,000, he did not know where it was. Standing there behind his fake-plywood Formica desk, in the hard light and hum of air conditioning, he stared after me. "Good luck," he said in a sniping voice as I went through the glass door, which swung to on the conditioned air with a soft exhaling.

In the San Joaquin Valley summer night, far out beyond the neon lights, crickets jittered and a dog barked in the wash of silence between passing cars. Alone in his office, the manager still stood there, hands on his barren desk, with as much vindictiveness in his face as a man can afford who believes that the customer is always right. Under the motel sign, the light read VACANCY.

2

I HAD arrived in Delano late in the evening of the last night of July, and was to meet Cesar Chavez for the first time the following morning in the office of his assistant, Leroy Chatfield. The whole staff had just returned from a retreat at St. Anthony's Mission, in the Diablo Range, "a holy place," Mr. Chatfield said, "where we tried to figure out how to make life miserable for rich people."

Chatfield is a gaunt, mild-mannered man with the white hair of a summer child and the wide-eyed, bony face of a playful martyr; at thirty-four, he is one of the brightest and most resourceful of a bright and resourceful staff. Before coming to Delano three years before, he had been Brother Gilbert of Christian Brothers and a teacher at Garces High School, in Bakersfield; but it was Cesar Chavez, he said, who gave him his education. As Chatfield spoke of Chavez and the farm workers, his face was radiant; Mrs. Israel, struck by this, said, "You really love these people, don't you, Leroy?" It was a straight question, not a sentimental one, and it made him blink, but he did not back away from it. "Oh, yes," he said quietly. "I mean, you don't *meet* people like that . . ." His voice trailed off and he shrugged, at a loss, still smiling.

While Chavez was meeting with some visitors from

Martin Luther King's Southern Christian Leadership Conference, Mrs. Israel and I were taken on a tour of the Union offices, which are small and cluttered and busy. Chatfield introduced us to Union vice-president Dolores Huerta, to Chavez's administrative assistant, the Reverend James Drake, to staff lawyers Jerome Cohen and David Averbuck, to Philip Vera Cruz, a Union officer and head of the Filipino membership in the absence of assistant director Larry Itliong, and to Helen Chavez, who is in charge of the credit union office. Mrs. Chavez, Chatfield told us, is very quiet and very strong, with a hot temper that rarely surfaces. "Sometimes," he said, "she has less faith than Cesar in non-violence." Chatfield's disarming innocence and his gift for understatement have made him very effective as a Union negotiator, and since he is also a good speaker, he often represents the Union when Chavez himself cannot make a public appearance.

Most of the offices are decorated with posters of Union heroes. Robert and John Kennedy are everywhere, and some of their portraits are black-bordered and hung with flowers, as in a shrine. A huge blue-bordered picture of Gandhi contrasts strangely with blood-red posters of Emiliano Zapata, complete with mustachio, cartridge belts, carbine, sash, sword and giant sombrero, under the legend VIVA LA REVOLUCIÓN. Here and there are Union emblems, a square-edged black eagle in a white circle on a red background, over the letters UFWOC or the word HUELGA, which means "strike." Chavez says that the impact of a black emblem in a white circle on a red field was discovered by the Egyptians. Some people like to think that the eagle appeared to Cesar Chavez in a dream; some say it came to

Chavez's cousin Manuel, whose inspiration was the label on a wine jug of Gallo Thunderbird. The truth is that the emblem Chavez wanted was an Aztec eagle, which he asked Manuel to design. With the assistance of Richard, Manuel sketched it on a piece of wrapping paper, and they squared off the wing edges so that "the damn thing would be easier to draw," not only for Richard and Manuel, but for the many strikers who have since sewn homemade flags for use on the picket lines.

Manuel and Richard Chavez were on the point of setting off for New York by car to help with the faltering boycott; Manuel was waiting in Chatfield's office when we returned. He is a powerful, volatile man with a high forehead whose supreme confidence in his own ability to reverse the New York tide was not meant entirely in fun. "I'm going over to New York," he said. "How far is it? I'll be back in three weeks."

The Union boycott of California table grapes, which began in New York City in January 1968, has since been extended to other cities; if it can be sustained, it will be the first successful nationwide boycott in the history of the American labor movement. At first the boycott, led by young strikers who sought and got the support of local militants of the New Left, was unquestionably effective; in New York, for example, there were no grapes to be found in June and early July. BOYCOTT JEOPARDIZES ENTIRE GRAPE CROP read the *California Farmer*'s headline of July 6. "No question that the boycott of California grapes," wrote the Sunkist *Newsletter* for August, "unethical and illegal as it may be, is currently effective." The anti-Union press spoke somberly of the boycott, which, if successful, could be applied to any product; consumers were exhorted in patriotic language to fight for their food freedoms to the last man. But toward the end of July, boxes of green Thompson seedless grapes labeled HI-COLOR began to flood the New York market. The HI-COLOR label belongs to the Earl Packing Company, a subsidiary of the Di Giorgio Fruit Corporation, with which UFWOC has a contract, and which is therefore specifically exempt from the boycott. But Di Giorgio was not harvesting table grapes in 1968, which meant that its label was being used illegally by the non-Union growers. Manuel Chavez had just heard that a worker had seen HI-COLOR labels in the vineyards of Bruno Dispoto; Sabovich and Kovacevich, in the fields around Arvin and Lamont, southeast of Bakersfield, were also suspect. But the true culprit was evidently the Di Giorgio Fruit Corporation itself, which had permitted the use of the exempted label in an effort to subvert the boycott.

Or so it seemed to Cesar Chavez, who appeared suddenly in Chatfield's doorway. "I just had a talk with Robert Di Giorgio in San Francisco," he said to Chatfield. "I told him this was irresponsible and dishonest. I told him, 'You want a fight, you're going to have one!' " Hearing himself talk this way, his intense expression gave way to a gleeful smile and he rubbed his hands. At the same instant he caught sight of Mrs. Israel and came forward to embrace her. Warmly, within seconds, he welcomed us both to Delano, said goodbye to Manuel, apologized for being so busy and excused himself. "I see you later, hey?" A moment later his head reappeared in the doorway. "There's a very ancient saying," he said somberly, raising one finger. " 'Never trust a grower!' " The same gleeful smile lit up his face again as it disappeared.

．　．　．

In the days that followed, I was able to piece together the story of how Chavez became an organizer. Chavez, who described most of it himself, picketed the cotton fields at Corcoran for the National Agricultural Workers Union in 1946, when he was nineteen, and watched the union fail. Subsequently he would mutter about the frustrations of the poor to his wife, Helen, and his brother Richard, but he saw no way to put his outrage into action until 1952. That year he and Richard lived across the street from each other in San Jose, and worked together in the apricot groves. The Los Angeles headquarters of Saul Alinsky's Community Service Organization wanted to set up a chapter there, and among the names given to the CSO organizer by the parish priest, Father Donald McDonnell, was that of Cesar Chavez.

"I came home from work and this gringo wanted to see me. In those days when a gringo wanted to see you, it was something special; we never heard anything from whites unless it was the police. So anyway, Helen says, 'Oh no, it must be something good for Mexicans—money and a better job and things!'" Chavez's expression conveyed what he had thought about promises of something good for Mexicans. "You see, Stanford University had people nosing around, writing all kinds of screwy reports about how Mexicans eat and sleep, you know, and a lot of dirty kind of stuff, and Berkeley had its guys down there, and San Jose State—all the private colleges; they were interested in the worst *barrio,* the toughest slum, and they all picked Sal Si Puedes."

"What?"

"Sal—"

" 'Escape If You Can'?"

"Yah. That's what that *barrio* was called, because it was every man for himself, and not too many could get out of it, except to prison. Anyway, we were sick and tired of these people coming around asking stupid questions. I said to hell with him. Well, he came that day again and said he would come back in the evening, so when I got home I went across the street to Richard's house, and in a little while this old car pulled up and this gringo knocked on my door, and Helen told him I was working late or something. As soon as he left I came back and said, 'What happened?' and she said, 'He's coming tomorrow,' and I said, 'Well, I'm not going to be here tomorrow either.' So I came home from work and just dumped my lunch pail and my sweater and went over to Richard's house, and the same thing happened again. Helen said he was coming back tomorrow, and I said I wouldn't see him, and she said, 'Well, this time you tell him that, because I'm not going to lie to him any more.'

"So he came and talked to me. I was very closed, I didn't say a thing. I just let him talk. I'd say 'Yes' and nod my head, but half the time I was plotting how to get him. Still, there were certain things that struck me. One of them was how much I didn't like him even though he was sincere. I couldn't admit how sincere he was, and I was bothered by not being able to look at it. And the other thing was, he wore kind of rumpled clothes, and his car was very poor. And his flawless pronunciation of the Mexican language— that *really* impressed me. It's minor, I know, but I was impressed.

"Well, he wanted a meeting as soon as possible, and I said, 'How many people do you want?' and he said, 'Oh, four or five,' and I said, 'How about twenty?' 'Gee, that'd be great!' I had my little plan, you see. So I invited some of the rough guys in the *barrio,* and I bought some beer and told them how to handle it: when I switched my cigarette from my left hand to my right, they could start getting nasty."

The memory of his own behavior made Chavez frown. "These damn people used to talk about forty- or fifty-year patterns, and how did we eat our beans and tortillas, and whether we'd like to live in a two-bedroom house instead of a slum room, things like that. They try to make us real different, you know, because it spices up their studies when they do that. I thought this guy meant to snoop like all the rest. We didn't have anything else in our experience to go by; we were being pushed around by all these studies. So we were going to be nasty, and then he'd leave, and we'd be even. But I knew all the time that this gringo had really impressed me, and that I was being dishonest.

"So he came in and sat down and began to talk about farm workers, and then he took on the police and the politicians, not rabble-rousing either, but saying the truth. He knew the problems as well as we did; he wasn't confused about the problems like so many people who want to help the poor. He talked about the CSO and then the famous Bloody Christmas case a few years before, when some drunken cops beat up some Mexican prisoners down in L.A. I didn't know what the CSO was or who this guy Fred Ross was, but I knew about the Bloody Christmas case, and so did everybody in that room; some cops had actually been sent to jail for brutality, and it turned out that this miracle was thanks to the CSO.

"By this time a couple of guys began to get a little drunk, you know, and started to press me for some action. But I couldn't give the signal, because the gringo wasn't a phony.

I mean, how could I—I couldn't do it, that's all. So some of them got nasty and I jumped in and said, 'Listen, the deal's off. If you want to stay here and drink, then drink, but if you can't keep your mouth shut, then get out.' They said I had chickened out, so I took them outside and explained. There were a couple of guys that *still* wanted to get this gringo, but anyway, the meeting continued, and he put everything very plainly. He did such a good job of explaining how poor people could build power that I could even taste it, I could *feel* it. I thought, Gee, it's like digging a hole; there's nothing complicated about it!" Sixteen years later, as he recalled this moment, there was still a note of discovery in Chavez's voice.

"You see, Fred was already an organizer when Alinsky hired him. I guess some of his theories came from Alinsky, but I learned everything from Fred. It was Fred who developed this technique of house meetings—Alinsky never used them.

"Anyway, I walked out with him to his car and thanked him for coming, and then I kind of wanted to know—well, what next? He said, 'Well, I have another meeting, and I don't suppose you'd like to come?' I said, 'Oh yes, I would.' I told the others I'd be right back, and I got in his car and went with him, and that was it.

"That first meeting . . . I'd never been in a group before, and I didn't know a thing. Somebody asked for a motion, and I didn't know what the hell they were talking about. I tried to get answers from my friends, and none of us knew. We were just a bunch of *pachucos*—you know, long hair and pegged pants. But Fred wanted to get the *pachucos* involved—no one had really done this—and he knew how to handle the difficulties that came up, and he didn't take for granted a lot of little things that other people take for granted when they're working with the poor. He had learned, you know. Finally I said, 'What about the farm workers?' and he said that the CSO could be a base for organizing farm workers, and it was a good prediction, not exactly as he envisioned it, but it came about."

Chavez laughed. "I was his constant companion. I used to get home from work between five and five-thirty, and he'd say, 'I'll pick you up at six-thirty, give you a little time to clean up and eat,' and I'd say, 'No, I don't want to clean up and eat, pick me up at five-thirty!' So he would be waiting when I got home from work, and I'd just drop my lunch pail and rush right out. I was observing how he did things, how he talked to people and how patient he was, and I began to learn. A lot of people worked with him, but few learned what I learned. I think the reason was that I had more *need* to learn than anybody else. I really *had* to learn. So I'd pay attention to the smallest detail, and it became sort of a—well, I'd use the word 'game' if it didn't throw a wrong light on it. It wasn't a job, and at the same time it was very, very important, trying to understand these things and then apply them."

Chavez first joined the CSO as a volunteer in a voter-registration drive: the organization of Mexican-American bloc voting was the first lesson in his understanding of a power base. "Most of the volunteers were college people, or had good jobs—very few were farm workers. I had a part-time job in a lumberyard. Voter registration depended on as many evenings as you could give, and soon so many people stopped showing up that we had to find a new chairman every day. Finally I was the only one who went with Fred every night, so he made me chairman.

"So here I am in charge, and where do I start? I can't go to the middle class, or even the aspiring middle class, for my deputy registrars; I have to go to my friends in Sal Si Puedes. So I round up about sixteen guys"—at the memory he began to smile—"and not one of them can qualify as a deputy registrar, not *one*. They can't even *vote!* Every damn one of these guys had a felony!" He laughed. "Well, they could still knock on doors, you know; they put out a lot of energy. They were my friends, I grew up with them and knew what they were up against, and I always thought they were in the right except when they got sent up some place to do their time."

A few months later, at Fred Ross's recommendation, Chavez was hired by Saul Alinsky as a staff member, at $35 a week. After six months in San Jose, he took over Ross's CSO chapter in nearby Decoto, and two months after that, he was asked to start a new chapter in Oakland. He was still so poorly educated that he could scarcely read; he was small and thin and looked much younger than his twenty-five years, and he lived in terror of his own house meetings. He would drive back and forth in front of the house where a meeting was to be held, then dart in and sit in the corner until forced to identify himself as the organizer. But his first big meeting in Oakland was a turning point, and Fred recognized it; in 1953 he put Chavez in charge of the whole San Joaquin Valley.

In the next few years Chavez established chapters in Madera, Bakersfield, and many other towns. He was already a good organizer, and he got better as he developed techniques of his own. He learned to beware of established precepts, to cut around the entrenched local leadership, to avoid philosophizing in favor of clear illustration and example ("You have to draw a simple picture and color it in," he says), and above all, he recognized that organizing requires time. He estimates that 40 to 50 percent of the farm workers are illiterate in English and nearly so in Spanish. "You have to spend time with people, that's all. If a man's interested, it makes no difference if he can read or write; he is a man."

In the early fifties the Cold War wave of reaction that congealed around McCarthyism was prospering in the Valley, which since the thirties had been hypersensitive to anything radical or "Red," and a man who encouraged Mexican-Americans to vote was an obvious subversive. Cowed by local patriots, his own people in the Madera chapter began investigating Chavez for symptoms of the dread Communism, then backed off, abashed, when he challenged them to do so in his presence, not behind his back. The experience taught him the great folly of expecting gratitude, and more important, how pathetically afraid poor people were. Subsequently he had to return to San Jose and rebuild the CSO chapter: in the absence of strong leadership, the people had retreated into their apathy.

Nevertheless, the CSO was gaining strength, and its new power was reflected in the increased expense accounts of its staff. Politicians and professional people attached themselves to the organization for prestige purposes, and meanwhile the leadership was opposing Chavez's impractical demand that they try to organize a union of farm workers. At meeting after meeting Chavez spoke out against the new luxurious habits and the softening of purpose, the "erosion" that he speaks of to this day as the thing most to be feared in his own union; to symbolize his protest, he showed up at meetings unshaven and tieless—he has been tieless ever since—and refused any further increase in his own salary. "That salary was almost an insult," he remarked, still cross about it, and I asked him why. "Well, there were certain rules I set myself as an organizer," he said, "and I had to obey them. To come in a new car to organize a community of poor people—that doesn't work. And if you have money but dress like they do, then it's phony. Professional hunger." He grunted in disgust. "You can be hungry and have money in the bank, or you can be hungry and have nowhere to go. There's a big difference."

Union vice-president Dolores Huerta is a pretty, sad-eyed girl who does not look like the mother of seven children; like Chavez, she is a veteran of the CSO, and she shares his high opinion of Fred Ross. "He is the only one who ever had faith in us as people," she says, "who thought we could manage our own union, once we had the chance."

Mrs. Huerta knew Ross before she first met Chavez in 1955; at that time she was an organizer attached to the CSO headquarters in Los Angeles, and Chavez was organizing in Oxnard. "I had heard a lot about him from Fred Ross— Cesar this and Cesar that—but I didn't really get a chance to talk to him the first time I met him, and he didn't make much of an impression on me. I forgot his face. I knew he was a great organizer, but he never showed it; it came out in the reports. He was very unassuming, you see—did a lot of work but never took any leadership role. The first time I really heard him speak was at a board meeting in Stockton in 1957; he had to respond to sharp questions from an attorney, and I was very impressed by the way he handled it. You couldn't tell by looking at him what he could do; you had to see him in action to appreciate him. He was a different guy in those days, so quiet and easygoing, never got into a fight; he just did the work. In 1958 they made him director of the whole national organization, but even then he wasn't the forceful leader that he is now." Recalling this, Mrs. Huerta laughed. "Of course," she said, "everywhere he worked, tremendous things happened; those things didn't just happen by themselves. The rank and file began to see Cesar as the real head of the organization long before the leadership did. The reason he finally quit was because the CSO would not involve itself in forming a farm workers union, and Cesar knew that a union was the only chance that the farm workers had."

For a year and a half, between August 1958 and November 1959, Chavez had organized the farm workers of Oxnard against the inequities of the *bracero* program, which was being abused for the growers' benefit by both the Farm Placement Service of the California Department of Employment and the Bureau of Employment Security of the U.S. Department of Labor. Work cards issued to domestic laborers by the FPS proved useless when any *braceros* were available—according to Public Law 78, the reverse should have been true—and Chavez, knowing that pleas for justice would be useless, documented hundreds of cases of illegal job discrimination by taking groups of jobless workers to fill out work cards, day after day, and keeping a record of the results. Then he staged field sit-ins—his men went out and stationed themselves opposite the *braceros* who had taken their jobs—and a protest march, at the end of which the cards were burned in a gesture of contempt for the corruption of the hiring program. The press was invited to the fire.

All of these maneuvers anticipated tactics that Chavez

would refine in his own union, and they worked; in the glare of publicity, the domestic workers returned to work. They were eighteen hundred strong, and loyal to Chavez, and they held firm when he demanded better wages and conditions. The growers met his terms, though not officially; concealing their names, they would call up and say "please send me the workers. I'll be waiting by the church in a yellow pickup." "This is when I really learned," Chavez says, "that the growers weren't invincible." He now feels that he could have got a union shop, but his CSO job did not permit him to negotiate a contract. For fifteen months he had worked twenty hours a day, his weight had shrunk to one hundred and twenty-nine pounds, and he watched in despair as the Packinghouse union of the AFL-CIO took over what was, potentially, the first effective farm workers union in California. Under mechanical trade-union direction, an organization which had been built on dedication soon disintegrated.

According to Manuel Chavez, his cousin offered a year's service without salary to the CSO if the organization would support a new union of farm workers. At a CSO convention in Calexico, in March 1962, the board voted down Chavez's plan for the last time, and Chavez rose and said simply, "I resign." People immediately jumped to their feet and started arguing with one another, as if Chavez weren't there. He couldn't resign, they decided. But he had, and he and Dolores Huerta and Fred Ross went across the border to Mexicali to get something to eat. They were all very depressed. Chavez told me later that he had been "heartbroken"; he had known that he would have to quit, but it was the CSO that had changed his life.

Even before he left Calexico, Chavez was offered a well-paid job as organizer for AWOC (Agricultural Workers Organizing Committee), a farm workers union set up by the AFL-CIO in Stockton during his own successful organization of the workers in Oxnard, but he wanted no part of trade union methods, and refused. He spent two weeks cleaning up his work, and on March 31, his birthday, disappeared.

With Helen and his children, Chavez went to Carpinteria Beach, southeast of Santa Barbara, on the last vacation he has ever had time or money enough to take. For several years, in his seasons as a migrant, his family had picked tomatoes in nearby Summerland, and he had grown fond of this beautiful coast. The decision in the mid-fifties to rebuild the CSO chapters in the Central Valley, the decision to fight the *bracero* program at Oxnard, and the decision to base his farm workers association in Delano—the three projects Chavez regards as the most crucial in his life as an organizer—were all made at Carpinteria.

After six days on the coast, the Chavezes went straight to Delano, where his wife's family lived, and where Richard Chavez, now a carpenter, was head of the Delano CSO; Chavez himself had first worked in Delano's vineyards and cotton fields in 1937, when he was ten. Chavez has said that he picked Delano because he knew that hard times were ahead, and his family would not starve there, but Dolores Huerta has another theory. "Cesar picked Delano because Richard was there, that's all." Richard, a soft-voiced man with a mandarin mustache and the Oriental eyes of the first Indians to cross the Bering Strait, agrees. "We were inseparable," he says. "Except for his CSO years in East Los Angeles, we've never been apart."

Another good reason for picking Delano was the composition of the work force. There are seventy-odd grape ranches in the Delano area, with an estimated 38,000 acres of the table-grape vineyards, and grapes, unlike most crops, require tending of one kind or another—pruning, tying, girdling, cultivating, spraying, etc.—for almost nine months of the year. Because of the long work year, and because some of the jobs are semiskilled, the farm workers of Delano are less transient than most, and many stay all year round.

The growers are doubtless right in their contention that Delano's grape workers, who average $2,400 a year, are the best-paid farm workers in California, and apart from the hope that their dues might support their union, it seems strange that Chavez should have chosen the vineyards as his first battleground. But the very fact that so many workers were nonmigratory simplified their organization and made them more effective as a bargaining force. Furthermore, the most desperately poor are not necessarily the most desperate; unlike the man who has glimpsed a spark of hope, the destitute are often too defeated to revolt. Finally, Chavez preferred to start with a crop that was visible all year round. "You can't picket bare ground," he says. "There's a bad psychological blow in all that emptiness."

In Delano, Helen Chavez got a job picking grapes at Di Giorgio's huge Sierra Vista Ranch, and Cesar, baby-sitting his youngest children in the car, took a three-day trip to "absorb" the Valley, from Marysville, north of Sacramento, to Tehachapi, in the south, crisscrossing the flat Valley floor on the long straight roads. Then he returned to Delano and picked peas, the first of a long series of part-time jobs that helped support the small beginnings of his union.

At first Richard Chavez did not appreciate what his brother was trying to do. He had not been a farm worker for a long time, and had small interest in a farm workers organization. "I had a job in construction and worked hard," he says. "I was a journeyman carpenter by that time, and I had my wife and child. So I didn't want to believe in what he was doing." He nodded his head. "But way down deep, you see, I believed."

As for Manuel, he was making a good salary as a car salesman in San Diego; when Cesar asked him to join the new association, he flatly refused. " 'Neither of us are farm workers any more!' he yelled. 'We got away!' And Cesar said, 'Just because we got away does not mean we can abandon all the others.' " Finally Manuel agreed to join him for one month; he has never gone back. As one of the most effective organizers in the Union, he finds it simple to explain to people why they should be responsible for the farm workers. "I learned how," he says, "when I had to explain it to myself."

Apart from Helen, the only person who believed in *la causa* from the very start was Dolores Huerta. When Chavez left the CSO in 1962, she told him she would be honored to work for him—the verb is hers—and after 1962 she was a lobbyist for his National Farm Workers Association at the state capitol in Sacramento. A less optimistic supporter was the Reverend Jim Drake, who had arrived in the Delano area in the same month as Chavez, on his first assignment as a migrant minister; he ran into Chavez soon thereafter in the course of his efforts to help migrant workers in Tulare County. Drake was familiar with the farm labor situation because he had grown up in California, but he knew nothing about Cesar Chavez. "Cesar was very quiet and just mentioned that he had quit his job to start organizing farm workers around Delano. I was doing the same thing, more or less; I had been assigned to Delano for a six-week training period, and I'm still here."

When Chavez first got to Delano, the cheapest rental he could find was on Kensington Street, a block north of where he lives today. He had a small garage, which he used as a headquarters; it was so hot in there, Drake recalls, that all the ink melted down in the mimeograph machine that he had lent Chavez. "Everything was so oppressive that first summer; everything he wanted to do just seemed impossible. He had so many kids, and they had almost nothing to eat, and they had that old 1953 Mercury station wagon that burned much too much gas and oil; it belonged in a museum even then. So I really thought this guy was nuts. Everybody thought so except Helen, even Helen's family. I had a car and a credit card, but I couldn't really help much besides that. They had no money, but whatever they had, they shared. I'd bring a lunch with me, but it was very important to them that I eat with them, and they were so gracious that I'd finally give in.

"What impressed us most at the Migrant Ministry was that even though Cesar was desperate, he didn't want our money. He made it clear right from the start that whatever organization he got going would be entirely independent; he didn't want any Teamster money or money from the AFL-CIO or any other money that might compromise him."

"Cesar had studied the structure of the CSO," Mrs. Huerta says, "and he tried to correct its mistakes in NFWA: mainly, he wanted the people who did the work to make the decisions. He wanted the workers to participate, and he still does, because without that, the Union has no real strength. This is why he would never accept outside money, not until the strike began: he wanted the workers to see that they could pay for their own union." Very early in his struggle, Chavez turned down a private grant of $50,000 that was offered without conditions; he felt that the gift would put pressure on him to obtain immediate results. "Manuel and I almost quit," Richard Chavez says.

In his first hard year, when his own $1,200 savings were all spent, Chavez became so desperate that he had to go to people to beg food, like a monk seeking alms. This was hard on his pride, as he admits, but he sees it as a blessing. "Then and later," he has said, "we got some of our best members by asking for food. The people who give you their food give you their hearts."

Chavez got up early every morning and worked until midnight, taking a survey up and down the Valley to find out what farm workers really wanted. With his son Birdie (Anthony), who was then four, he went from door to door and out into the fields, distributing eighty thousand cards that asked the workers how much they thought they should be earning. At that time the average wage was 90 cents an hour, and it is a measure of their despair that most of the workers said that what they deserved was $1.10 or perhaps $1.25. Occasionally a man would say that he deserved $1.50 or even $1.75, or he might scrawl a note of encouragement or hope on his card. These people Chavez visited in person, and many became the first members of his association.

"His consistency and perseverance really struck me," Jim Drake says. "A disability case, a worker injured on the job— he would stay with that worker day and night, day and night, until he could locate an attorney who would take the case for nothing, or find some way of settling it that was of benefit to the worker. That's how his union was built: on plain hard work and these very personal relationships. It was a slow, careful, plodding thing; the growers didn't even know he was in town. Even when the strike started they had no idea who Cesar Chavez was, but the workers did. Day and night they came to his house, because his office was his house: he simply built up this basic trust. He ran a series of house meetings and never talked about forming a union, just an association of concerned people, because there had been unions and unions and strikes and strikes, and every one of them had failed. He learned how to keep books from a government manual, and he set up a credit union. He talked about co-operatives and everything, but he never used the word 'union' until 1965, when the strike began."

The early members of the Union were people of exceptional faith, and one of the first was a man named Manuel Rivera. He had come to Chavez in 1963 with the complaint that his labor contractor not only refused to tell him what his hourly wage was for work he had already done, but had kicked him out of the truck when he protested this and let him walk back to town. The police had shown no interest in his case. Chavez learned that Rivera's old car had broken down for good, and that after three days in Delano, the Rivera family was still waiting at the bus station. The Chavezes took the whole family into their own small house, and lent Rivera the now defunct Volvo that sits outside the Chavez house; later, he found them a place to stay, and when Rivera had saved a little money, a cheap car.

When Rivera asked how much he owed him, Chavez answered that he didn't owe him anything; he owed help to other farm workers. Rivera returned Chavez's old car, all polished up; then he disappeared and Chavez forgot him. But six months later he showed up again. Over Chavez's protest, Rivera paid union dues for all the months since Chavez had taken him in, and on the job he spoke so fervently of Chavez that he brought in over one hundred new members. "That spirit was what we were looking for," Chavez says, "and it is our strength."

The first real meeting of the National Farm Workers Association took place in Fresno in September 1962. Here the bold red flag with its black Aztec eagle in a white circle was first revealed by Manuel Chavez, its designer, who ripped down a paper that covered it on the wall. The flag was enormous, sixteen feet by twenty-four. Some of the stunned membership thought that the red looked kind of Communist; others that it looked like a Nazi banner. "It's what you want to see in it," Chavez told them, "what you're conditioned to. To me it looks like a strong, beautiful sign of hope." Finally Manuel, who is rarely at a loss, sprang up and shouted, "When that damn eagle flies, the problems of the farm workers will be solved!" and the day was won.

Ten months later, all but twelve of the two hundred and twelve dues-paying members at that meeting had lost faith in their association. Manuel Chavez still has his 1963 NFWA card with its green eagle; on it is printed: DELANO LOCAL NUMBER 2. CESAR CHAVEZ, GENERAL DIRECTOR. MANUEL CHAVEZ, SECRETARY-TREASURER. Manuel laughed. "I guess Cesar was one local and I was the other. We were the membership, too. It's a good thing Richard was still a carpenter; he was kind of supporting us." In this dark period Chavez could have taken a $21,000-a-year job as a director of the Peace Corps in a four-country region of South America, and it is a considerable tribute to his faith that he refused it. He was penniless, his wife's family was upset, and Helen herself, besides managing the office-home, took care of their eight children. "It was rough on Helen," Drake remembers, "and she got cranky sometimes, but in her own way she was great."

Chavez held on and kept on organizing, and by August 1964 he had a thousand members. "I knew sometimes I was taking the workers' last penny, but it gave NFWA an awful lot of character. They paid just on faith that in the future something would happen," he has said. The dues, then as now, were $3.50 a month.

A number of the new members, including Julio Hernandez, a green-card Mexican who is now a Union officer, came from the town of Corcoran, twenty-five miles northwest of Delano, where on October 4, 1933, five thousand cotton pickers, many of them Mexicans, went out on strike. The Corcoran strike, which spread up and down the cotton fields of the San Joaquin Valley, eventually involved eighteen thousand workers, and was the most significant farm labor rebellion since the IWW protest that culminated in the Wheatland Riot of 1913.

As was customary in the Depression, wages had been drastically depressed by advertising for many more workers than could be used, then letting men with starving families underbid one another for jobs that paid as little as 15 cents an hour. In the thirties the trade unions had small interest in the farm workers, and the cotton strike, like many farm strikes of the period, was led by the Cannery and Agricultural Workers Industrial Union (CAWIU), which was unabashedly Communist in its organization. The growers armed themselves, and after evicting the strikers from their camps, followed them to a rally at the union hall in Pixley, just north of Delano. There, for want of a better plan, they opened fire on the crowd, killing two workers, and a third worker was murdered in Arvin the same day. Eleven growers were arrested, and eleven acquitted.

Like the evictions, the killings served to harden the strikers' cause, and the uprising, which lasted for twenty-four days, won a small wage increase for the workers. But like the Wobblies, the CAWIU leaders were flogged, tarred and feathered, and finally jailed, in fine vigilante tradition, and their union perished like all the rest. (Vigilantism, a kind of organized mob rule that has characterized California racism since 1859, was easily turned from the "yellow peril" to the "Reds." In the thirties it was often led by the American Legion, which boasted in print of taking the law into its own hands and routing out "all un-American influences." In the late thirties, vigilantism was organized by the growers behind a front called the "Associated Farmers," which made no secret of its admiration for the fascism in Europe and engaged in open terrorism against strikers. Its activities were exemplified in the lettuce strike of 1936, when the unopposed vigilantes took over the whole town of Salinas.)

At the time of the Corcoran strike, the ethic of the status quo was expressed most eloquently by an assistant sheriff:

> We protect our farmers here in Kern County. They are our best people. They are always with us. They keep the country going. They put us in here and they can put us out again, so we serve them. But the Mexicans are trash. They have no standard of living. We herd them like pigs.*

Like the signs of Chavez's childhood that read NO DOGS OR MEXICANS ALLOWED, such public statements are unfash-

* Department of Labor Bulletin No. 836 (1945).

ionable today, but the man who said it is probably still alive, and so are his opinions.

With the new surge in membership, Helen Chavez left the cotton fields to take charge of the credit union, and Dolores Huerta moved permanently to Delano to take over the bookkeeping and membership. Gilbert Padilla, a former CSO man who was to become an important leader in the Union, was assigned by the CSO to work with Jim Drake on the problem of the state-run Kern-Tulare labor camps, which the efforts of Drake and Padilla and a lawyer named Gary Bellow finally closed down. "The state was making a big profit on those camps, which were just slums," Drake says, "and when the workers found out about that profit, it wasn't hard to organize a rent strike." The tin shanties, considered temporary even in the thirties, have been replaced by modest housing.

Drake was persuaded by Padilla to join his Tulare workers with Chavez's association, and the merger took place in February 1965. "It wasn't much of a merger," Drake says, "because I only had about a hundred people. But this was when I became involved directly in Cesar's work."

In this period the old grocery store at Albany and Asti streets was acquired, and Chavez and his family sanded and painted it. Mrs. Huerta remembers that first office with great pleasure. "It had an old cement floor, but we waxed it and everything—it was beautiful! And Cesar was so proud of his new desk—he wouldn't let anybody touch it." The red desk, now in Helen's office, had been built by Richard: "I'm really a cabinetmaker by trade, so I made him this desk. He was very proud of it, but it was just a cheap pine desk, you know."

The first strike raised by NFWA took place in March and April 1965, when Epifanio Camacho, representing the rose workers of McFarland, came in and asked Chavez for help in a strike for higher wages. All the workers pledged to go out on strike, but on the morning it was to begin, Dolores Huerta found four workers getting dressed to go to work; she moved her truck into their driveway, blocking their car, and hid the key. Later that morning, representing the Union, she went to the company office; there the foreman called her a Communist and kicked her out. When the pay raise was granted, the strike was broken by the rose workers themselves, who voted to go back without a contract.

During the summer an NFWA strike at Martin's Ranch, led by Gilbert Padilla, won a pay raise for grape pickers, and this small victory, boosting the morale of the new union, encouraged it that September to join in what has become known as the California grape strike, by far the largest and most important farm strike to develop in California since the cotton pickers walked out at Corcoran.

I could not pretend to be nonpartisan about the grape strike, but I was anxious to be as objective as possible, and that first morning in Delano I paid a call on Bruno Dispoto, in the first of a number of attempts to hear and understand the position of the growers. Leroy Chatfield had suggested that I interview a grower named Jack Pandol, whose steadfast conviction that UFWOC answers to Moscow has contributed a good deal to the general sympathy accorded to Cesar Chavez by the press. "Pandol does our work for us," Chatfield said, grinning. "By the time he is finished, we don't have to say a word." Bruno Dispoto had not identified himself with the far-right wing, despite a reputation as the most violent of the growers in his hostility to the Union.

The Delano offices and storage sheds of Dispoto Brothers are located on Glenwood Street, on the west side of the railroad tracks. The outer office, which is entered from the shed platform, has been set up with an eye to consumer relations: there was a bowl of green Thompson seedless grapes and a stack of complimentary car stickers, bright orange-and-black, which bore the counterrevolutionary legend DON'T BUY NEW YORK PRODUCTS. The warm welcome was offset somewhat by a very large man in cowboy boots who was sitting just inside the door with his legs stretched out on a desk. He glowered inhospitably as a secretary showed me into Bruno Dispoto's office, a room in the corner of the building adorned with a photograph of a train and a bowl of plastic fruit.

Mr. Dispoto arrived in a few minutes and sat down behind his desk, under whose glass top, facing the visitor, was a sign reading "AVOID *TENSION*." From the start he was pleasant and hospitable, the antithesis of *El Malcriado*'s propaganda grower in planter's hat, dark glasses and jackboots, clutching a black stogy and a whip; on a busy day, he took more than an hour to accommodate an interviewer who would probably be critical in print of his own hard-won way of life.

Dispoto is big, open-faced and balding, with small eyes and big active hands; as he talks, he sniffs through his nose like a boxer. He declared immediately that the strike and boycott had not bothered him a bit, that all the growers were enjoying one of the finest grape deals in years, from the Coachella Valley right on northward. During my visit this claim was substantiated by a call from a New York buyer who had ordered eight thousand boxes the previous week and needed more. "You see?" Dispoto exulted as he hung up. "I can't *supply* all my orders! *That's* how the so-called boycott is working in New York!"

According to Dispoto, the only growers bothered by the Union were the ones who had signed contracts with it. Di Giorgio and Schenley, he said, had had to give up table grapes because of the Union's failure to supply workers, and Di Giorgio had been forced to shut down its vineyards at Sierra Vista and Borrego Springs. "At Sierra Vista they used to give work to a couple of thousand people; now there's just one—a guard. If Mister Cesar Chavez were sincere, if there had been performance on the contract, he could walk down Main Street and say hello to any grower, but he has less support now in the work force than at any time since he started. Hell, they could put me under Union contract in ten days if they could get my workers. In the harvest season I'd have no choice, because your table grape is perishable, a semiluxury item. There your money sits on the vines, and you're susceptible to all kinds of risks—we're the biggest gamblers in America! But he hasn't got the workers. This boycott in the East shows how desperate he is; it's the final proof that the strike here in California has been a dismal failure."

The man in cowboy boots came in and leaned against the wall, and Bruno Dispoto introduced his brother Charlie, who acknowledged my name with the same glowering gaze with which he had greeted me outside. After a moment, deciding to follow his brother's lead, he permitted his mouth to fall open in a kind of smile.

Like Bruno, Charles Dispoto was born in the New York area; he started out in life as a shoeshine boy. Four years ago he gave up the contracting business to join Bruno in California and take up farming, which he described as "the same rat race." Frowning again, less in displeasure than bewilderment, he stared at his brother, who was discussing the New York market ("New York is the biggest and has got to be the best; you go out in the country, like Louisiana, the product don't have to be so good"); insecticides ("You can't use these things indiscriminately, because the Public Health people come down on you. Damage to cattle and crops—you got to watch out for damage suits"); and his private airplane, which he flies himself to visit Dispoto holdings in northern California and Arizona.

I could not help but notice that Dispoto made no mention of the threat of pesticides to people, notably farm workers. Still, he was articulate and persuasive, and presented the case for the growers very well. With most of his problems—the cost-price squeeze without government price supports, spiraling taxes, large overhead, the risk of bad weather and a perishable crop—I was familiar and sympathetic, since I live all year on Long Island in a farming community in Suffolk, the biggest agricultural county in New York State, and have listened to the problems of my neighbors. Today's farmers in Suffolk are predominantly of Polish origin, with an Old World heritage of potatoes, and they correspond closely in their attitudes to the Yugoslav and Italian immigrant families of Kern County, who carried their experience of the Mediterranean vineyards west to California. The Di Giorgios have become absentee landlords, but it was a Di Giorgio from Sicily who developed the first vineyards in the region a half-century ago.

Like the San Joaquin Valley immigrants, the Suffolk farmers came mostly in the twenties, as common laborers or near bond-servants to Yankee farmers or to a relative who had already established a small holding, and their own farms were acquired and built painfully, with "sweat equity." Those who made it are a tough, bitter breed; they will not give an inch, and their intransigence is understandable. Having climbed out of poverty the hard way, they feel threatened by and harsh toward the poor who have not escaped. Anxious to consolidate their new security, they are politically conservative, and as in California, tend to evoke the specter of Communism at the slightest threat to the status quo. Thus, the New York farmers claim that the migrants, 98 percent of whom are black, are incapable of collective bargaining on their own behalf and should therefore be denied the protection of the State Labor Relations Act, lest Communist influences take over.

Mr. Dispoto was saying that Delano's grape pickers had a higher hourly wage and enjoyed more benefits and protective laws than any farm workers in the nation. This is like saying that American blacks have no cause for dissatisfaction, since they own more clothes than those in Africa, but probably it is true: in 1967 the average hourly wage of farm workers in South Carolina, for instance, was 89 cents. But it is also true that the 1967 average income of the farm worker in California was less than $1,500, or not even half of the annual income beneath which a family is statistically assigned the status of poverty. This is because the work is seasonal, and heavily dependent on harvest time; the hourly wage does not count for much when a man may find work less than six months in the year.

In Suffolk County the main crop is potatoes, the harvest of which is now almost entirely automated. The county's dwindling number of migrant workers labor mostly in the packing sheds, and some of the potato processors have signed contracts with the Teamsters, Local No. 202. The contract assures a dues-paying member of some basic protections, such as workmen's compensation and grievance arbitration, but the hourly wage and the minimum workweek are set so low (twenty-four hours per week, except during the harvest season, September through November, when it is twenty-six) that in August 1968 a union-protected picker was guaranteed no more than $38.40 per week, except in "circumstances beyond the Employer's control," including Acts of God and machinery breakdown, when he would make even less. The sense of the contract, under the "Management's Rights" clause, gives an idea why employers in New York and California are not frightened to do business with the Teamsters:

Sec. 7. The Management of the Business and the direction of the working forces, including but not limited to the right to hire, schedule hours and shifts, assign employees to shifts, suspend, promote, transfer or discharge for proper cause, and the right to relieve an employee from duty because of lack of work or for other legitimate reasons, is vested exclusively in the Employer. The determination and establishment or modification of performances standards for all operations is reserved in the Management. In the event of change in equipment, Management shall have the right to reduce the working force, if in the sole judgment of Management such reduction of force is fairly required, and nothing in this agreement shall be construed to limit or in any way restrict the right of Management to adopt, install or operate new or improved equipment or methods of operation.

Nothing herein contained shall be intended or shall be considered as a waiver of any of the usual, inherent, and fundamental rights of Management whether the same were exercised heretofore, and the same are hereby expressly reserved to the Employer.

The New York State model-housing code specifically excludes migrant housing; as a result, its labor camps are unbelievably filthy. New York farm workers in general have no written contracts, no unemployment insurance, no minimum workweek guarantees; in addition, migrant workers are excluded from social security and workmen's compensation (i.e., disability insurance, which they need badly; though farm workers comprise only 7 percent of American labor, they suffer 22 percent of the fatal work accidents, from machinery, pesticides, and other causes), not to speak of many other basic accommodations—toilet facilities on the job are an example—which all other workers in America accept as a matter of course. Finally, the state minimum-wage law is commonly evaded by a system known as "downtime": when a machine breaks down or a truck is delayed, or when, for any reason, the employee is not actually working, he may be laid off during the workday, or not put on the payroll until noon.

In other words, a man who shows up on the job and is ready to work for fourteen hours may return to camp with $5 or $6—less than the exorbitant sums deducted from his pay by white employers and black labor contractors for crowded, filthy quarters, dangerous transportation, wretched food, and cheap wine sold at double the price, without a license. Since in many cases the migrant cannot read or write, he probably suspects—probably correctly— that he has been cheated as well as overcharged. At the end of his lonely exile he will, if he is lucky, make his way back to Arkansas or Virginia or Mississippi, not with the savings for his family that he had been promised, but dead broke or in debt.

Walter—he never told us his middle name—a middle-aged (in appearance much older) Negro migrant in the infamous Cutchogue Labor Camp, told me that he didn't like it at all; he made it quite clear, drunk though he was (he had been idle, yet confined like an animal to the fenced-in camp for five weeks with no other diversion), that he hated it; that he lived in fear of the crew leader, the processor, the white community outside, and the migrants he worked with. As if trapped in the basement of a burning building, he cried for help: "Tell 'em! Let 'em know what goes on! Tell it so they listen!"*

I live near Bridgehampton, in Suffolk County. After the harvest in the fall the main street of the town and the outlying highway are wandered by black outcasts of both sexes who are too broke, sick or drunk to make their way home. Sodden people with Twister wine in paper bags sit in big broken cars outside the liquor store; black faces haunt the winter dumps with the rats and gulls. When one has seen the shantytowns off the Bridgehampton–Sag Harbor Road and the labor camps in the scrub woods and hollows, it comes as no surprise that in the last two years, six farm workers in the state died in three separate fires when their rickety housing went up in flames; the most recent fire occurred in January 1968 in Bridgehampton, taking the lives of three black workers and injuring others. In the eighteen months before the Bridgehampton fire, that labor camp had been repeatedly condemned by county inspectors for multiple violations of safety and health standards (including the use of the unvented kerosene heater that caused the deaths), and nothing was done; the local justice of the peace had repeatedly granted delays in court action. The Suffolk County Human Relations Commission, a private

* Jack Cook, *Catholic Worker*, July 1967.

organization that works hard to call attention to the migrants' plight, admits that almost nothing has been accomplished.

A Suffolk County psychologist predicts a high crime rate among migrants due to childhood psychosis based on frustration, loss of hope and "withdrawal as the child becomes aware of his place in the world." This withdrawal leads to the apathy which the employers interpret, according to need, as "laziness" or "contentment with their lot." A friend of mine who works with migrant children in my own village has met some who have never seen salt water; the ocean, three miles south, and the bay, three miles north, are beyond their reach.

Most good Americans, like "good Germans," have managed to stay unaware of inhumanity in their own country. Yet almost every state uses seasonal farm workers for one harvest or another, and most of them come in migrant streams from Texas and Florida; the heaviest concentrations gather in the coastal and north-central states, especially Wisconsin and Michigan. Everywhere, their condition is appalling. Despite recent wage increases, the relative economic position of the farm workers, like that of the ghetto poor and other destitute groups in whose "progress" we so fervently wish to believe, is worsening, mostly because migrant children, from nutrition to education, are the most deprived human creatures in America. But we who eat the food the migrants pick can't bear to examine their plight honestly, because their misery refutes the American way of life. For instance, pickle cucumbers—one of the most difficult stoop-labor crops, the vines being close to the ground and tough—are harvested in Wisconsin. Yet the arguments, in 1966, of the Wisconsin Better Government Committee against an increase in the minimum wage included the statement that migrants enjoyed "more freedoms than the average American" and that the legislature should be "extremely cautious in legislating away the freedoms of one of the few remaining free groups in this country." Infant mortality among these free spirits is 125 percent higher than the national average; the accident rate is 300 percent higher; the life expectancy for migrants is forty-nine years.

(Our need to delude ourselves has lessened very little since 1920, when writers could speak of the migrant's miserable life journey as "a few rainbow-tinted years in the orchards of California." The light-hearted "gasoline gypsies" were envied by one and all: "Many orchardists have erected dance pavilions and laid out croquet grounds . . . to add to the pleasure of the tired help after a long day's work under the rays of the torrid sun.")

The patriotic emphasis on the word "freedom" only makes the Wisconsin hypocrisy more sickening; one prefers the honest brutality of Mr. Louis Pizzo, a New Jersey farmer whose qualities won him a membership on the Governor's Migrant Labor Board. Forbidding VISTA volunteers to enter his fields, he bellowed, "See those people in the field? Well, they're nothing, I tell you, nothing! They never were nothing, they never will be nothing, and you and me and God Almighty ain't going to change them! They gave me the bottom of the barrel and I'd fire them all, clean them from the fields, if you'd get me someone else!"

Bruno Dispoto claimed a good relationship with his workers; he even went so far as to acknowledge, toward the end of our long talk, that there was right on both sides of the fence. I asked why, in that case, it would not be useful to discuss mutual problems with Chavez; after all, Chavez was not out to destroy the industry that gave work to so many of his people. For the first time Mr. Dispoto's face lost its affability, and I got a glimpse of the Bruno Dispoto of yore. "It would be of *no* use to me to talk with *Mister* Cesar Chavez! If we talk to a union, it's going to be the Teamsters or somebody!"

Mr. Dispoto seemed to realize that his mask had slipped, and he hurried to account for himself: only the week before, the Delano Chamber of Commerce had met to discuss Delano's "image gap" in the eyes of America. "Anyway"— he was smiling again—"I'm management, not labor." I asked if he had ever met Chavez and he said that he had, once, on the picket line. "Those days were kind of hysterical." He attempted to laugh, as if in recollection of grand college years, but the mirth gave way quickly to a frown of concern. "Mister Cesar Chavez is talking about taking over this state—I don't like that. Too much 'Viva Zapata' and down with the Caucasians, *la raza,* and all that. Mister Cesar Chavez is talking about *revolución.* Remember, California once belonged to Mexico, and he's saying, 'Look, you dumb Mexicans, you lost it, now let's get it back!'" He glanced at me to see if I shared his outrage, and after a moment I inquired how he had come by such inflammatory information. He said that Chavez's true intentions were revealed regularly by "my colored pastor." Dispoto was referring to the Reverend R. B. Moore of St. Paul's Baptist Church in Delano. This minister, the only black man in the Kiwanis Club, was cited as an example of democracy in Delano, which Dispoto described as one of the most integrated towns in all America, where people of many nationalities live in concord. These happy reflections restored his good humor, and he made the kind offer of a complete tour of his vineyards and labor camps the following day. "We've got nothing to hide. You can talk to my workers, and we don't tell them what to say."

The next afternoon, with Mrs. Israel, I followed Dispoto eastward through the farmland. Vineyards gave way to the dark green of citrus groves, then reappeared again. In a little while Dispoto's car turned off onto the dirt road of the ranch, where it met a police car on its way out. The two vehicles stopped side by side, idling in the midday dust while their occupants consulted; then the police car moved on again, and we trailed our host down the ranch road past plantings of red Ribier grapes, still unripe, to an area well away from the highway. Here a small crew of workers had begun the harvest of green Thompson seedless. Families of workers in straw hats and bright handkerchiefs peered at us from the shadow of the vines, and their foremen and box checkers were jollied by the boss, who appeared to know many of his people by their first name. Carts had been supplied for lugging the grapes down the rows, and in the background, like a new green sentry box, stood a portable toilet, the first I had seen in the vineyards and—though I was to stay nine more days—the last.

Strolling up and down his rows, Mr. Dispoto consumed grapes without hesitation; three or four days after spraying, he said, there are no ill effects. In this, of course, he is mistaken, unless a heavy rain has intervened. The sulphur dust that burns away the mildew spores and the chlorinated hydrocarbons that wipe out hoppers and mites are very damaging to the human system. Still, washing food in the Delano area is of doubtful benefit, since according to researches conducted by the University of California at Berkeley, so much residue from chemical sprays and fertilizers has leached down to the water table that even the ground water is grossly polluted and should be considered highly dangerous to infants. Nearly half of all Americans already drink water that is "inferior" or worse by public health standards, but in few places has contamination gone so deep as in Delano.

Mr. Dispoto introduced us to his foreman and to his son, a good-looking boy of about sixteen. The cheerful harvest atmosphere was not lessened by Mr. Dispoto's own good humor, which graced his explanation of the interesting details of grape culture; he offered to answer any questions that we cared to ask. Mrs. Israel asked immediately if Dispoto Brothers was using HI-COLOR labels on their product, and Dispoto acknowledged that he was; in fact, he had supplied grapes to Di Giorgio's Earl Packing Company for several years. He denied that the use of HI-COLOR, which circumvented the boycott, accounted for the prosperity of his company; only 15 percent of his crop, he said, was labeled HI-COLOR, the rest going out under his own label, MARY JO, so called in honor of his wife, Mrs. Mary Jo Dispoto. Whether or not he felt uneasy about the use of the HI-COLOR label, it was fortunate that Mr. Dispoto was frank about it, since we passed a large stack of HI-COLOR boxes on the way over to the labor camps.

On this property Dispoto Brothers operates two camps, one old, one new. The new camp, Mr. Dispoto confessed, was not as nice as the new camp at Giumarra, which is considered a showpiece in Delano. Anyway, it would not open until the following week, when the harvest workers would arrive in numbers; he was not at all anxious to show it off.

"We just utilize it during harvesting," he repeated. Its housing, which we passed in the course of our tour, looked bare and institutional, thrust up rudely out of a barren area in the green flats.

The old camp is occupied by those few workers who remain at the ranch all year; unlike most growers, Dispoto charges no rent for the rooms. Since the majority of the non-migrant Mexicans have families and live in Delano, or Pixley or Earlimart, the camp inhabitants are chiefly old Filipinos, the last of the wave imported to California in the 1920's. These men had believed that they would soon make enough money to send home for their women, but few of them ever did. Some were lucky enough to get back to the Philippines, but many more linger on in labor camps like this one, up and down the state. The lonely fate of these Filipinos rivals the history of the Nisei Japanese as one of the most pathetic episodes in the progress of California.

Mr. Dispoto treated us to soda pop from a dispenser in the old labor camp's new mess hall and joined us in a sample meal of fish, meat, several vegetables, salad, butter, bread, dessert—everything, in fact, but soup and nuts. It was a typical workers' meal, he said, and in truth it was very good. The workers themselves, unfortunately, were not present to eat it, since all but a few were still in the fields when we arrived. A few old Filipinos came and went, however, and Dispoto asked one of them to show us his quarters. This man seemed to be in charge of the camp, and had a small room to himself. He was embarrassed that nudes and Virgins were shoulder to shoulder on his walls, but he seemed less embarrassed than Mr. Dispoto, who became increasingly less hospitable as we snooped around. Mrs. Israel, who wandered off by herself, reported later that the men's quarters were cramped and dirty, the washroom filthy. I myself saw the old dining room, now the recreation room; it was still dingy and windowless, and must have been awful.

In fairness to Mr. Dispoto, it should be said that the most wretched worker camps are in my own state of New York; some of these have been described as "the worst slums in America." But a few years ago, after a surprise visit to three labor camps in the Salinas Valley, Secretary of Labor Willard Wirtz said, "I'm glad I hadn't eaten first. I would have vomited." This could scarcely be said of the Dispoto camp, or, to my knowledge, of any ranch camp in the area, but it could have been only a few years ago, before the publicity brought to California by the grape strike put pressure on the state to enforce at least a few of the protective laws in which the growers take such pride.

3

ON August 2 I drove down to Lamont, a farming town southeast of Bakersfield, where a small vineyard off Sandrini Road was to be picketed. The Lamont-Arvin–Weed Patch fields, celebrated by John Steinbeck in *The Grapes of Wrath*, are the southernmost in the San Joaquin Valley; here the grape harvest, which had scarcely begun in Delano, thirty-five miles to the north, was virtually complete.

At dawn, the hot summer air was already windless, and a haze of unsettled dust shrouded the sunrise. Trucks were unloading empty grape boxes at the ends of the long rows, which, in the early light, threw a grid of shadows on the dusty service lanes; the grape leaves looked almost fresh in the thin dew. Standing beside their pickups, the growers and foremen watched my strange car from a long way off.

As I drew up behind the waiting vehicles, two men in the middle of the road began to argue. One said, "You don't want to do that, Abe! You don't want to do that! You do that and they'll know they're getting to you!" But the other, small and bespectacled, stomped over to my car. "You on our side?" he demanded. His companion, a husky, dark-haired man in his late twenties, came over to calm him down. Politely, to elicit my identity, he introduced the small man, Abe Haddad; "Barling's my name," he added, hand extended. "Most people around here call me Butch." He glanced at Haddad, who glared at me, unmollified. "Our dads are partners in this field," Barling explained.

I asked him how they had known they would be picketed this morning. "How did *you* know?" he countered. I said that I had learned it from the Union office. "Well, we have a spy system too," he said, "but their system is a hell of a lot better." He indicated the unpicked vines near the public road, where his pickers would work within easy reach of the voices from the picket line. The pickets, he said, would arrive around seven-thirty, when the pickers were well settled at their work. If even one worker could be persuaded to walk off the job and give his name to the U.S. Department of Labor agents assigned to the area, then a labor dispute would be certified and a strike declared: an official dispute gives the Union a legal basis for prosecution, since to use green-card labor to break a strike that has been certified is against the law. "I think me and Johnson's are the only ones left around here that don't have a certified strike," Barling remarked, but in fact he was the last; several people had walked off the Johnson Farm after work the day before.

Plainly, Haddad and Barling felt less cheerful about the strike than Bruno Dispoto, but they agreed with Dispoto that Chavez had lost ground with the workers. "As far as your local help here," Haddad said, "they don't want no part of him. They wish he'd get the hell out of here," he added, looking wistful. I asked why. "Because they're makin more money here than they could ever make with the Union!" Haddad said.

"The Union, they only work a forty-hour week," Barling said, "so even with their wage increase they make less money." Like Dispoto, they cited the sad case of Di Giorgio (pronounced locally "Die-George-y-o"). "On your Union ranches, sure, the wages are just as good, maybe better, but they don't let 'em work the hours, work the days. Why, Di Giorgio's was cryin on the radio for plum pickers and they couldn't get 'em. The Union can't supply the help! The Union is tryin to run a farm like a factory, and you can't run a farm like a factory! To the grower, it makes the costs so high that he's out of business—that's why Di Giorgio's ain't pickin a single table grape this year. They just can't make it under Union conditions."

Haddad described how, at Di Giorgio, there was a Union irrigator assigned to each irrigation pipe line in the vineyards, although all the lines together could readily be maintained by one or two men. "You can't afford that," Barling said. "Di Giorgio's old Sierra Vista Ranch, up there in Delano, they used to hire maybe three thousand people in harvest time; now all that's finished, gone. They're hiring just one man now—a guard."

The death of the Sierra Vista Ranch is a symbol to the growers of what could befall them under a UFWOC contract, but their version is less than half the truth. The Friant-Kern Canal, which reached the Delano area in 1951, saved the fledgling grape industry, and federal water, almost the whole cost of which is borne by the taxpayers, is the sole reason that the Delano grape growers are still in business. To protect the huge public investment in the rerouted rivers that water the San Joaquin Valley, the Bureau of Reclamation decreed that farms of over 160 acres—or 320 acres if the farmer was married—had to develop their own water, which the one-family farms could no longer afford to do after the water table sank. But in customary deference to the large grower, use of the public water for unlimited acreage was granted if the company offered its excess land for sale after ten years. Extensions at the 4,400-acre Sierra Vista Ranch were granted freely at the company's request, and would doubtless have continued indefinitely but for the bad publicity about the arrangement which grew out of the grape strike. Even before the further extensions were denied, Di Giorgio had decided to sell the property, which is now farmed by a dozen different growers. The harvest workers hired at Sierra Vista numbered two thousand at the most; a large portion of that number must be hired to this day, because the vines are still in production.

When Haddad had gone, Barling acknowledged that the boycott had hurt: the 15 percent of the market lost, he said, was equivalent to 15 percent overproduction—in effect, his profit. "Today the market is three dollars a box—I'm breaking even. Next week I could be going backwards." Unlike Haddad, he was still able to laugh a little at his own helplessness.

In their reaction to the grape strike, the difference between Barling and Dispoto is the same as between the smaller grower and the large, and even the small grower is far better off than the man with the family farm. Two thirds of California's farms have fewer than 100 acres, and even without the pressure of a strike, the family farms are going under; the state has lost sixty-one thousand farms— nearly half—in the last decade. Since 1960, more than a quarter of America's family farms have vanished, but it is the family that vanishes rather than the farm; farmland, absorbed by the large growers, has decreased only 4 percent in the same period. The small farm with small capital and small margin can afford neither the labor force nor the new machinery of automation that keep increasing the advantage of the factory farm: 7 percent of California's farms employ 75 percent of the hired labor. Rarely do the small farms co-operate in their production and distribution facilities, which are notoriously archaic and inefficient, or join forces to support the price of their smaller crop. Big growers, such as Dispoto, or huge corporate enterprises, such as Di Giorgio, which have mutual interests (and often joint directorships) with banks, land monopolies, canneries and railroads, are known as "agribusiness," and they are far more dangerous to Barling than Chavez's union. With their marketing volume, they can underbid the small grower and still make money; it is they who set the prices. Furthermore, the small farmer's crops, often worked by himself, must compete with crops produced by low-wage labor; Union wages would actually benefit the small farmers, whose National Farmers Union supports UFWOC demands. But the small growers are dominated by the large, and as a result they will fall one by one to the farm factories which are waiting to absorb them.

Across the road, irrigation pumps watered the second potato planting of the year. Barling said that thirty years before, when his dad was raising potatoes, it cost $250 to $300 to grow one acre; since then, everything from land taxes to the cost of tractors had nearly doubled, but the price of potatoes had remained the same. The figures of this cost-price squeeze are identical in the potato country of Long Island.

We stood around for a while, awaiting the strikers. Before long Barling said, "Here they come now." A caravan of ancient cars had appeared on Sandrini Road. They drew off the pavement, and fifteen or twenty people got out, scratching and stretching. One of the cars had a bumper sticker with the small silhouette of a man raising a rifle above his head, and the legend UNIDOS CON LA RAZA. Carrying horns and HUELGA banners, the strikers split into two groups, stationing themselves opposite the two main crews of pickers.

"Well, this is a pretty good-looking group," Barling said, starting across the highway. "Sometimes we get a lot of these guys with long hair and beards." He grinned bitterly through his early-morning stubble. " 'Course, *we* know they're grape pickers," he added. "Don't get me wrong."

For the first time and the last, we laughed together. Barling crossed the public road. Arms folded on his chest, legs wide apart, he took up a position where his workers could get a good look at the boss.

Up and down the road, red strike flags fluttered, the only brightness in the sunny haze that stretched away to the brown shadows of the Tehachapi Mountains. Not all the flags had a white circle, but all had a handsewn version of Manuel Chavez's eagle, black and barbaric. The flags were festive, and in the air was that feeling of the arena which precedes a bugle note and the commencement of a blood sport. Already the voices of the picket line were calling to the workers: "*¡Venga! ¡Véngase! ¡Compañero!*" "*¡Huelga! ¡Huel-ga!*"

To Chavez, the picket line is the best school for organizers. "If a man comes out of the field and goes on the picket line, even for one day, he'll never be the same. The picket line is the best possible education. Some labor people came to Delano and said, 'Where do you train people? Where are your classrooms?' I took them to the picket line. *That's* where we train people. That's the best training. The labor people didn't get it. They stayed a week and went back to their big jobs and comfortable homes. They hadn't seen training, but the people here see it and I see it. The picket line is where a man makes his commitment, and it's irrevocable; and the longer he's on the picket line, the stronger the commitment. The workers on the ranch committees who don't know how to speak, or who never speak —after five days on the picket lines they speak right out, and they speak better.

"A lot of workers make their commitment when nobody sees them; they just leave the job, and they don't come back. But you get a guy who in front of the boss, in front of all the other guys, throws down his tools and marches right out to the picket line, that's an exceptional guy, and that's the kind we have out on the strike.

"Oh, the picket line is a beautiful thing, because it does something to a human being. People associate strikes with violence, and we've removed the violence. Then people begin to understand what we're doing, you know, and after that, they're not afraid. And if you're not afraid of that kind of thing, then you're not afraid of guns. If you have a gun and they do too, then you can be frightened because it becomes a question of who gets shot first. But if you have no gun and they have one, then—well, the guy with the gun has a lot harder decision to make than you have. You're just—well, *there*, and it's up to him to do something."

One observer has described the picket-line phenomenon very well. The strikers seemed to him "the only people I had seen in months who seemed positively happy and free from self-pity. In their response to me, they had been friendlier and more open, by far, than most of the people I meet, though my speech and manner must have struck them as very unlike their own I wondered why they had trusted me; then I realized that, of course, they hadn't. It was themselves they had trusted, such people do not fear strangers. Whether he wins *La Huelga* or not, this Cesar Chavez has done, or rather, has taught his people to do for themselves. Nothing I know of in the history of labor in America shows as much sheer creativity . . . as much respect for what people, however poor, might make of their own lives once they understood the dynamics of their society."*

In the first months of the strike, during the autumn of 1965, local sheriffs and the state police of Kern and Tulare counties followed the strikers everywhere they went. At that time many of the ranch foremen carried guns, and shotgun blasts, destroying picket signs and car windows, echoed the violence on the picket line. The growers, startled when several hundred harvest workers walked out in the first few days, meant to see to it that this strike was broken as quickly as all the rest, and they set about their business with a will. Under the benevolent gaze of the police, they marched up and down the picket lines, slamming the strikers with their elbows, kicking them, stomping their cowboy boots down on their toes; they cursed them, spit on them and brushed them narrowly with speeding trucks. On September 23, while picketing the house of a scab labor contractor in Delano, a small striker named Israel Garza was knocked down repeatedly by a grower named Milan Caratan before the police, warned by Chavez that he could not control his outraged strikers if this continued, removed Caratan from the scene. The police reported to the Fresno *Bee* that they had dispersed the crowd "when one picket fell down."

* Edgar Z. Friedenberg, in the *New York Review of Books*.

The strikers, committed to nonviolence, accepted this treatment in the expectation that arrests would soon be made, but those arrested were invariably strikers, who were taken into custody for such offenses as public use of bull horns, public use of the word *"huelga,"* and in one case, public reading of Jack London's "Definition of a Scab." Union protests and filed complaints to the authorities were politely accepted, then deferred or disregarded. But on October 19, when the sheriffs jailed forty-four pickets, including several ministers and Helen Chavez, merely for shouting *"¡Huelga!"* a rumble of concern was heard across the nation. Chavez, who was speaking at Berkeley, announced the mass arrest to his student audience. "Don't eat today," he told them. "We need your lunch money." The Berkeley students took up a collection of $6,700.

In Delano, where the strike began, the most aggressive of the growers were the Dispoto brothers. Not satisfied with traditional harassments, they threatened the strike line with Doberman pinschers and sprayed it with sand, spit, obscenities and poisonous insecticides: the volunteers and clergymen were especially loathsome to Bruno Dispoto, who called them "creeps," "fairies," and worse. To this day, Union people are amused in a puzzled way at the huge fury of the Dispotos, who are both very large in comparison to most Mexicans and Filipinos, and were not ashamed to take advantage of their size. Chavez says his ribs still ache from the elbows of Bruno Dispoto, and Dolores Huerta recalls being picked up off the ground by Charles and shaken; had he not been cowed by the outcries of some Filipino strikers, Mrs. Huerta says, he would have hit her.

"It was Bruno who ran one of our pickets down," Chavez remembers. "Backed into him and knocked him down. We tried to take him to court, but the cops wouldn't do anything. And Charles Dispoto, the brother, he beat up Hector Abeytia, who is crippled—he has an artificial leg. Hector was once on the Governor's Farm Labor Committee, but we still had to raise hell all over the state before we could get the local police to make an arrest. They fined Dispoto ten or fifteen dollars."

Of all the tactics of harassment, the speeding trucks were the most dangerous, but repeated complaints got nothing more from the police than the statement that no crime had been committed. Inevitably, a striker was not quick enough and was run down.

> On or about Oct. 15, 1966, at the packing shed located at Garces Highway and Glenwood St. in the City of Delano, County of Kern, State of California, at or about the hour of 10 A.M. of the same day, defendant Lowell Jordan Schy, acting within the course and scope of his employment, did maliciously, deliberately, and willfully assault and batter plaintiff by driving a flatbed truck, California license number W49–554, over plaintiff's body . . .

The plaintiff was Manuel Rivera, the man whom Chavez had befriended a couple of years before. Rivera, who became permanently crippled, nearly lost his life. In 1965 he had been one of the first workers to walk off the job and join the strike; despite his accident, he has never regretted it. He still holds a job at Schenley, and is grateful for the security that the Union gives him. "In the old days they just fire you any time they want," he told me. He is a cheerful man, with curly gray hair and a great smile; the day I talked to him, he was sitting in his small bungalow not far from Union headquarters, against a pink wall decorated with wedding pictures and a portrait of the Virgin. "As a leader, Cesar is the best of any; he is not playing games with us," Rivera said. "He is not capable of selling us out."

Schy, the man who crippled Rivera, was not a trucker but a salesman; he got angry when the drivers refused to cross the picket line (one driver was shamed out of it when his two sons, supporters of Chavez, came to the picket line and shouted at him) and decided to man a truck himself. Having recklessly run down Rivera, he rolled up the windows of the cab and subsided into a funk.

Chavez had left the scene a few minutes before the accident; Helen Chavez phoned him at the office and he came rushing back. Schy was actually yelling for Cesar Chavez to come and save him, but Chavez could not reach the truck door through the angry crowd. Finally he crawled under the truck bed and surfaced again at the running board of the cab, where he rose like a vision before the startled mob. But the people were cursing his nonviolence; they wanted blood, and Chavez was in their way. Chavez yelled that they would have to get him too, then, and finally the people in front calmed down enough to listen, and he brought them back under control. He escorted Schy to the packing-shed offices, where he confronted the owner, a grower named Mosesian. "That was the maddest I ever got," Chavez says. "I really let him have it. I told him, 'You people value your damn money more than you value human life!' " Mosesian was sheepish and sorry, but subsequently a warrant was sworn out for the arrest of Manuel Rivera for obstructing traffic; in Kern County courts, this was considered good and sufficient cause for delaying the case indefinitely. Though the case is still pending, Rivera has received no compensation of any kind, and Schy is still unpunished.

The episode caused a Filipino member of the Union named Alfonso Pereira to lose faith in the nonviolent philosophy. He told Gilbert Padilla that he was old and despondent and wanted to trade his life for that of a grower. He was not a striker, and when Padilla sent him home Pereira said, "You'll be hearing from me." He got into his car, drove around the lot to pick up speed and then launched himself at a trio of growers by the roadside. All but one jumped clear; the victim, John Zaninovich, got away with a broken hip. Unlike Schy, Pereira was dealt with swiftly by the courts; he went off without regrets to spend a year in jail, happy in the relief of a lifetime of bitterness.

"Almost everybody closely associated with the strike agrees tactically on nonviolence," Jim Drake says. "A percentage of that group agrees philosophically. But you can agree philosophically and still lose your temper. That time Manuel Rivera was run over, the police were very Gestapo-like, more so than ever before. They were marching with their clubs, up to the picket line, practically goose-stepping. And everybody thought Rivera was going to die; he was lying there helpless. So they wanted to get the cops and the driver. The driver was yelling for Cesar! He was really frightened and he wanted Cesar to come and save him. Afterward one of the strikers, carrying a gun, walked up to Cesar and said, 'Good-bye, it's been nice knowing you'; he said how enjoyable it had been to work with Cesar and the Union. So Cesar said, 'Where are you going?' and the man said, 'I'm going over there to kill that guy.' So Cesar put his arm around him and said, 'Let's take a little walk.' The point is, in a situation like that you forget your philosophy. I've been on the picket line ten different times when I didn't even know myself; you just see red and you have to do something."

The public attention attracted by these episodes made the chamber of commerce nervous about Delano's "image," and to avoid the loss of local support, the growers were forced to moderate both their violence and their public statements, which thereafter were released by Mr. J. G. Brosmer, a man who is more or less identical with a public relations outfit called the Agricultural Labor Board. As a result, the police in the San Joaquin Valley have been able to withdraw most of their surveillance, which had become expensive.

In the Coachella Valley, a rich, irrigated desert region southeast of Palm Springs, the old ways are still in favor. The harvest strike in the Coachella Valley was declared on June 17, 1968. "We met at three-thirty every morning and were on the picket line by four-thirty or five," Jim Drake recalls. "For ten days straight, we worked from three until midnight in 120-degree heat. I was kind of acting as Cesar's bodyguard, eating and sleeping with him, and I was fighting to keep up with him; he puts out a lot of energy on the strike line. But every morning in the Coachella, between five and six, I would be shaking; that's how certain I was that something was going to happen."

A number of things *did* happen, many of them violent. Manuel Chavez showed to a local sheriff the tire marks of a truck that had swerved onto the shoulder and brushed two strikers, and was duly informed that no crime had been committed. "Sure, I believe a little bit in nonviolence," Manuel says, "but not all the way. Sometimes you got to put on a little pressure." Manuel later caught up with the trucker, who thereafter, as Manuel put it, became "neutral."

A few days later a picket was struck by a car, then dragged into the vineyard and beaten. In turn, the growers accused UFWOC of "sensationalism, terrorism and violence," including harassment of nonstriking workers, in the fields and out. A lot of these charges were true; the majority of the strikers could not be kept under control.

After twelve days Chavez withdrew his picket captains, sending them off to boycott in the Eastern cities. The strike no longer justified the risk of violence, having been broken effectively by a federal court order obtained in Los Angeles by Giumarra. On the grounds that the law was unconstitutional, the injunction forbade the U.S. Immigration Service to enforce the Justice Department regulation which prohibits introduction of green-card Mexicans into fields where a labor dispute has been certified, and the workers who had sacrificed high harvest wages to walk off the job were replaced immediately by scabs trucked in from Mexicali, fifty miles away. (After the harvest was completed, the courts decided that this law was constitutional after all.) In addition, the court ordained that picketers must stand two hundred feet apart, where they were at the mercy of foremen and contractors. Finally, the Coachella City Council closed the park where the farm workers' meetings had been held. (Chavez was so outraged by this fresh evidence of Establishment collusion that he yelled publicly, "That's gringo justice!"—the only time, he now says sheepishly, that he can ever recall having used the word "gringo" in anger.)

Still, Chavez regards the Coachella campaign as a Union victory. "We waited and we waited, and we hit them right at the beginning of the harvest of the Thompson seedless, and then we pulled back. We struck for twelve days, hard, and then pulled back. The whole thing cost us pennies, but it cost them two and a half million. [This was also the estimate of the growers' magazine, *California Farmer*.] And then one morning they came out with their picketing injunctions—by that time they had laws against everything we did, against *striking*, almost—but we were gone. We had left the night before. The people are all over the state, working now; we'll meet again in the Coachella in October, when the pruning starts."

Jim Drake agrees. "The growers say Coachella was a failure because we got no contracts there, but we got a lot of new members, and we learned a lot. I grew up down there in Thermal, and I was very pleased by the spirit of the workers, because the Coachella is a frightened place; it's like organizing Mississippi. And next year I think we'll win."

Despite the absence of police in the San Joaquin Valley, or perhaps because of it, there remains an atmosphere of impending violence between the opposing sides. Butch Barling pointed out the two Labor Department officials and a heavy man in a white shirt who leaned against his pale-blue car, arms folded. This was Joseph Brosmer of the Agricultural Labor Board, the organization set up, in effect, to protect the growers from themselves. Brosmer was present to make sure that "no growers get overly excited. Some of your growers," Barling said, "lose their tempers fairly easy, particularly if they are picked on or aggravated at, or so on and so forth." The very idea had him breathing hard, and he glared vindictively at the small brown people who were threatening his way of life. " 'Course, this is what they *like*. If you blow up," he said, struggling not to blow up himself, "the more trouble you have. If you just *stand* there, and just *take* it"—he actually gritted his teeth—"and just don't *do* anything, well . . ." He broke off, red in the face, to get his breath, and his voice calmed again. "Well, you're better off."

Barling introduced me to Mr. Brosmer, who, discovering my profession, asked me if I was aware of the fact that a worker who had only been employed one second could walk off the job and give his name to the gentlemen over there—he pointed at the Department of Labor people—in order to certify a labor dispute. "This situation," he observed, "tends to lend itself pretty well to plants." When I had absorbed the truth of this, I was asked if I was aware of the fact that the farm workers' election in 1966, which had forced Di Giorgio to sign a contract, had been won for the Union by green-carders—"the same type of individual they're now trying to keep *out*," Mr. Brosmer emphasized, in case I had missed the paradox. "The same type of individual that won their election for them is now not good enough to come into the country!"

Brosmer was sensitive about the press. When Barling remarked, "I'll bet I got six people out there now who are Union already," Brosmer corrected him. "I think you ought to rephrase that, Butch; I think you ought to say that they are *members* of the Union." Barling hastily agreed with the distinction, which is here recorded only in the interest of fairness, since it was much too subtle for me to catch. Brosmer gazed at me in a knowing manner, nodding his head, and I nodded back at him. He is a sandy, sleepy-eyed short man with an expression of patient irony on his face, and he stands habitually with his arms folded on his chest, like someone in a supervisory capacity. At the moment he was supervising poor Barling, who was already glancing at me with suspicion and grew increasingly nervous as the morning wore on.

Approaching the strikers, I was stopped by the picket captain, a blond husky man with glasses. He had seen me talking to the growers, and he asked for my credentials. "I want to know if you're friend or enemy," he said. I told him that on a public road I was under no obligation to identify myself. "I'm asking, anyway," he said, neither rudely nor politely, and I obliged him, because if he could not stop me from asking questions, he could stop me from getting answers. This picket captain was the Reverend Nick Jones of the Migrant Ministry, the Protestant group that tends to the needs of migrants in many states and does a poor job of it, in Jones's opinion, everywhere but in California. Despite a mild, boyish appearance, Nick Jones is blunt and businesslike; a little later, when I pointed out to him a sign that read NO TRESPASSING: SURVIVORS WILL BE PROSECUTED, he went straight to his car and got out an old camera, and after placing a stout Mexican lady striker with a bull horn in the foreground, recorded the sign for propaganda purposes.

This lady, whose name was Mrs. Zapata, wore a big cone-peaked straw sombrero with a pink rim. The sombrero was festooned with Kennedy buttons, an AFL-CIO badge, a GRAPES OF WRATH-DELANO button, a small picture of Jesus, and a purple feather. In the long rise and fall of loudspeaker rhetoric, she talked nonstop most of the morning. She told the workers not to be afraid of the *patrón;* that they, the strikers, had known hunger too, and were seeking to better the lot of the poor; that all workers must organize and fight so that their children would not have to work like animals, as they had. "*¡Véngase, señores!*" she bawled. "*¡Para su re-specto y dignidad!*" Her entreaties were carried to the work-ers on waves of "*¡Huelga! ¡Huelga!*" from the picket line, and the workers glanced at her uneasily and kept working. Now and then Mrs. Zapata was drowned out by a passing truck, which would blare its horn from a half mile away and continue blaring at the strikers after it had passed, its dust cloud rolling off into the fields. These trucks were driven at high speeds, skimming the road edge just behind the strikers, and the Filipinos called out warnings to one another. Once I had to jump myself, and each time I was shaken by the passing blast of air. Then the strike cries would resume again: "*¡Huelga!*"

Through strong police support and the faithful obedience of the local judiciary, the growers have broken the picket-ing effort almost everywhere—a bad mistake, as it turns out, since the consumer's boycott, which the Union adopted as an alternative, has hurt them far more than local picket-ing, and attracted attention and support from all over the country. Most of the first-line strikers were now working on the boycott in the Eastern cities; what was left was a skeleton crew. The male strikers were mostly aged Fili-pinos; the women mostly Mexicans out of work or conva-lescing.

One pretty woman told me that she had been knocked unconscious by sprayed chemicals while picking grapes in the Coachella Valley a few weeks before. She was a green-carder from Mexico City, Magdalena by name and beau-tician by trade, who had come to make quick money during harvest time. She was gaily attired in a green shirt with huge polka dots, a yellow bandanna, lavender slacks and fake red hair, all set off by a small silver Virgin on a chain, and she was cheerful about her ailments, which included nose bleeds, bad headaches and sore lungs. It still pains her to breathe; she cannot go near the smell of sprays without suffering a recurrence of her symptoms. Overhearing her, a striker told me that her experience was very common. "I been workin on the ranches all my life," he said, "and I'm tellin you, they don't give you *nothin* for protection, no, man! Only in the Union. That's why Cesar Chavez is a great man." Magdalena nodded.

"*¡Huel-ga! ¡Huelga, huel-ga!*"

"*¡Véngase! ¡Alegría!*"

"*¡No tiene miedo del patrón, señores! ¡Véngase!*"

The old Filipinos beckoned with their arms, or waved red banners back and forth, like fans. When they saw a country-man among the work crews, they would switch from poor Spanish and English and cry out to him in their native Tagalog. They could not talk to him about his children since few Filipinos have any, but they could reach him by appealing to his self respect and dignity.

"*Mag labas cayo, cabayen!*"

"*¡Huelga! ¡Huelga, muchachos! ¡Huelga, compañeros!*"

"*¡Venga, venga! ¡Alegría, ale-gree-ee-e-a!*"

Jones told me that the Union had held a rally in Lamont to tell the people to stay in the fields, since there weren't enough jobs on the Union ranches to go around: what UFWOC wanted was a token exodus to certify the strike, and thereby give legal status to the boycott. Other workers were helping the Union from inside, through slowdowns and minor subversion. "I was around at the packing sheds yesterday, and a lot of field-packed grapes that come in ready to go to market just aren't ready," Jones said with a small smile. "Either they're green or the mildew hasn't been cut out or they're badly packed." He shrugged. "The brothers don't like the work conditions, so they do a bad job. Then the growers make them repack all night without pay, and that makes them even madder."

Jones was optimistic about the progress of the strike. The Johnson ranch had been struck the day before; no workers had walked off the job during the picketing, but a whole group had come into the farm workers' office afterward. This was the last ranch in the area. "If we get the base here, we can start sweeping, take a lot of ranches farther north. Those guys aren't going to make us boycott —they'll sit down and negotiate."

"*¡Esquirol!*" a woman shouted at the workers. "*¡Esquirol!*" I asked her what the word meant, and she said it was a term used for scabs. "*Es un animal,*" she laughed, making an ambiguous writhing motion with her hand, "*ni aquí ni allá.*"

Jones introduced me to Bill Chandler, a Union organizer who had previously worked in Texas; Chandler is married to a Mexican girl whose family's history as migrant laborers is no better and no worse than most. "They used to migrate as far north as Colusa, in November, and then catch the cotton on the way south. So Irene never had a real chance to go to school. Her brother can't really read or write. In her first year working, as a kid, she fell off a cotton truck and was in a coma for a week. In Bakersfield. And the doctors refused to help her because the family was Mexican and had no money. For a week they ran around here trying to find a doctor who could help them, and then they went back to El Monte, where there was this *bruja*, this lady with healing equipment, who did something, and Irene got better. Gloria, her older sister, got pneumonia, and the same thing happened: they went running from doctor to doctor to doctor, and the doctors refused to look at her without being paid for it, or give her medication, and after a week of that, she died."

On the strike line, the perfunctory yells and catcalls gained sudden momentum; the red flags danced as both bands of pickets gathered like a flock of birds in a single spot. Down a row of vines, perhaps fifty yards away, a work crew had run out of boxes, and while they waited for a truck, they turned toward the picket line and sat down to listen. The strikers' big gun, in the person of Mrs. Zapata, was moved into position, and while she huffed and blew into her bull horn, warming up like a musician, a Filipino shouted futilely at the work crew in an old, hoarse voice that could scarcely be heard. Most Mexicans do not speak English, and this man's Spanish was not up to the job. "¡Veng!" he cried. "Come on, you! All of you! ¡Veng! Come on! Leesten, you!" He wore a red HUELGA kerchief tied to the band of his plastic straw hat, and his purple button read DON'T BUY SCAB GRAPES. Over the strikers' heads, the red flags swished, blood-red against the blue sky; some of the flags were agitated vertically, in excitement.

"¡Para respecto, hombre!" Nick Jones yelled. "Come on!"

The squatting workers were still listening; they argued among themselves. Then one stood up and started for the picket line; after a few steps he retreated, to argue some more. A second time he started down the road, more confident now, motioning over his shoulder for his friends to follow. Though several got to their feet, they did not come. When the worker reached a point perhaps ten yards from the property line, he looked back and saw that he was all alone. He was no more than eighteen, small and thin, with a red-and-white kerchief tied around a homely narrow head. He stared at the dancing banners of the picket line— "*¡Véngase! ¡Venga!*"—and at his boss, Barling, and Joseph Brosmer and at the two federal officials, then glanced back again at the *campesinos* he had left. Then he sank slowly to one knee and picked at the spray-poisoned earth. Bravely he forced a smile, to suggest he was playing a game; he glanced back again to where he had come from.

"*¡Venga! ¡Véngase! ¡Nosotros también . . . hombre!*"

The boy waved a thin, ragged arm at the workers who had not come. By now work had completely stopped; the original crew had been joined by others. But in a little while the crews dispersed; they were going back to work. Soon the long row was almost empty, stretching away southward into the dusty sky. The boy got up.

"*¡Muy macho! ¡Hombre!*"

He hesitated, then spun away, cringing at the howl of disappointment from the pickets; shoulders hunched, he hurried down the row. Staring at the ground, kicking at clods, he lifted both hands high into the sky, thumbs outward, and without turning, waggled a good-bye with his fingers at the picket line.

"*¡Macho! ¡Mach-o-o-o!*"

The picket line subsided in discouragement; it seemed to know that the boy had dissipated any pressure that might have been built, and that this morning was a failure. But Mrs. Zapata, nothing daunted, merely moved a few rows away where, using the bull horn, she burst into song. "Nosotros venceremos" ("We Shall Overcome") was followed promptly by "Huelga general" ("General Strike"):

"¡Viva la huelga en el fil [fields]*!*
"¡Viva la causa en la historia!
"¡La raza llena de gloria!
"¡La victoria va cumplir!"

A big woman came to the edge of the fields and shouted violently at Mrs. Zapata. Through the bull horn, Mrs. Zapata notified the workers that she knew this broad only too well and that she was entirely shameless, *sin vergüenza*: in fact, she owed Mrs. Zapata $15, which she refused to pay. The woman, calling Mrs. Zapata a bitch, shrieked out an invitation to cross the property line, at which time she would be paid in full. In response Mrs. Zapata saluted her with one finger without letting up on the bull horn; to cross the property line, as the workers knew, was to get arrested.

Laughing, the picket line disbanded, and the strikers got into their old cars and drove away. I reminded Barling of a promise he had made to let me go into the fields once the pickets were gone and talk to his workers. He looked unhappily at Brosmer. "I think that would be useless, Butch," Brosmer said. "I think it would be better to wait until you finish your day." To me, he added, "People have a natural-born curiosity, and you may only talk to two, but every goddamn one of 'em is going to stop working to watch. It's just human nature." Barling nodded in discomfort; he could not look me in the eye. "I think I'd have to agree with Butch," Brosmer continued, "that you'd better hold off going in there until Butch finishes his working day."

Apologetically Barling said that after work he would take me in and let me pick out any worker I wanted to talk to, and I asked him why, now that the strikers were gone, it would not be all right to walk into the fields by myself. "I guess we're not communicating," Brosmer said before Barling could speak. "You would be a disruptive factor." Barling said, "That would probably be all right. Just so long as I don't get disrupted." He seemed a little surprised by Brosmer's insistence. "No," Brosmer said, "I think you're making a mistake."

"Well, let's go, then," Barling said ambiguously, looking at no one. He set his jaw and started for his truck, and I stuck with him and got into it. "You're making a big mistake," Brosmer called, with no pretense of indifference.

We drove down a side road into the fields. It was nearly noon, and the truck raised big clouds of hydrocarbon dust. Barling swung off into a service lane that crossed the rows of vines, and stalled the truck at the edge of a crew of workers; here he was set upon by an Anglo foreman and his Mexican labor contractor. The only part of the field that was still unpicked was on the most vulnerable corner of the public highway, and the strikers had gone. "I got a hundred fifty people here," the labor contractor said. "We pick that in a hour." But the grape boxes were all gone. "We ain't set up to do it," the foreman said. "We got to get in here first thing in the mornin, before they can get here."

"I ain't *never* goin to get out of here," Barling said, "if them damn people don't leave me alone." His voice was tight and his face red, and he stamped over to the water truck to cool off. "Where are the paper cups?" he shouted. "We're supposed to have paper cups!" The labor contractor pointed at the DO NOT BUY NEW YORK PRODUCTS sign on Barling's bumper. "We could not buy them," he pleaded. "They made in New York." To Barling's credit, he was genuinely embarrassed. "I guess that's kind of a farce," he admitted, fooling with the community tin cup. "Makes us feel like we're *doin* somethin." With distaste, he drank from the tin cup, then shouted at his foreman that the corner would not be picked the next day, but "first thing Sunday." This was for my benefit; rightly, they did not trust me. But Barling is a poor actor, which was one reason why I liked him; I was certain that the vulnerable corner would be picked "first thing Saturday," and I said as much to Bill Chandler later, when I ran into him at the Union meeting. Chandler arranged to have the pickets at the Lamont office at six o'clock the following morning, but by the time they reached Sandrini Road, the corner was already picked and the workers gone.

Now the contractor's big wife came up, and I recognized her as the woman who had shouted at Mrs. Zapata. Actually, she was attractive, full of bullshit and coy swagger, with the infectious laugh of the born con artist. "Did you see that bitch give me the finger? Did you see that?" She tried to look offended and aggrieved, but burst out laughing. She guided me, by no accident, to a worker named Francisco Garcia, a big sincere man on his knees. Garcia was cutting grape bunches, and behind him, his family watched me in apprehension, huddled in the hot shadows of the vines. The contractor's wife said that Garcia had joined the Union two years before in Delano and had quit almost immediately; as she spoke, Garcia slowly drew a Union card out of a thin billfold and pointed out his name to me with a cracked fingernail. "He was at Schenley, pickin wine grapes," she continued. "They only let him make fourteen dollars, and then they sent him home. This is why they can't get anybody to walk out of this field; he told them all about it."

Garcia confirmed this. "I was only in Union two week,

one week," he said. "You put too much grape in the gondola, they get mad; you don't put enough, they get mad." He shook his head.

"That's because it's unionized," the woman said. "You can only pick so much and no more, and everybody got to do just the same."

Another worker told me he was making $3 an hour: $1.50 base wage, plus 25 cents a box. "I don't know what they want over there," he said, jerking his head northward toward Delano and the Union. "T'ree dollars is good money." I said I supposed the Union contract offered other benefits besides the wages, and he looked worried. "Maybe they other benefit—I don't know."

Because Garcia was obviously sincere, I later relayed his complaint to Dolores Huerta, who shrugged. "I'm sure he's right. It was kind of a mess there for a few weeks, until we got a system going." Leroy Chatfield, who had seen crews filling the heavy carts called gondolas before the Union came, shook his head at the ugly memory. "I couldn't believe how those people drove themselves—they were *running!* They *had* to run if they wanted to keep their jobs! If a man in the crew was slower, he was almost set upon by the others! The young green-carders, here to make quick money, were the fastest, which was pretty hard on the domestic workers doing an honest day's work."

Down the rows I spotted a red-and-white sweat rag, wrapped on a head bent down behind the leaves. I waited a little while, then asked Butch Barling if I could talk to the worker of my choice, and he fell into step beside me. Sure, he said, which one? If he didn't mind, I said, I'd like to operate alone: it might be more spontaneous. He grunted and let me go. But the contractor's wife was on to me in moments. "*That* young kid?" she called. "There weren't any boxes, and he said, 'I'm going to have some fun with them while I'm waiting'; that's why he walked out there and sat down."

The boy was deep under the vines, which reach no higher than to the chest of a six-foot man. In the shadows, in the filtered sun, the soft bloom on the big bunches of green grapes gave them a soft glow. Crouched there, he stared up at me. He did not speak English. "*Buenos días,*" I said; he did not so much answer it as repeat it, in a hushed voice full of fear. Perhaps he thought I had come for him, like Death.

In bad Spanish, I asked him please not to be afraid, then asked why he had changed his mind an hour before. I had expected a few frightened murmurs, but he spoke right out, in passion and in pain. He was a green-carder, on vacation from an insurance job in Mexico, and he could speak frankly because in harvest time no one was fired. His voice grew louder. Besides, as an insurance man, he would only be there for two more weeks before his vacation ended. The insurance man poked his head out of the row before continuing in a lower voice. ¡*Sí!* He was in favor of a union! "The ranchers have no concern for us! These people"—he waved contemptuously at the Mexican strikebreakers— "they do not understand anything! Everybody should have a union!" Persisting, I repeated my question: Why had he not walked out an hour before? The boy picked at the dust on his sandaled toes. "The whole world was awaiting me," he murmured, "and I became afraid."

Like Bruno Dispoto, Butch Barling was eating his own grapes; one federal man, observing him do this earlier, had sworn that he would not touch one of those things until it had been washed five or six times. In the pickup Barling was still tense, and backed rapidly out of the lane. To get him to slow down a little, I complimented him on the skill of his reverse driving, at which he set his jaw, smiled in strange satisfaction and increased speed. We headed for a ranch building on the far side of the fields, where Joseph Brosmer was awaiting us.

In my absence Butch had come to a few conclusions. Before we left the field he said that Chavez was not a reasonable man, and this was why he was meeting so much resistance. The boys in Delano all agreed that if they had to go union, they would go Teamsters, because a man could do business with the Teamsters. He denied any racial overtones in the resistance to Chavez. "You never find any more democracy than you get right here in agriculture. We got a lot of Mexican fellas and we're all buddies, and we're out here tryin to do a job and make a livin for ourselves. In agriculture you probably have the least amount of discrimination anywhere; the grower negotiates with Mexicans every day, right out there in that field!"

But Union people are convinced that what the growers resent and fear most is any real power for *chicanos*.

"Man, they don't like Cesar," Nick Jones had remarked. "And behind the dislike for Cesar is the whole Mexican thing: a man they called 'boy' is standing up and asking to negotiate. As Cesar says, pride is one of the biggest things to beat down in a rancher before you can get a contract."

"Let them have their pride," Chavez himself says; "what we want is the contract. This is what they fail to understand. We are not out to put them out of business because our people need the work; we are out to build a union, and we'll negotiate half our lives to get it. If we can get better wages and conditions for the workers, we are willing to give up something. But the growers choose to make it a personal fight, so we have to do something to save their face. It's not hard to understand why they feel the way they do, because they've had their own way for so long that they've got the habit of it. So things can't look as if we are getting a victory and they are not."

A man at the ranch agreed with Barling. "We have a nice relation with our people. They're good people, making good money. Everyone is as happy as a person can be, doing this type of work. I'm not saying it's white-collar; it's hard work. But I'd say there's more people in that field out there than Cesar Chavez represents altogether." He paused for a moment, not certain he had made his point. "When you see those big gatherings at the park—I mean, a Mexican is just like an American, everybody likes a carnival. I like to go myself. When the growers in Arvin have a picnic, we all go. And when the Mexicans have a picnic, *they* all go."

In answer to my parting question, Brosmer denied that there was any prospect of the growers' negotiating with Chavez, whom he referred to as "Cesar." Cesar didn't represent the people; if he did, there wouldn't be any choice. It wouldn't be what-do-we-sign, it would be *where*-do-we-sign. The pickers, he said, worked for the growers of their own free will; they weren't coerced. Perhaps hunger coerced them, I suggested, and Joseph Brosmer scoffed. "When is the last time anybody went hungry in this country!" he exclaimed, sincerely incredulous. I didn't bother to point out to Brosmer that ten million Americans, at last estimate, are suffering from malnutrition, and that a state of true famine has been described for parts of the Mississippi Delta.

In Delano, at noon, I heard a waitress in Foster's Freeze deplore the loss of jobs at Di Giorgio's Sierra Vista Ranch; also, she said, the boycott had put a number of small family vineyards in the Delano area out of business. This is true, and the Union regrets it. The failing vineyards are not those being struck, but the farms of 100 acres or less that are worked by a single family. The product of these farms must compete on the market with cheap-labor grapes in high volume, and the boycott depresses the price past the point that a small farm on small margin can afford.

The waitress was a kindly woman with a big honest smile, and she felt sorry for Chavez, who was, she said, "the tool of higher-ups." A woman in White's Laundry, on the other hand, was sure she had no opinion; in a town as fractured as Delano, it didn't make sense for "people in trade" to express their views on anything.

In the late afternoon I found Chavez in the shade of the Pink Building with the Young Adult Leadership Group, a delegation of high school students from East Los Angeles. His door is never closed to anybody, and to workers and young people it is open wide. On his busiest day, Chavez seems unhurried; he is altogether where he is. "He would talk to a small child for two days if someone didn't go and get him," Jim Drake says. When I asked him once about a magazine interview in which his responses to the reporter seemed too easy, Chavez nodded. "He was in a hurry," he said, "so I was too."

The students were mostly Mexican-Americans, with a

few whites and blacks. Some were straight and some wore long hair and hippie beads, but all were interested in helping the Union by picketing the East Los Angeles *mercados*. "We had a great reception in East L.A. when we went down to get the vote out for Senator Kennedy," Chavez told them. "I went to many polling places and talked to the ladies and the men, and they knew all about the Union. We made a *lot* of friends there. They send us food now, and some have come to visit us in Delano. Anyway, don't let them kid you about those grapes coming from Arizona or Mexico; in East L.A. they shouldn't be selling any grapes at all." He grinned. "They should only be selling tacos and tamales, things like that." The students laughed, all but the blacks and whites. One boy asked for a comment on a TV film about Chavez that had appeared on California stations a few months before: "Did you like it?" Chavez took a sip of Diet-Rite Cola; he looked uneasy. "Oh," he said finally, "I don't know." He looked up at the boy. "I didn't see it," he explained apologetically. His ignorance of the show was so unfeigned that the students, delighted, laughed. They decided that the film was superficial, and Chavez shrugged. "People come and they try to do something in three or four days," he said.

Chavez talked to them about race prejudice and the problems he had had in his own union with the *chicanos,* as Mexican-Americans refer to themselves. "The *chicanos* wanted to swing against the Filipinos. We don't permit that against anyone. I told them they'd have to get somebody else to run the Union. You don't take a vote on those things, whether to discriminate or not. You don't ask people whether they want to do that or not—you just don't do it."

In his audience, the black, white and brown students were quiet. He regarded them. "That doesn't mean you can't be proud to be what you are. In the Union we're just beginning, and you're just beginning. Mexican-American youth is just beginning to wake up. Five years ago we didn't have this feeling. Nobody wanted to be *chicanos,* they wanted to be anything *but chicanos.* But three months ago I went up to San Jose State College and they had a beautiful play in which they let everybody know that they were *chicanos,* and that *chicanos* meant something and that they were proud of it." He paused again. "In a conflict area like here in Delano, you have to be for your people or against them. We don't want to see anybody on the fence. I walk down the street here, and I get insulted almost as many times as I get a friendly wave. And that's the way it should be; you have to be for or against. If you aren't committed one way or the other, then you might as well lie in the weeds."

The newborn pride in being a *chicano,* in the opinion of most people, is due largely to Chavez himself.

The students told Chavez about the hostility of the police in East Los Angeles, especially against the Brown Berets, a group of young Mexican-American militants who style themselves after the Black Panthers and have inherited some of the repression that Panther spokesmen have brought down on themselves. A boy said, "The Man is even worse in El Monte and Whittier—it's getting real nasty down there." A girl said, "The Man is after everybody now. I think they're out to crush the whole *chicano* movement!" Discussing the police, the young voices became tight and worried, and in their haste to confide their worry to Chavez, who looked worried himself, they interrupted one another.

"Them thirteen that were arrested—"

"Club you, man. They club you!"

Chavez was nodding. The students were discussing the arrest for "conspiracy" of people who protested against the wretched schools of East Los Angeles, where over half the student body drops out or is kicked out. He feels it is only a matter of time until brown communities start exploding like the black ones. "Those police clubs will organize the people," he said quietly. "You can't organize the people without a good reason. When we were picketing, if they'd ignored us—" He shook his head.

When Chavez had excused himself, the students chattered excitedly among themselves; they had come a long way to see him, and he had pleased them. One black student who kept himself apart from the *chicanos* seemed surprised at the effect Chavez had had on him. "I didn't think he would be so down-to-earth," he said, looking at the door through which Chavez had gone.

Already a few students had acquired VIVA LA CAUSA buttons and HUELGA scarves. One of the hippie contingent, in wild beads and green Che fatigue shirt, was pinning on a GRAPES OF WRATH-DELANO button. "We'll show these guys," he said, referring to the growers, the Establishment, the Man. "Cesar don't believe in violence, but we do." From the Man's point of view, this kid had everything going against him—dark skin, long hair, fantasy dress, a life style and a sense of humor. Fists on hips, he tossed his chin toward his fellow students, who had dropped their tense discussion of the police like a used piece of gum, and squealed, jostled and flirted their way to their bus. "The Young Adult Leadership Group," he said with a low whistle, as if to say, "Like, man, there is no hope."

4

ACH Friday night a Union meeting is held at Filipino Hall, a green makeshift edifice on Glenwood Street, just opposite the lumberyard. Originally the hall was headquarters for the Agricultural Workers Organizing Committee, the AFL-CIO farm workers group set up in Stockton in 1959 which gained local wage increases and improved conditions but got no further than the unions of the past toward legal contracts and the right to collective bargaining. AWOC membership consisted mostly of bachelor Filipinos, who had no better home to go to; only the staunchest Mexican-Americans had bothered to sign up. In addition to an accumulating and justified mistrust of Anglo unions, which worked with the labor contractors and employers and encouraged race discrimination, the bloody history of farm workers' strikes in California had made the *chicanos* so wary or apathetic that both AWOC and Chavez's National Farm Workers Association avoided the word "union" in their titles.

On September 16, 1965, the anniversary of Mexican Independence Day, NFWA voted to support an AWOC strike for a wage increase that had started a week before; six to eight hundred AWOC workers, led by organizers Larry Itliong and Ben Gines, had struck about half the Delano growers, and NFWA decided to strike the rest, including the huge holdings of Di Giorgio, Schenley and Giumarra. Chavez, who did not think that his painfully constructed association was ready yet for a big strike ("You can't organize and strike at the same time," he says), reminded the members that they must be prepared for great difficulties and privation. But fainthearted people would not have joined him in the first place; he listened with mixed joy and apprehension as the parish hall of Our Lady of Guadalupe resounded with the fierce speeches, rallying cries, roars, song and acclamation of over twenty-five hundred workers, including an old man who had seen the two workers killed at Pixley, in 1933. Chavez tried to fire the crowd with the urgency of nonviolence, and asked for and received permission to seek outside help, since the NFWA would be responsible for any strikers; inevitably, people would be evicted by the growers and would need food and shelter. Many of the Filipinos had already been kicked out of barracks where they had lived for twenty years.

On September 20, eleven hundred members of NFWA went out on strike. Chavez, seeking funds and volunteers, spoke at a number of colleges, and appealed directly to the clergy as well as to CORE and SNCC, whose members had experience with confrontations and police, and could act as picket captains until the farm workers were trained. He was immediately denounced by the local clergy and even by the local chapter of the CSO. (The Delano CSO was led by a police captain, Al Espinosa, who moonlights as a labor contractor; the chapter's action was repudiated by the national organization.)

Response to Chavez's appeal was mixed, even in the colleges. Once he was actually pelted with eggs and tomatoes, but by this time he was so exhausted that he scarcely noticed. He kept right on with his speech. Apparently his inert manner was taken for beautiful cool, because the booing changed to wild applause, which he scarcely noticed, either; he just kept droning away. "I made a lot of friends there," he says, still slightly puzzled.

For the most part Chavez is impressed by young students and by what they represent in America. He shares the feeling of so many that there is more hope of an American renaissance in the young radicals of the present, in their insistence on honesty and love of man, than there has been in whatever generation we may think of as our own; that they are citizens, not just consumers. Their philosophical poverty and abrasive attitudes should not obscure the fact that these people are forming the front line in a *necessary* revolution; they have heroes like Che and Malcolm, who died for a cause, and they long for that dramatic liberation from the nation's shame that confrontations represent. But Chavez points out that the young radicals are a distinct minority, like the blacks and browns; their criticism of the System is too searing for the majority to accept.

"The trouble with activists is that movements grow old for them very quickly, and they move on," Chavez said, in 1967. "These students are the first people who have ever come to us without a hidden agenda. They just want to help us—to be servants—and that's a really beautiful thing."

That first December of the strike, with more courage than hope, Chavez attempted to address a hostile crowd at Bakersfield Junior College, where he was asked, among other things, when he had last paid dues to the Communist party. The moderator disallowed the question, but Chavez asked for permission to answer it; he had nothing to hide, he said, and would answer any question whatsoever. Apparently frustrated, his hearers crowded to the stage and began shoving him, and the police were called in by his hosts to get him out of there. One of the few voices that rose in his defense, or so it is said, belonged to Marshall Ganz, an ex-SNCC worker with hard experience of Mississippi; Ganz, who had been an honor student at Harvard, was so impressed by Chavez that he joined the cause right on the spot. ("It might have happened that way," Ganz says doubtfully. "I like the story anyway." Ganz is a soft-spoken, mildly cynical man who wears a big modern mustache; as an early volunteer who stayed, he is very close to Chavez.)

Besides the SNCC and CORE people, a number of clergymen of all faiths came to man the picket lines, along with volunteers from other groups, such as Students for a Democratic Society and the W. E. B. Du Bois Clubs, as well as an assortment of students and hippies of uneven quality, some of whom were less help than hindrance, wishing mainly to expiate their own guilts and frustration in angry identification with *la causa*. Some of the female volunteers brought the new freedoms to Delano, and even the more innocent girls not already paired caused consternation in the homes of the farm workers who drank beer with the volunteers in the People's Café. A few volunteers were an embarrassment to the Union in their public use of drugs; for others, being jailed was fashionable or a proof of commitment. Since the Union felt obliged to pay their bail, these jail-bent individuals, many of whom were new arrivals, became a serious financial burden.

The hippies had less taste for jail, and Chavez liked them. "I don't know much about them, really, but I do know that they are peaceful and that they are truthful, and that attracts me very, very much." But pot heads and flower people were of limited use on the picket line, and others were too adolescent or idealistic to be effective, spending their energies philosophizing at the People's Café.

"We don't let people sit around a room crying about their problems," Chavez says. "No philosophizing—*do* something about it. In the beginning, there was a lot of nonsense about the poor farm worker: 'Gee, the farm worker is poor and disadvantaged and on strike, he must be a super human being!' And I said, 'Cut that nonsense out, all right?' That was my opening speech: 'Look, you're here working with a group of men; the farm worker is only a human being. You take the poorest of these guys and give him that ranch over there, he could be just as much of a bastard as the guy sitting there right now. Or if you think that all growers are bastards, you're no good to us, either. Remember that both are *men*. In order to help the farm workers, look at them as human beings and not as something extra special, or else you are kidding yourself and are going to be mighty, mighty disappointed. Don't pity them, either. Treat them as human beings, because they have just as many faults as you have; that way you'll never be in trouble, because you'll never be disappointed.'

"I had that sentimentality myself; I'm probably as big a sucker as anybody you've ever met. But you have to learn a *real* sense of their human worth, not a phony one, because there are a lot of phonies among workers, too. Some of them really exploited those volunteers"—Chavez raised hands in prayer, rolling his eyes—" 'Oh, we are so *poor!*' " He gazed at me, pained and disgusted, as if I might explain how people could behave that way. "I told them, 'Stop that damn nonsense!' But most of the workers disliked being pitied: 'Gee, I may be poor, but I got a lot of dignity, and I don't need to be felt sorry for.'

"We were all equal, and everybody had to work; there were no special jobs. And some came around to this, and some didn't. We told the volunteers they had to work *harder* than the farm workers because they understood more, and the ones that kept oversleeping or sitting around —well, we got rid of them. Right out."

This harsh talk is deceptive. "He didn't act nearly as fast as the rest of us wanted," Leroy Chatfield says. "He agonized about those kids for months. But when he *did* move"—he made a quick executionary flick—"*man!* Like a knife!"

Chavez can be stern, but he is never brutal, even in anger. While I was in Delano, he reprimanded one of his Anglo aides for speaking impatiently to a *chicano* girl on the office staff. "When someone rebukes you heavily," the culprit told me later the same day, "you remember it, you carry a scar; Cesar did it so softly that I couldn't focus on it while it was happening. I feel bad, but I won't carry a scar."

In effect, Chavez serves as father of the Union family, praising, teasing, needling, cajoling, comforting, and gently chastising to maintain a balance in this huge and complex household; like all families, this one has its fights and feuds, its drinkers and malingerers, but injured vanities waste more of his time than anything else. "That's why Gil Padilla is so good," Cesar says. "He's not subjective, he doesn't take things personally."

Chavez, who was coming from Los Angeles, would be late for the Friday night meeting, and since Larry Itliong was on the boycott, in St. Louis, the people were welcomed to the hall by one of the Filipino leaders, Philip Vera Cruz. Subsequently, progress reports were made by various officers of the Union. Some spoke in English, some in Spanish, and afterward a Spanish or English translation was supplied by David Fishlow, a former Peace Corps volunteer, and editor of *El Malcriado*. The speakers were lined up against a background of piled cartons of dry cereal donated to the Union mess hall, which adjoins the auditorium. An American flag stood to one side, and on the bare wall was a sign that read:

COMRADES OF THE FIRING LINE
WITH THE HELP OF GOD WE'LL PREVAIL
OUR STRIKE PLACARDS ARE OUR PRAYER

The meeting was opened by Jerome Cohen, a Union attorney out of Berkeley. Cohen is an intense man whose eyes are usually red-rimmed with fatigue, and his staccato speech is punctuated by a nervous popping noise accomplished by banging one open palm on the cupped fingers of the opposite hand. He favors basketball sneakers, untucked candy-colored shirts and casual shaving, and looks ordinarily like an All-American boy trying to pull himself together after a rude awakening in the wrong house. Hands popping, he paced up and down before the audience, exhorting the workers to report on the several complaints which UFWOC is currently filing against the growers.

Cohen spoke first of the use of the HI-COLOR label, which threatened the boycott effort in New York. In permitting other growers to use this label, he explained, Di Giorgio was intentionally subverting the Union, and this was illegal by the terms of the contract. A worker in a green shirt stood up to report that he had seen HI-COLOR at Dispoto, and Cohen asked him to come in the next day to prepare a signed affidavit. Next he discussed the failure of the growers to protect the workers from dangerous pesticides, and the necessity of reporting illness or injuries immediately, so that legal action could be taken while the worker was still in the area. From here he progressed to the chronic and illegal absence of chemical field toilets, which is not only disagreeable for the worker but a public health hazard. The girls in the audience looked shy and the men laughed when Cohen brought up this subject, but they stopped laughing when he spoke of the serious kidney ailments that women can develop from going too long without relieving themselves. Finally he discussed a report of "slave labor" demanded by a grower in Lamont who was allegedly forcing people to work without pay all evening in the packing sheds repacking grape boxes that were unsatisfactory; another report said that Giumarra was recruiting greencarders without telling them, as the law demands, that they would be used as scabs. In all these matters, Cohen needed firsthand evidence and affidavits.

Next, the Reverend Jim Drake reported to the members on the progress of the boycott. Drake is a big man whose brusque manner defends a warm, sensitive friendliness. He was the first outsider to join forces with NFWA, cooperating with Chavez from 1962 until 1965, and joining him full time thereafter. Drake's car has had all its windows blasted out while it sat outside his office, and Drake himself has been assaulted in the street by an irate grower. "I got a lot of credit for my nonviolence," Drake says, laughing at himself, "but it wasn't so hard. He only came up to here on me"—indicating his rib cage—"so all he could do was pummel."

Drake spoke of the progress, or lack of it, in the twenty-five cities where grape strikers had been sent; in Cleveland, Detroit and New York, he announced, the mayors had supported the boycott. But in New York the boycott was seriously threatened, not only by false labeling—aside from HI-COLOR, California grapes were being marked "Arizona"— but by a false letter sent out to all the food chain stores on a United Farm Workers letterhead announcing that the boycott was now over. The audience laughed when Drake referred to Delano's retaliatory boycott of New York products: if Delano boycotted Detroit, a worker called, "den de growers couldn't buy no more beeg car!" Finally Drake spoke of Senator Eugene McCarthy, who had come out in support of the boycott on July 26: McCarthy had said that state and federal agencies were siding unfairly with the growers. Now the growers of Delano had challenged McCarthy to a debate and McCarthy had answered that the time for debate was long since past: it was time to negotiate. At this, the Anglos in the audience cheered loudly, and the workers looked at one another. In the California primaries all of these people had worked hard for Senator Robert Kennedy against McCarthy, and few had really understood what Drake had said. After a moment's delay they joined modestly in the cheering, out of politeness.

The next speaker was Tony Orendain, the Union treasurer, a former wetback who had come to California by way of Texas. Orendain is a handsome Mexican with luminous brown eyes and a bold mustachio; he dresses with flair and speaks laconically. The local efforts by the growers to stop the boycott in Eastern cities he dismissed as the "kicks of a dying man." Orendain was followed by a Filipino striker who stood up to report on the day's picketing: in his opinion the workers had been afraid to come out at Haddad-Barling because the federal men had seemed so friendly with the bosses. Next Dolores Huerta, just back from San Francisco, reported on the correction of contract abuses at Almadén and Gallo wineries, which had signed contracts with the Union in 1967. (The Almadén contract—the best that the Union has—was the first with a company outside the San Joaquin Valley.) Mrs. Huerta had also spoken to the insurance companies about their prejudice against farm workers, especially Mexicans and blacks, and had gotten the companies to let Leroy Chatfield advise them on more equitable compensation policies.

Shortly after nine o'clock Cesar Chavez was glimpsed in the doorway at the back of the hall. A murmur arose, and a scraping of wooden chairs as the people all got to their feet. The Mexicans, especially, smiled and laughed, and a slow clapping started which became a rhythmic beat. Chavez remained where he was, a little hunched, looking annoyed. In the hallway he had told Dolores Huerta he knew that the brothers would clap and that he hated it, and that if this meeting was not so important he would not enter. In most men this would be a pose, but in Chavez it is a passion: one of the rare times I ever heard him speak illtemperedly was in response to a request over the telephone that he come somewhere to be honored. "I have told you so many times," he snapped. "I do not accept personal awards."

Now he came forward, starting to speak almost before he

reached the platform. "I have asked you so often not to do this," he said. "Please don't do this. I am one of you. And when you stand up and applaud me, I don't feel one of you. Please don't do this." The workers are proud of him and wish to express it, but Chavez knows that their pride comes partly from the growing notoriety of their cause across the country and partly from the courtship of Chavez by famous men.

Chavez told the audience in detail about the meeting in Los Angeles with the Teamsters. "We"—in speaking of Union business, he avoids use of the first person—"asked them for money, we asked for permission to come before their locals and tell our story; we also asked for help in setting up a meeting with the owners of the chain stores, to support the boycott." Here he paused to explain. "You see, we have to put pressure on the chain stores to put pressure on the growers to negotiate. We asked that labor really show its solidarity, and they agreed."

Sensing a resistance in his audience, Chavez fell silent. It was plain that the members still disliked the Brotherhood of Teamsters, which two years before, in collaboration with the growers, had attempted to destroy NFWA, Chavez's small union. In the first months, the Teamsters had joined the other big unions in a show of labor solidarity behind the new strike, which they doubtless thought would fail, like all the rest. Their self-interest was excited by NFWA's first contract, signed with Schenley Industries; if America's one million farm workers could actually be organized, a whole new source of dues had been opened up.

The Schenley farm in Delano was such a small part of its enormous operation that a defense against Chavez's boycott, in late 1965, scarcely seemed worth the bad publicity that his volunteers, spreading out from Delano after the harvest, were giving to the Schenley trade name all across the country. The volunteers were young veterans of the picket lines, and they were sent off to thirteen cities without funds of any kind, riding the rails and living by their own resources. At their destinations, they would contact CORE and SNCC and other sympathetic activists and set up a boycott of the liquor stores.

"People are frustrated by taxes, high prices, everything else," Chavez says. "If you can give them a clear-cut, boy-cottable issue, they can take out that frustration. After a while a good boycott gains momentum. That one at Schenley, we were really atrocious. We picketed unions and we picketed churches, we stopped railroads and broke the law a million times—all-out." He shook his head. "We made a lot of people unhappy. We had sit-ins at the warehouses, and there was one beautiful picture of a little girl wearing a poncho sitting on the pavement down in Los Angeles, in the middle of about thirty huge trucks"—he frowned as he said "huge," drawing out the word as a boy might, as if the hugeness was excruciating—"and over here a line of fifty policemen. We had another one of a nun blocking the trucks. No one is going to run over a nun, you know; you'll run over a priest maybe, but not a nun." Grinning, he mimicked a fierce nun: " 'I dare you! Run over me!' " He sighed. "Yeah, we fought 'em hard, and it was rough. We weren't afraid of them; they came, and we took them on. At that time we had fifty organizers. I mean, they weren't trained organizers, but they were people," he said, putting an admiring emphasis on this last word.

The Schenley fight was costly for the farm workers. Hundreds of poor people sacrificed their jobs to strike, and the first autumn exhausted the strike fund. Cars, gasoline, even food and housing were inadequate, despite numerous small contributions. In this critical period the NFWA Service Center was awarded a grant from the Office of Economic Opportunity of $265,000 for community development. Chavez refused it. With the strike on, he said, there was nobody free to administer the money. (Learning of the proposed grant, the Delano City Council asked the OEO to review it: "Cesar Chavez is well known in this city, having spent various periods of his life in the community, including attendance at public schools, and it is the opinion of this council that he does not merit the trust of the council with regard to the administration of the grant." The council fabricated the record of school attendance to suggest acquaintance with Chavez's low character, but Chavez was never in Delano except in harvest season; he never went to school there in his life.)

With the help of the Migrant Ministry and of individual clerics, militants and plain citizens, the strike was kept going, and meanwhile the labor movement was organizing slowly in support. In September, the AFL-CIO offered NFWA the use of AWOC's Filipino Hall; in October, the ILGWU contributed funds for a workers clinic, which was tended by a volunteer nurse. Out-of-town doctors gave free services; no local doctor ever volunteered. The Teamsters refused to cross the Schenley picket lines, and the Longshoremen refused to load Schenley products at the dock. In mid-December, Walter Reuther of the UAW marched with Chavez and Larry Itliong down the streets of Delano and spoke out in defense of the Schenley boycott: "We'd rather not do negative things like boycotts, but when the growers refuse to sit down at the bargaining table, there is no alternative." Reuther gave AWOC-NFWA $5,000, and pledged the same amount every month until the strike was finished. The AFL-CIO was underwriting AWOC by $10,000 a month, and collections had been taken up by the Clothing Workers, Seafarers, Packinghouse Workers, and other AFL-CIO unions, as well as by church and student groups, but the combined sums did not pay for the strike, which was costing $40,000 a month: the difference was made up in hardship. After the harvest season, when many of the volunteers left Delano to spread the boycott around the country, the pressure eased a little, but the winter of 1965–1966 was extremely bleak.

In early winter, Chavez went east on a fund-raising tour, and in his absence the morale in Delano sank so low that Richard Chavez took money from the meager treasury to give a beer party at the People's Café; it seemed to him that this was necessary to avoid a mass defection of the volunteers. "Big Brother gave me hell for that," Richard recalls. "He gave me hell." By this time Chavez himself had given up smoking and drinking, and his growing strictness about Union comportment extended to such matters as newspaper reading in the office and unnecessary telephone calls, which annoy him to this day: "Goddamn it, we run up a monthly phone bill of three thousand dollars, and then some lady comes into the office who needs a new pair of shoes or something, and there's no money for her!"

By March 16, 1966, when the Senate Subcommittee on Migratory Labor of the Committee on Labor and Public Welfare conducted hearings in Delano, NFWA-AWOC had carried on by far the longest farm strike in California history; it had asked for and received great sacrifices from its members and volunteers, it had attracted national attention, and it was on the verge of total defeat. But the chairman of the subcommittee was Democratic Senator Harrison A. Williams, Jr., of New Jersey, who had been the farm workers' best friend in Congress since 1959, when the subcommittee was established. "Any thoughtful person," Senator Williams has said, "who observes the poverty and total wretchedness of the lives of migratory farm workers and their youngsters will never leave the work of trying to improve these lives until it is done." Williams was accompanied by Senator Robert Kennedy, whose commitment was more complicated, and by Republican Senator George Murphy of California, there to see to the prevention of cruelty to the rich. In the course of the hearings the strikers were blessed with the unanimous support of the seven Catholic bishops of California, led by the Most Reverend Hugh A. Donohoe of Stockton, who personally appealed for collective-bargaining rights and a minimum wage for farm workers. (A few months later Congress passed an inadequate minimum-wage bill that covered a small percentage of the farm workers; oratory on the bill revealed an uncommon concern for social justice on the part of congressmen from the Pacific states, which were already paying farm workers the equivalent of the minimum wage —$1 an hour at that time—and were anxious to see other states lose a competitive advantage.)

Though badly in need of any assistance he could get, Chavez addressed Senator Williams' subcommittee with his usual frankness. "Although we appreciate your efforts here, we do not believe that public hearings are the route to solving the problem of the farm worker. In fact, I do not think that anyone should ever hold another hearing or make a special investigation of the farm-labor problem.

Everything has been recorded too many times already and the time is now past due for immediate action.

"Or some people say education will do it—write off this generation of parents and hope my son gets out of farm work. Well, I am not ready to be written off as a loss, and farm work could be a decent job for my son with a union. But the point is that this generation of farm labor children will not get an adequate education until their parents earn enough to care for the child the way they want to and the way other children in school—the ones who succeed—are cared for. . . . All we want from the government is the machinery—some rules of the game. All we need is the recognition of our right to full and equal coverage under every law which protects every other working man and woman in this country.

"What we demand is very simple: we want equality. We do not want or need special treatment unless you abandon the idea that we are equal men."

The appeal of the bishops was the first formal step of the Catholic Church toward endorsement of the farm workers; the support of the senators gave new hope to their fight for the protection of the National Labor Relations Act. (As originally written, in 1935, the Wagner Act had included farm workers, but when it came out of committee two months later, they had been excluded. At that time Democratic Representative Vito Marcantonio of New York was unable to find "a single solitary reason why agricultural workers should not be included under the provisions of this bill," but the majority opinion, as expressed by Democratic Congressman William P. Connery, Jr., of Massachusetts, while "in favor of giving agricultural workers every protection," opposed him: "If we can get this bill through and get it working properly, there will be opportunity later, and I hope soon, to take care of the agricultural workers." Since 1935 the Wagner Act has been amended four times, but the farm workers are still waiting. The amendments include the antilabor Taft-Hartley and Landrum-Griffin acts of 1947 and 1959, respectively, which would effectively cripple a new union before it could get established; protection of the NLRA, as constituted at the present time, would be much worse than useless to the farm workers unless they won at least temporary exemption from its strike-killing provisions.)

On March 17, the day after the hearings, Chavez set off on the celebrated workers march, or *peregrinación*, from Delano to the capitol steps in Sacramento.

The *peregrinación*, which was born as a protest against Schenley's spraying NFWA pickets with poisonous insecticides, was inspired in part by the Freedom March from Selma, Alabama, but like Chavez's fast just two years later, it also had religious reverberations: its emblem was the Mexican patron saint of the *campesinos*, la Virgen de Guadalupe, and the *peregrinación* arrived at the capitol steps on Easter Sunday. The theme was *"Penitence, Pilgrimage and Revolution."* Chavez felt from the beginning that the march should be penitential like the Lenten processions of Mexico, an atonement of past sins of violence on the part of the strikers, and a kind of prayer. But Luis Valdez, then director of the Union's propaganda theater, El Teatro Campesino, was a nonbeliever, and Marshall Ganz and other volunteers were Jewish, and none of them saw the slightest reason for atonement on the workers' part— weren't the workers the victims? Like most of the Anglo volunteers, Ganz disliked the Catholic aura that the Virgin of Guadalupe would give, and so did the scattered Protestants among the Mexicans, including Epifanio Camacho, the rose worker from McFarland, who had been nominated, with Robert Bustos, as co-captain of the march. "The question was brought up at a special meeting," Dolores Huerta told me; she laughed uneasily at the memory of those bad days. "We put the Virgin to a motion, and virginity won." At this, Camacho resigned his captaincy, and Manuel Vasquez, a farm worker from Earlimart, was nominated as *jefe* in his place.

After a ritual confrontation with local police, some sixty-seven strikers set off on the three-hundred-mile march to Sacramento and a ritual confrontation with Governor Edmund G. ("Pat") Brown. The progress of the pilgrimage was slow and ceremonial. As Chavez anticipated, it received a good deal of support and participation from people who gave food and shelter to the marchers, whose blisters and other medical needs were ministered to by the Union nurse, Peggy McGivern. Most of the marchers had reconciled themselves to the Virgin of Guadalupe, including Luis Valdez; his Teatro Campesino staged nightly propaganda skits. A statement of aims, the "*Plan de Delano*," based on Zapata's manifesto, the "*Plan de Ayala*," was distributed everywhere along the way.

The talented Valdez, whose company is now a self-sustaining group on national tour, has written eloquently of the *peregrinación* in *Ramparts*.

> The Virgin of Guadalupe was the first hint to farm workers that the pilgrimage implied social revolution. During the Mexican Revolution, the peasant armies of Emiliano Zapata carried her standard, not only because they sought her divine protection, but because she symbolized the Mexico of the

poor and humble. It was a simple Mexican Indian, Juan Diego, who first saw her in a vision at Guadalupe. Beautifully dark and Indian in feature, she was the New World version of the Mother of Christ. Even though some of her worshippers in Mexico still identify her with Tonatzin, an Aztec goddess, she is a Catholic saint of Indian creation—a Mexican. The people's response was immediate and reverent. They joined the march by the thousands, falling in line behind her standdard.

Like many Americans, Valdez has lost faith in the American Way of Life.

> There is no poetry about the United States. No depth, no faith, no allowance for human contrariness. No soul. . . . Our *campesinos* . . . find it difficult to participate in this alien North-American country. The acculturated Mexican-Americans in the cities find it easier. They have solved their Mexican contradictions with a pungent dose of Americanism, and are more concerned with status, money, and bad breath than with their ultimate destiny.

At the capitol steps a crowd of ten thousand arrived in the Easter rain, but of these, only fifty-odd *originales* had made the entire twenty-five-day march from Delano. The fifty were lost in the multitudes of latecomers, and Bustos and Valdez got hold of a microphone and demanded a place on the platform for the *originales*. A number of prominent people had attached themselves to the march in its last hours, and it says a lot about *la causa* that they were not allowed to rule the day. (Eugene Nelson, a picket captain assigned to the Schenley boycott in Houston, had begun on his own an abortive organization of Texas farm workers that was later salvaged by Gilbert Padilla and Tony Orendain. At the end of a similar march from Rio Grande City which ended in Austin on Labor Day of the same year, the politicians took over; the *campesinos* who had walked four hundred miles never said a word.) But it turned out that Governor Brown had fled, forsaking dignitaries and *originales* alike in favor of a weekend at Palm Springs with Frank Sinatra.

In the stress of all this publicity, Schenley had capitulated; the announcement of the first great farm workers' victory was made from the capitol steps. Chavez had taken time out from the march to tend to the Schenley negotiations with William Kircher, director of organization for the AFL-CIO, to whom he assigns main credit for the Schenley victory; Kircher and and Paul Schrade, head of the West Coast UAW, were among the many trade union sympathizers who participated in the start or finish of the march.

Though the best of them survived that ugly winter, the young volunteers had taken a bad beating. After hard work and poor suppers, many went to sleep on concrete; in addition, they were treated with hostility not only by the growers and the townspeople but by the *la raza* element at their own side, and even by Al Green, at that time the AFL-CIO head of AWOC, who was sorely offended by the bearded civil rights–peace element among them, and by such sympathizers as Stokely Carmichael of SNCC, who had made a brief late-evening visit to Chavez in December. To Green and his associate, Ben Gines, these volunteers, like the support that NFWA had obtained from SNCC, CORE, SDS, and the W. E. B. Du Bois Clubs, made Chavez himself suspect, and he was anxious to withdraw AWOC support. (Doubtless Schenley would have cracked before it did, had it not been so frightened of an alliance with a "leftist" union.)

For three months, though his own salary was docked, Larry Itliong, then AWOC's strike director, gave shelter to Chavez, but in March, just after the *peregrinación*, Americanism triumphed, and NFWA was purged from Filipino Hall. Right-wing publications had made much of the fact that some of Chavez's people were unembarrassed by "Marxist" affiliations, past and present, and doubtless there was pressure on Green from labor's huge apprentice middle class, which has historically adopted the values it once fought as soon as its own security was consolidated. Even some of the farm workers, hearing the peace views of the volunteers on the picket line, were asking Chavez if the union they had joined was Communist: most Mexican-Americans are still innocent enough to be blindly patriotic about the country which has used them so poorly.

The contract with Schenley, signed in June 1966, provided an hourly wage of $1.75 (it had been $1.40), and a union hiring hall; not counting Hawaii, where the International Longshoremen's and Warehousemen's Union had won contracts for pineapple workers, it was the first such contract ever negotiated in the history of American farm labor. Already the Union had turned its attention to Di Giorgio's 4,400-acre Sierra Vista Ranch in Delano, and had set up a boycott of Di Giorgio foods (White Rose, S & W, Treesweet). Di Giorgio, the "Gregorio" of *The Grapes of Wrath,* is or was the world's biggest shipper of fresh fruit, and the Teamsters, who had supported the NFWA picketing in the fight against Schenley, signed with the company what is known in labor circles as a "sweetheart" contract— one less beneficial to the workers than to the employers and the union. "We were striking Di Giorgio," Chavez said, "and we had won negotiating sessions; when the sessions were recessed over the weekend, the employer got together with the Teamsters and attempted to void the proposed contract, in total disregard of the fact that our people had been organizing there for a long time." The Teamsters announced their representation of the workers, and Di Giorgio set up a sudden election in which workers could choose between the Teamsters, NFWA, or no union at all. This first election, which was inconclusive, was finally invalidated by the American Arbitration Association, which recommended that a second election be held.

Between the elections—held on June 24 and August 30, 1966—was a long hot summer of accusations, violence, reprisals, injunctions and arrests. Among the arrested was Chavez himself, along with the Reverend Chris Hartmire, head of the California Migrant Ministry, and ten workers who had walked off the job at Di Giorgio's Borrego Springs Ranch, east of San Diego: having talked the workers into striking, Chavez, Hartmire and a Catholic priest, Father Salandini, accompanied them to the ranch to retrieve their belongings and were arrested for trespassing. To their chagrin and satisfaction—for the trespassing had been an open provocation—the arrested were stripped naked and chained together by sheriff's deputies who got carried away, as policemen will, in their eagerness to please those in power. As in the case of Governor Brown's refusal to meet with the strikers, the resultant publicity retrieved what had at first appeared to be a setback, and removed the growers further still from the sympathy of the public.

With their long history of "sweetheart" contracts—alone among the unions, the Teamsters had supported the retention of the *bracero* program, widely recognized as an anti-labor and promanagement device—the Teamsters had Di

Giorgio's full support, and this cynical alliance persuaded Chavez that in order to survive, he had no choice but to merge NFWA with AWOC, under the banner of the AFL-CIO. "We were an independent union at the beginning. We were not part of the AFL or anybody else, because we didn't want interference in the way we thought things had to be done. Too many mistakes can be made by unions trying to organize workers, and too much money would be an obstacle, at least in the beginning, because people who give it can tell you what to do with it. We didn't want to be in the same trap that the poverty programs are in today, with so many restrictions that they can't use the allocated money effectively. Money for money's sake is nothing." But thanks to the Teamsters, the price of independence had become defeat.

At this point, AWOC organizers Ben Gines and Pete Manuel defected to the Teamsters, giving as their reason that the merger had been set up by Chavez, Itliong and Kircher without consulting the AWOC and NFWA memberships, and that in any case, trade unionism had been abandoned for the civil rights–peace movement.

The merger took place in August, and the battle that ensued was vicious. The AFL-CIO declared that the Teamsters were controlled by gangsters, and the Teamsters swore that the new organization, now called the United Farm Workers Organizing Committee, was influenced if not actually run by the international Communist conspiracy. In this view the Teamsters had the strong support of the John Birch Society, which is currently being sued by Larry Itliong for referring to him as a "veteran Communist."

The strikers, still excluded from the protections of the National Labor Relations Board, were not legally obliged to observe fair labor practices, and they didn't. Enjoined from effective picketing at Sierra Vista, they held nightly prayer meetings outside the labor camps, setting up a simple shrine in the back of Chavez's old Mercury station wagon; the workers, some of whom had been recruited by Di Giorgio from as far away as El Paso and Juarez, Mexico, were proselytized when they came out to pray. Chavez also talked to the workers via a bullhorn strapped to the side of a low-flying plane, the pilot of which was a priest, Father Keith Kenny. Meanwhile, Di Giorgio was rooting out Union sympathizers, and one foreman and his wife were fired on hearsay evidence, after having worked at Sierra Vista for twenty-four years. Mrs. Ramirez witnessed an episode in which a security guard pulled a gun on a striker; when a girl volunteer protested this and tried to make a citizen's arrest, she was thrown to the ground "real hard" by Di Giorgio's personnel manager, Richard Meyer; when another striker tried to help her up, Meyer struck him over the head, then accused the strikers of starting the fight.

"Mrs. Ramirez" is a fictitious name; her real name can't be given because she and her husband are still blacklisted. "We work three days here, four days there, and get fired again," she told me. "We're trying to put our son through college, but we're so far behind on our bills, I don't think we'll *ever* catch up!" Mrs. Ramirez has a beautiful strong cheerful face, and she actually laughed heartily as she said this. "It's like climbing a glass mountain—you go up a little bit and then you slide all the way down!" She laughed again at the awful comedy. Her husband, an Army combat veteran with thirty-four months' service in World War II, watched his wife with admiration, unable to understand how she could laugh; he too, has a strong decent face, but his expression is vaguely bewildered. He told me how one boss made him fire a man for having a KENNEDY sticker on his car bumper: " 'Look, you're the foreman, you just find some excuse to fire him, that's all. Find somebody else that don't speak English.' " Workers who don't speak English are either defenseless "illegals" or too innocent to protest about unpaid bonuses or pay-check deductions for non-existent social security or workmen's compensation.

"I mean, you're working there because you been *promised* so much," his wife interrupted, as if her husband's complaint about unpaid bonuses might strike his listener as unreasonable. "They shouldn't promise it if they don't mean to pay it."

In Mr. Ramirez's opinion, eighty percent of the workers on all the ranches were pro-Union, though few would dare admit it; the rest were anti-Union out of ignorance.

"That's right," his wife said. "Like my neighbor, she don't read *anything*, not even the paper, she don't understand what's going on, none of them people do, they just believe what the growers tell them." Mrs. Ramirez had just found a new job picking cucumbers. Yesterday, she said, the workers on her crew had had to drink out of corroded rusty cans, and there was no toilet; she had worked for nine hours without relieving herself. It amused her that the growers could not afford portable toilets. "Pandol and Dispoto have airplanes," she said. "Another guy, Lucas, he has race horses." I asked her how she felt about the growers, and she seemed surprised by the question. "Oh, they're nice enough, they're not *mean* or anything," she reassured me, and her husband nodded in agreement; she spoke as she might have spoken of ill-behaved boys. "Sure, some of them can be a little bit rough, but most are pretty decent so long as you don't say nothing."

From the front stoop of his house, Mr. Ramirez pointed out the backyard of a neighbor who charged "illegals" a big fee for shelter in his shacks and chicken coops. Sometimes Mr. Ramirez and his friends report the "illegals" to the Border Patrol. He dislikes doing this, he says, because these Mexicans are poor people too, but otherwise, real American citizens had no chance. His face, as he spoke, was ridden with a guilt that is not his.

The final election, held at Sierra Vista on August 30, 1966, was supervised by the American Arbitration Association, and anyone who had worked for fifteen days or more at Sierra Vista in the previous year was eligible to vote. The Teamsters already had a large California membership of workers directly dependent on agriculture, which is a $4 billion industry in California, and the workers in the packing sheds voted to join the Teamsters, 94 to 43. But the field workers, some of whom had heard about the election from as far away as Mexico and came at their own expense to vote, won the election for UFWOC by 530 to 331; some of these people had participated in as many as three previous strikes against Di Giorgio, all of them broken in a few days. In the light of what the growers are still saying to this day, it is significant that only nineteen workers of the near-thousand whose votes were accredited cast a ballot for no union.

But UFWOC's credentials as a radical organization were no longer good enough for many of the young New Left volunteers, many of whom had been Freedom Riders and

SNCC workers disenfranchised by Stokely Carmichael's declaration of independence from the honkies; they felt strongly that American labor had sold out long ago to the Establishment, and that in merging with the AFL-CIO, Cesar Chavez had sold out, too. After the election on August 30, a number of white volunteers went home. They did not understand that a revolutionary is a man who brings about a revolution, not a boy in a Che Guevara T-shirt, and that the workers, to whom Chavez owed his first responsibility, had no home to go to if they lost the game.

Unlike some of the volunteers, the farm workers held fast; their endurance and faith in Chavez were astonishing. "Mexico is a poor land with a great deal of suffering," Drake explains. "A great deal of the natural suffering has been ritualized, institutionalized, especially in the work of the Franciscans. Mexicans didn't respond much to the missionaries who came with the conquistadors, but when Junipero Serra, the first Franciscan, landed at Acapulco and walked barefoot to Mexico City, this was something they could understand. Mexicans believe that from suffering you get strength rather than death. This is expressed in penitential acts and especially in the Eucharist. When we celebrate the Eucharist in a field or beside a picket line, with real grapes and real bread, it has the kind of earthy meaning that it had in the Indian villages before all the cathedrals were built. Of the strike, people are saying, 'We've always suffered. Now we can suffer for a purpose.'"

Nine days after the Sierra Vista election, field workers walked out of the vineyards at Perelli-Minetti and demanded representation by the United Farm Workers. As a result, Perelli-Minetti (Tribuno wines) signed a "sweetheart" contract with the Teamsters and was boycotted immediately by Chavez. After a long winter of Teamster-style dispute—in February 1967 the Teamsters kicked and beat a UFWOC picket named John Shroyer in San Francisco—the Teamsters reversed their policy and came to terms with Chavez. UFWOC granted the Teamsters' representation of the workers in the commercial sheds in return for the field workers, including those at Perelli-Minetti, whose union contract was summarily transferred to UFWOC. (Mr. Fred Perelli-Minetti now complains that he was sold out by the Teamsters, and of course he is right.) Gallo, Almadén and Christian Brothers, as well as other large California wineries, had not waited to be boycotted: because they advertise nationally, the big wineries are far more vulnerable to boycott than the growers of table grapes, and by September 1968, when Paul Masson signed, almost all of them had contracts with UFWOC.

The table-grape growers, on the other hand, had maintained a united front. Unquestionably they were heartened by the election in November 1966 of Governor Ronald Reagan, who had spoken out against the grape strike from the start of his campaign, and since that time, in Chavez's words, had tried to "destroy the movement by using the state as an apparatus to break our strike." In that same month, UFWOC won another representation election, 258 to 38, at Mosesian-Goldberg; this was the last election permitted by any grower. In the Delano area, not one of them has signed, though there is good evidence that many of the smaller farms would do so if they dared. A grower in the Coachella Valley has said as much to Chavez personally; another, in Delano, made several wavering phone calls while I was there. A third has said that he could not sign for fear of being denied the use of the distribution sheds in

Fresno, which are owned by the head of the California Grape and Tree Fruit League. These small growers are vulnerable to economic reprisal and social ostracism—one wonders which Americans fear worse—and so must continue to pay for an intransigence that only the big growers can afford. Table grapes in California are a $180-million industry, and presumably the big growers can hold out for a long time; if they do so long enough, they will be able to swallow up the farms of their small neighbors, who are going under one by one.

In July 1967, with the Teamsters agreement imminent, Cesar Chavez entered upon a brief fast of thanksgiving.

"I had done this once before, you know, just for four days, very quietly. That first time wasn't really a fast, it was more of a hunger strike, and this second time started out as a kind of a penance. We had made an agreement with Perelli-Minetti, and this was the end of that awful fight with the Teamsters—this was really one of the most difficult periods for me. And so anyway, we met with the Teamsters on a Friday, and I think the contract was supposed to be signed on a Tuesday, and so as a kind of thanksgiving you know, I decided on a four-day fast, and at noon on Friday I had my last meal. I still didn't know too much about fasting; the conditioning is the toughest part. You have to condition yourself mentally. If you're not prepared, I don't think you can do it. So . . . it went well for four days, but then it turned out that they couldn't meet on Tuesday. And they couldn't meet the next day, and they kept prolonging it, and from that point on, it became a . . . well, I said to myself, I've fasted, and I can't eat until we sign that contract. No one knew about the fast; the twenty-five-day one was the only one anybody knew about, the rest were very personal.

"By the end of ten days I was wrecked. Sick. Not from hunger, just mentally and physically. Weak. I kept working, I came to the office, but the last couple of days I just dragged myself, because I didn't have any strength, mentally or physically. Even the day we finally signed the contract, I had to drag myself out there, I was so sick. And some of these growers are really tough, you know, and *bitter, bitter*"—he shook his head, letting his voice fall to an awed whisper, as if bitterness so terrible should not be spoken of aloud—"but they must have seen my face, because they didn't talk much. It was like in the movies, when the children of the deceased get together with the attorney to divvy up the will—it was as cold as that. I didn't speak a word. They spoke to Jerry Cohen and Jerry would speak to me, and I would speak to Jerry and Jerry would speak to them. I hadn't planned it that way, I was just so sick I couldn't speak to anybody. I just wanted to sign the contract and get out of there. Afterward one of their attorneys wanted to talk to me, but I didn't want to talk to anyone. I just nodded my head, I just wanted to get out of there and go home to bed. And after a couple of days in bed I was okay."

After the victory at Perelli-Minetti, Giumarra was made the target of the boycott. In December 1967, during the Giumarra boycott, Chavez and his wife made a four-day trip to Mexico, to see if a break in the green-card impasse could be made with the Mexican government. But the politicians there would not believe that Chavez did not wish to end the green-card visa that brought so many dollars into Mexico; they were openly suspicious of his un-*macho* manner and his unwillingness to drink or smoke, and one drunken official went so far as to suggest to his face that he did not "enjoy women." The Chavezes were glad of the chance to see Mexico's great archaeological museum and the pyramids outside the city, but otherwise their trip to Mexico was a complete failure.

Though Al Green had retired at the time of the merger, the spiritual consolidation of AWOC and NFWA is still less than complete. In Filipino Hall, it is very noticeable that the Filipinos sit on the right-hand side and the Mexicans on the left. The Mexican-Americans have always outnumbered the Filipinos, which is usually the reason given why Cesar Chavez was made director. The Filipinos have remained loyal to Larry Itliong, the assistant director; two other Filipinos, Philip Vera Cruz and Andy Imutan, are on the board of directors. The old Filipino bachelors with their sad, smooth faces and half-hidden bright black eyes have little to cheer about, but they are proud that AWOC, not NFWA, led the original strike in 1965. While they admire Cesar Chavez, they haven't much faith in a union dominated by Mexican-Americans. "Look at Cesar's followers," one says, as if the hopelessness of these *chicanos* must be self-evident. On the other hand, the Mexican-Americans say, no doubt correctly, that without their help the AWOC strike would have been just another failure.

Like most racial friction, the origin of Filipino-Mexican discord can be traced to economics. In the early history of American California, the Indians inherited from the mission farms were paid half of what other workers got, and their protest against this treatment was a factor in the general massacre that took place in the two years between 1850 and

1852, when the Indian population in California, already low, was reduced from an estimated 85,000 to about 31,000 (the remnants, mostly Digger Indians, continued to be exploited on the farms, and contemporary descriptions of their squalor and misery have been echoed for a century by the few honest observers who have entered migrant labor camps). This free-enterprise solution to the Indian problem caused a temporary labor shortage, but the advantages of the discriminatory pay scale in keeping labor groups at odds with one another were already obvious, and the device has been used effectively ever since. When the Filipinos arrived in force in the 1920's, they were paid even less than the Mexicans, who were already in a very poor bargaining position; most were wetbacks who could be and often were deported before payday came around, or when they protested too strenuously about anything. Traditionally, the two groups have competed for available work—usually stoop labor, because preference in the tree jobs is usually given to the Anglos—and ever since, Mexicans have been saying that Filipinos are lazy, while Filipinos claim that Mexicans are dirty, or vice versa. Like the blacks and Puerto Ricans of New York and Newark, they work at cross-purposes against the common enemy.

Chavez speaks warmly of the Filipinos and worries constantly that their quiet nature, which he admires, will deny them a fair voice in Union affairs. But by making his people aware of what they are doing, Chavez has brought the two groups much closer together. With the Puerto Ricans, they have a common heritage of Spanish domination and Catholicism, and are loyal to one another on the picket lines or in any crisis. Still, they are not yet the "brothers" of Chavez's dream.

"I hear about *la raza* more and more," Chavez told me. "Some people don't look at it as racism, but when you say *la raza*, you are saying an anti-gringo thing, and our fear is that it won't stop there. Today it's anti-gringo, tomorrow it will be anti-Negro, and the day after it will be anti-Filipino, anti-Puerto Rican. And then it will be anti–poor-Mexican, and anti–darker-skinned-Mexican.

"In the beginning we had a lot of trouble with it in the Union. We had a stupid guy who began to whip up *la raza* against the white volunteers, and even had some of the farm workers and the pickets and the organizers hung up on *la raza*. So I took him on. These things have to be met head-on. On discrimination, I don't even give the members the privilege of a vote, and I'm not ashamed of it. No. The whole business of discrimination can't exist here. So often these days, the leaders are afraid, and even though they feel strongly against racism, they will not speak out against it. They're like married people who stay together, saying, 'It's because of the kids'—that's an awful thing, you know. If the leadership is united, then it can say, 'All right, if you're going to do things that way, then you'll have to get rid of us.' You have to speak out immediately, the first time.

"Anyway, this guy was talking to people and saying he didn't like Filipinos taking over the Union. So a small group came to me and said that a lot of people were very mad because the Filipinos were coming in. And I really reacted. I said a lot of people would be mad if Negroes came in large numbers like that, and I said that they were going to accept the Filipinos, if I had to shove them down their throat." Chavez paused as if surprised, years later, at his own violence. "I told them, 'That's the way I feel.' And so they left. A couple of days later they said they wanted a big meeting. And I said, 'Okay, let's have a big meeting.' So at the big meeting they said they wanted to discuss discrimination; in other words, they wanted to take a vote to discriminate. And I said, 'Over my dead body. There'll be no such vote taken here, and furthermore, before you get rid of the Filipinos you'll have to get rid of me.' 'No vote?' they said, and I said, 'It can't be done. Those of you who don't like it, I suggest that *you* get out, because you're not doing anybody any good. Or even better, *I'll* get out. And I'll join the Filipinos. And we'll build a trade union, and work well together.' Well, I'd say ninety-five percent of the audience stood up and applauded. And this small group felt isolated.

"The employers, of course, have used this for years and years—one group set against the other. I explained this to the audience, and I told them that the Filipinos would be a tremendous asset—new ideas, new people. That's what a union is. And about six months later I got hold of the people who had been so against the Filipinos, and I said, 'Listen, I think we should get rid of those Filipinos.' And they said, 'Why?'" Chavez looked astounded, rolling his eyes; he laughed.

"Then we had a case where one of the big growers came out and started pushing one of the white volunteers around, and one of the *la raza* guys, Marcos Muñoz, jumped up and wanted to take on the grower. And I said, 'Let him get pushed around; he's just a gringo anyway.' And Marcos said, 'I'm really offended.' And I said, 'I said that purposely, because *you*'ve been offending *me:* any time you say anything about a human being just because he's white, it offends me.' 'Well,' says Marcos, 'I really feel badly to feel the way I do, but I can't help it.' I said, 'Well, then, if a grower wants to run over one of those gringos on the picket line, to hell with it; let it go.' So he said, 'Well, I can't.' I said, 'Maybe you don't really hate gringos, then; maybe you're just trying to make it up. Maybe you're just trying to be a big *macho;* maybe it's a way of showing how brave you are.' Then Dolores went after him, and Gilbert Padilla, and we said, 'When you go on the boycott, you know what's going to happen? There's going to be a fight. And there aren't any Mexicans out there, so you're going to find a lot of gringos helping you. But if you don't like 'em, you can handle the whole fight yourself.' " Chavez shook his head.

"He learned. Marcos is running the Boston boycott now; he's one of our best young leaders. And he's got a hell of a lot of gringo friends there helping him. No, I don't like to see any man discriminating. But when a *Mexican* discriminates—*oo.*" He winced. "That *really* cuts me. As a Mexican-American, I expect more of them than anybody else; I love them, and I guess I'd like them to be perfect."

More recently, Chavez has had to deal with resentment against his so-called "inner circle," which certain Union officers feel is dominated by the Anglos. To this, Chavez retorts that he knows who works hard and long and cheerfully, and that these people, whatever their race, are the ones he has to count on.

"The Teamsters never could understand how our farm workers would go out on strike or work for the Union without pay," Chavez told the audience in Filipino Hall. "They don't understand what we're trying to do, because it isn't part of their history. They just haven't done what we have done. Most unions haven't." Like his listeners, he seemed dampened by the mention of the Teamsters, and then he cried out, "People are getting sick of the growers pushing us around; people are sick of poverty . . ." But Chavez isn't good at rhetoric, in fact dislikes it, and once again his voice trailed off, as if he knew that this was wishful thinking; more than most, he is aware that people everywhere are callous or indifferent to poverty, and always have been. It is the paupers who get sick of poverty, if anything meaningful is to be done.

"Then," Chavez said, brightening, "we ordered twenty-five thousand new bumper stickers today." He grinned with real enthusiasm, raising his hands to outline the sticker design: "BOYCOTT, then the eagle in the middle, then GRAPES! In a beautiful color! It's going to pop your eyes out!" He sighed in admiration, shaking his head; he looked extremely tired. "So I think," he concluded, "that it has been a very good day."

In response to a question, Chavez spoke briefly about the Di Giorgio HI-COLOR crisis and concluded, "I want some recommendations from you on what to do in this case." One after another, the workers stood up to state their opinions, pitching their voices too softly or too loud in their struggle to overcome their shyness. Chavez himself translated their statements into Spanish or English: "I'm asked by a sister . . ."; "A brother suggests that we sue . . ."

A man who moved that Di Giorgio be boycotted was seconded by acclamation. Philip Vera Cruz, representing the Filipinos, stood up and cried fiercely, "I think we should fight him all the way! Thank you!" Mack Lyons, a laconic young black man who is workers' representative at Di Giorgio's Arvin ranch, spoke quickly and coldly in favor of a confrontation, and by now the hall was so excited that Chavez felt obliged to try to calm it. It was plain that he was stunned by the prospect of a new fight with Di Giorgio. Quietly he explained that a boycott would cancel out their hard-won contract, that this should be avoided if possible. "You must understand these things," he pleaded. But the workers were outraged by Di Giorgio's betrayal, and Chavez, who had reared this fighting spirit out of decades of defeat and ignorance and apathy, and who believed above all in participatory democracy, including the right of the poor to make their own mistakes, did not feel he could interfere. The vote to sue Di Giorgio was unanimous, and a motion to boycott Di Giorgio's S & W brand very nearly so. It was agreed that the next day, Saturday, Chavez, Mrs. Huerta, Jerry Cohen and Mack Lyons would meet with Di Giorgio's representatives. If no agreement was reached over the weekend, both suit and boycott would be carried out on Monday.

Hollow-eyed and worried, Chavez concluded the meeting with some comments on a member's request that an armed guard be stationed at the Forty Acres to prevent further damage to Union property: the member was referring to the burning of the cross. "I have told you many times," Chavez said, "that people who are violent will not be permitted to work in the strike. And so we are not going to go armed. No one goes armed." More quietly he said, "I've been getting threats on my life every day for the last six months, and I'm not armed, and I won't permit anybody with me to be armed."

An old Filipino, angry, jumped to his feet. "We spent our money there! Should we let them burn it?" The others cheered, and Chavez gazed around the room.

"You can vote right now to arm yourselves—" Chavez began, but before he could complete his threat of resignation, a woman stood up and spoke in his behalf. Concluding, she turned in a semicircle to plead with the brooding audience. "The whole world supports Cesar," she entreated, "just *because* of his nonviolence!" A man stood up. "I offer words from the Bible," he said. "Justice of God cannot be won by the sword. We must resist temptation to violence, especially when victory is certain."

The audience fell silent. Chavez, too, was silent. His tired face reflected anything but the certainty of victory. When it resumed, his voice came quietly, as if he had been speaking all along and only now had become audible again. "If you want a guard, and nobody wishes to guard it without arms, then I will guard it myself." He spoke very simply, and he meant it. "If they burn it, we can build again. But if a man is killed, who can revive him?"

"Here was Cesar," Luis Valdez has written, "burning with a patient fire, poor like us, dark like us, talking quietly, moving people to talk about their problems, attacking the little problems first and suggesting, always suggesting— —never more than that—solutions which seemed attainable. We didn't know it until we met him, but he was the leader we had been waiting for."

When the meeting was over, Chavez invited Mrs. Israel and myself to accompany him to a farewell party being given for a young lawyer who was moving to Los Angeles. He felt badly that he had been away since our arrival, and was extremely warm and gracious—a heroic effort, considering how tired and tense he really was. Outside on the steps, he permitted himself to become annoyed by the presence of a beer can on the railing, but by the time we were under way, down Glenwood Street, he was relaxed again and was able to laugh as he described how this stretch had looked before U.S. Highway 99 pierced the town. "The chamber of commerce would like people to believe that Delano is a sweet, simple American town where everybody loved his neighbor until us troublemakers came, but it was *always* a violent place; this whole stretch was gambling and prostitution, and people were killing each other left and right."

From the party, in a small cantina on Garces Highway, we went on to the Coffee Cup, on Main Street, to get something to eat; Dolores Huerta and Jerry Cohen came with us. Chavez likes the Coffee Cup and a Chinese restaurant, the Pagoda, because in neither place do people stare at him. Warmly he greeted Thelma, the waitress, asking if she was working hard tonight. She said that she was, and he sighed in commiseration. When Thelma went to fetch a menu, he told us that at the time of the Sierra Vista elections she was one of the few people on the east side of Delano who would say hello to him, and he admired her for her courage.

Ann Israel now declared that the party was on her, at which Chavez jumped right up out of the booth and peered out the window; from where he stood, through a gap in the warehouses, he could see across Main Street, High Street, and the railroad tracks to the Pagoda, on the far side of Glenwood. "It's open!" he said. "Let's go have Chinese food!" He turned to Thelma. "I'm going to spoil the party," he confided. "We're going to have Chinese food!" He smiled delightedly, and she smiled too. "Never mind," he called back to the waitress from the doorway. "This is *still* my favorite restaurant!" Thelma waved. She had been somewhere and knew something, and this small, warm man was no threat to her at all.

Outside in the summer darkness, Chavez checked the long night shadows of the parking lot. Once when he came here with Fred Ross, a man pointing a black object had jumped at him out of the darkness; the black thing turned out to be a camera. "Fred asked the guy, 'What the hell did you do *that* for?' and the guy said, 'I just wanted a picture.' " Chavez shook his head, looking from one face to the other as if in hopes that one of us might explain human behavior. "I was scared," he said fervently, looking scared.

At the Pagoda, Chavez asked the waitress if she was working hard tonight, and like Thelma, she acknowledged that she was. His sigh at the Pagoda was as genuine as the sigh at the Coffee Cup: he said he hated the sight of women on their feet and working late at night.

Over won ton soup, Chavez listened to Jerry Cohen's plans for next day's confrontation with Di Giorgio. Cohen, Chavez and Mrs. Huerta agreed that the Di Giorgio people were entirely untrustworthy. "They are animals," Chavez said quietly, using his worst term of opprobrium; the only other time I ever heard him use it was in reference to the old Mexican governors of California. Cohen, who is excited at his calmest, related his visit the day before to the Arvin area, where he had spotted HI-COLOR boxes in the fields of the Sabovich farm; he described how Jesse Marcus, a Di Giorgio foreman notorious for his hatred of the Union, had tried to run him off the road. It would do no good to file a complaint, he said: there was no justice in Kern County, where the cops and judges knew nothing about the Constitution, and cared less.

Mrs. Huerta remarked that the Delano police were still harassing her. She borrowed other people's cars as often as she could, but she still was stopped every time she turned around. Chavez recalled how he had been accosted repeatedly by the Secret Service at Robert Kennedy's funeral in New York. As usual, he had been dressed in his clean work clothes, and standing there among celebrities in formal mourning dress, he was clearly a suspicious character. "I guess I did not look right," Chavez said.

They talked a little bit about the assassination. Chavez had been in Los Angeles on the night of the primary election, but he did not see Kennedy. With a *mariachi* band on a flatbed truck, he was campaigning until the final minutes; then the band entered the downstairs ballroom at the Ambassador, where Kennedy had been headed when he was shot, and at this point the crowd began to chant, "We want Cha-*vez!*"

"So I left," Chavez said. "I felt uncomfortable." He had gone to the bar, where somebody bought him a Diet-Rite, but there a drunken girl began to yell, "Hey! This is Cesar!" so he fled the hotel entirely. Picking up Helen at the priest's house where they were staying, he went to a party for a Mexican-American who was running for the state senate, and he was just leaving when a cry came that Kennedy and a labor leader and a woman had been shot. Chavez knew that Mrs. Huerta had been with the senator in his suite before the victory speech, but he was not worried about her. "I was very sure that Paul Schrade had been shot, but not Dolores. I can't explain it; I just had this feeling, but I was sure."

Chavez sat up all night watching the news, and drove back to Delano early in the morning. Stopping at the post office about nine, he was shouted at by a carload of "the opposition. They yelled something horrible, something like they were so happy that he got it; I felt weak in the knees; I could hardly walk or even speak. I just stared at them and said, 'Gee . . . God—' And a lot of telephone threats started coming in. So I really didn't want to go to the funeral in New York because I was afraid there might be violence in Delano, but the membership took a close vote and decided I should go." At two-thirty in the morning, on the night he arrived, he was put on the "Kennedy vigil" at the bier; he was suffering from pains in his back, and he did not quite understand what he was doing there.

Mrs. Huerta and Leroy Chatfield had accompanied Chavez to New York. In St. Patrick's Cathedral they sat behind *la raza* leader Reies Lopez Tijerina, who wore a big sombrero that obscured Mrs. Huerta's view. She also rode on the funeral train to Washington, but Chavez didn't see much point in this. Of the funeral he said, "It was just what I expected—a lot of people." He flew straight back to California.

The conversation shifted to the subject of the Agricultural Workers Freedom to Work Association (AWFWA), an anti-Chavez organization which Cohen wished to sue for defamation. Intentionally or otherwise, the concept of "freedom to work" evokes the Taft-Hartley law (the Labor-Management Relations Act of 1947), which labor regards as a union-busting device masquerading as progressive legislation; among other things, Taft-Hartley rules against active support of a union boycott by another union, or what is termed a "secondary boycott." "Since Taft-Hartley," Chavez says, "labor solidarity just doesn't exist any more in the

United States. Other unions can help out indirectly, but the Longshoremen are about the only ones that quit when they see a picket sign. Not the leadership but the membership—the men. In San Francisco, if you carry a picket sign anywhere near the docks, everything stops. It's sort of a tradition with them: the membership will not work behind picket lines. It's a small union, and they couldn't help us with money, but back in '65 they stopped the grapes at the docks twice in one week and got sued for eighty-five or ninety-five thousand dollars."

Officially, AWFWA is run by Joe Mendoza, a former shoe salesman and radio announcer, and Gilbert Rubio, a former errand boy at UFWOC who, Chavez says without elaboration, was "finally asked to leave," but UFWOC people say that AWFWA's membership is made up chiefly of labor contractors and must be sponsored by the growers, since Rubio and Mendoza conduct their business without visible means of support; among the growers, the prime suspect was Giumarra.

"My scab cousin from Texas, I never even met him, and he runs to Rubio and Mendoza with bad stories about me," Mrs. Huerta said with a small, sad laugh of surprise. "Like, I travel around so much alone, and I don't take proper care of my kids." She shrugged. "What am I going to say?" she said, to no one in particular. "All of it's true." Again, she gave a characteristic peal of melodious sad laughter. Mrs. Huerta's children are called Communists in school, and life was made so miserable for the eldest child, Lori, that she was sent away to school in Stockton; her daughter Alicia, a beautiful child of seven who is a mascot at the Union offices, felt obliged to part with her best friend as they grew older because the parents of the friend were scabs; in a town as tight as Delano, friendship between seven-year-olds from rival factions is not a possibility.

In her gray-checked San Francisco suit with round white collar, Mrs. Huerta's sad face looked beautiful. From across the table, Chavez watched her with concern. There is a single silver strand in the Indian jet hair falling across his forehead, and a black mole on the brown skin just under the right side of his lower lip seemed to balance the gold tooth in his growing smile. She glanced up at him, looking flustered, and lowered her eyes again. Gently he began to tease her, and in a little while he had her giggling; in the shelter of a vibrant discussion between Cohen and Mrs. Israel, they played a game of words, like children.

Outside the Pagoda, Mrs. Huerta asked me never to leave Cesar by himself. "If you are alone with him, then see him to the door. He is so careless where he walks." Chavez seemed nervous to her; he was not his serene old self at all. He came over to say good night, and seeing her worried expression, he glanced at me with the hint of a question in his eyes. "See you later, hey?" he said.

5

ON Saturday morning, with Cohen and Mrs. Huerta, Chavez drove to the airport motel in Bakersfield to meet with the Di Giorgio lawyer, Don Connors, who was flying down from San Francisco; joining them from the 9,000-acre Di Giorgio ranch at Arvin would be Richard Meyer, the personnel manager, and Mack Lyons, the workers' representative. The Arvin ranch has a mixed crew of Mexicans, Filipinos, Puerto Ricans, blacks, and Southern whites (mostly children of the Okies who descended on California in the Depression), and any man that these groups could agree upon, Chavez said, and a black man especially, "*must be a nice guy.*" Dolores Huerta, who serves as the Union representative at most contract negotiations, is training Lyons as a negotiator, and she says he is very good, very cool. Lyons was chosen for the October 1966 sit-in at the Di Giorgio offices in San Francisco, for which he went to jail, and in 1967 he was a Union representative at hearings of the House Subcommittee on Labor and Education in Washington. There Lyons was patronized by his congressman, Hon. Bob Mathias, the former decathlon champion and one of a number of instant politicians—Ronald Reagan, George Murphy and Shirley Temple are best known—whose qualifications for public office would be thought negligible anywhere in the world but the superconsumer culture of California. Mathias told Mack Lyons, "You look like an athlete—ever play anything?" And Lyons said, "A little basketball—how about you?"

On the way south on U.S. 99, Mrs. Huerta remarked that Di Giorgio had surely sold the rights to HI-COLOR to hurt the Union. Cohen and Chavez were equally certain that the company had done it to make money and that Union strategy must be directed at its purse; at Di Giorgio, no one acted on principle unless a profit could be shown. Chavez granted that Di Giorgio was still battling the Union: the company felt that the contract had been forced on it and that therefore it was justified in sabotaging the Union in any way it could.

On large issues Dolores Huerta is perhaps Chavez's most loyal ally, but on small ones, she tends to be combative. Everyone was tense about the upcoming meeting, and she persisted in her arguments past a useful point, at which Chavez, less gently than usual, cut her off. "Dolores! What are we fighting about? Why do you argue with me so much? Goddamn it, Dolores!" he exclaimed, and Dolores cried out, "Don't swear at me, man!"

"Goddamn it, Dolores," he repeated, softly this time, "I lose my patience." He looked away, out the window.

Despite the 100-degree heat, Chavez kept his window rolled up tight. I took this as a sign of his preoccupation, and decided to find out, at the airport, if this U-drive car could be exchanged for a model that had air conditioning. Another sign of tension was Chavez's failure to comment on the things he saw along the highway. Ordinarily he delights in small phenomena and grotesqueries of all kinds, but this morning he noticed nothing. After a while he said,

"We can't take on another fight; we have more than we can handle right now." He sat there slumped in a wide-striped summer shirt of varying grays, wearing a big button issued in support of the movement to recall Governor Reagan. The button read:

THIS STATE IS
TEMPORARILY
OUT OF ORDER

Mack Lyons met us in front of the motel, and the UF-WOC people walked inside. I went over to the airport lobby, and after trying unsuccessfully to change cars, wandered back out into the Valley glare. In the driveway I ran into Chavez, all alone and looking gleeful. "We declared all-out war and they really hit the ceiling; they're trying to get Bob Di Giorgio on the phone!" Despite his worries in the car he seemed elated now that the battle was joined, and was looking for some fuel to keep him going. "You noticed any Diet-Rite around here?" he said. We could not find any, and he settled reluctantly for a Tab, disgorged by a huge outdoor dispenser.

We stood in the hot concrete shade while he drank Tab and discussed Diet-Rite.

"During the fast I would get thirsty, and one doctor recommended Diet-Rite Cola, which has no food value—only one calorie. 'Well,' I said, 'I better not take it; one calorie is one calorie.' It was the principle, you know. But when the fast ended, there were some ridiculous things I really craved. The doctors told me that getting off the fast, I would be—what's the word . . . euphoric?—but then it would be like a woman having a child, you know, I would get depressed. Well, the depression wasn't so bad, but I did get these crazy food cravings. Helen and I took a week off and were driving to the coast, and we had a nurse with us—Peggy McGivern, you know—and she asked me what I wanted: I could have anything but meat or very heavy stuff. 'Really?' I said. 'Anything?' She said yes. So I said, 'You're not going to believe this.' We stopped at a store and we bought Diet-Rite and matzos, packaged and produced by Manischewitz. And now I'm kind of addicted to them both."

We talked about the meeting the night before, which led to Chavez's favorite subject—organizing. When he talks of organizing he uses his whole body, struggling to clarify, to simplify, as if he were developing techniques to be used later.

"There has to be a real organization, a living organization, there has to be . . . people in motion, and they have to be disciplined." He laughed. "I don't mean, like, *marching*, I mean a trained instinct so that when the moment comes, we just turn around and *hit* it. That's real organization. If you organize for demonstration, all you have is demonstration. You must demonstrate, and then return right away to the real work. We're so flexible, yet there's so much discipline that we do things and don't even talk about them. We can go down the highway at eighty miles an hour and throw her into reverse gear and not even screech. For instance, we can be striking today, and tomorrow morning or a couple of days later we can move the effort into a boycott without missing a step. We have a motion and rhythm. That mobility makes a difference. It can be compared to a prize fight, where the whole idea is to be in balance so that however bad things get, you don't get knocked out, and you're always ready to take advantage of their mistakes. By instinct more than anything else, when we see them make a mistake we move right in, and this is true right down to the simplest striker on the picket line." He grinned. "That's why they call us the Vietcong—it's guerrilla warfare.

"Institutions can't afford these methods. The growers, for example, are in the business of growing grapes, and picking them, and shipping them and all the problems that go with that. We're in the business of building a union, and so we just have one thing to do: strike, boycott, whatever, is all part of that business. If we take them on in a strike, then we force them to do two things, fight on two fronts, but we continue to do one thing. And we are on the offensive, while they are defending something, so we can afford mistakes. We can make thirty mistakes in a day, you know, and unless the mistakes are very, very bad, we'll only pay for one or two. But they make just one mistake, and we punch right through their lines. Right through. And this is what happens, and it happens by instinct; it isn't that we sat down and diagramed it. It's just instinct. People know. The oldest and youngest picket, the dishwasher at Filipino Hall, knows what to do if he sees an opening. I estimate that we can make them spend fifty dollars to our one, and sometimes more. And we're still developing our tactics." He tried to look fiendish, and we laughed.

"You see, we have a great training ground for organizers. The good ones have some unexplainable attitude, I can't explain it but I can sense it, I can see it. Some of the organizers, they watch a guy for one day and then say, 'Oh, I've met a terrific leader,' or 'a potential leader,' but you can't tell that soon.

"People come along that have a great love of human beings and have never found a way to channel it. And then they go out on strike and transform that love into something effective—the whole question of human rights. Women have something very special this way; women have a lot of staying power. They're endowed with some real special thing by God, I think. Men, you know, we *want* it, let's *do* it, we want to finish it all up in seconds, but women just keep going. If you're full of *machismo,* you can't appreciate what women do, but if you're not, it's really beautiful. Sometimes they have to organize around their husbands because their husbands are *macho,* the head of the house, the *king,* you know, and to have his wife out on the picket line is degrading. And so she has to organize him, and the first thing you know, he's out there, too. We know that if we don't get the wife, we'll lose the husband, anyway. Sometimes we have a guy who's really full of love, and he wants badly to go out and do things, and his wife says nothing doing, and we lose him. We have lost many good organizers to their wives; some guys were broken in half, because they really wanted to work. But the strongest ones, the wives don't bother them too much. Or the husband doesn't give a damn, and the wife really wants to do something—in those cases, the husband can be reached. But if the guy wants to do something, and he doesn't want his wife out striking —well, that's difficult. We try hard to keep the family involved. It's a lot easier to say we don't want the women and the kids—they make too much noise at the meetings, so forget it. That's too easy. I think the women and children have a lot of determination, and they make some beautiful contributions."

. . .

Chavez talked for a while about gibberellin, the plant hormone that the growers pump into the fruit to make it fat and hard; the result looks and feels almost as good as plastic fruit, and it keeps much better than a natural grape on the trip across the country. "The next time you're in New York," Chavez said, "try a strawberry. Get a real big one, the nicest-looking strawberry you can find. Don't put any cream or sugar on it; just eat it. I mean, wash it first, because it may have parathion all over it. Then taste it. And after that, get a piece of cardboard and eat that too; they taste about the same." He grunted. "Here at Davis Agricultural College, at the University of California, they've decided that people don't really care about taste anymore, they can get that from the cream and sugar: what they care about is a big berry that *looks* nice. If you find a little puny berry that's really sweet, like berries used to taste ten years ago —well, probably that comes from Mexico or Latin America or France, maybe Arabia, but it doesn't come from this country. And the same thing is happening with grapes." American food corporations, he said, prepared cherries for the consumer by leaching out all their natural hues (and with them any nutrients the fruit might have) and shooting them full of artificial color.

Loss of quality in grapes means loss of sugar and taste. Possibly the agronomists at Davis are mistaken about what people want, since table-grape acreage in California, in the last ten years, has been cut nearly in half in response to a decline in sales, and a few growers would like to outlaw the use of gibberellin.

Though Lyons and Mrs. Huerta were still with the Di Giorgio people in the motel room, Chavez seemed in no great hurry to go back. We sat at a poolside table under a two-decker row of rooms, from where they could see and call him if he was needed. From the diving board a big pallid man with a small close-cropped head, wearing large orange bathing trunks—the sort of man who was probably called "Whitey" long before that name came into fashion—was performing big board-splitting jackknives for his wife and son. Ba-*whoom*-pha! Over and over against the shimmering flat asphalt of the airport, the man catapulated himself into the air, rising above the tight, hard shrubbery of the motel landscaping into slow orbit against the bare blue sky; at the moment of impact, his re-entry splash sizzled out on the hot jet howl of the straining airplanes. Thin-backed, thin-headed, in a row of two, wife and son attended dutifully. Now and then the woman glanced with birdy disapproval at a female sex threat in a lounge chair who every few minutes, like a sprung mechanism in a cuckoo clock, performed a loose circuit for the other guests and returned into her chair again.

The more Chavez watched the lonely performance of the woman, the more distressed he became. Chavez is un-American in his fondness for women—as people, that is, not sex trophies or appointments of the home—and he feels that in the American culture, where appearance means everything, women have no choice but to exploit their bodies. As someone has pointed out, the use and purpose of gibberellin is very much like the use of silicone to enhance women's breasts; we agreed that topless waitresses and *Playboy* girls are too much a consumer product to be sexy.

On the subject of sex, Chavez is both frank and shy, which is as it should be: to respect the mystery even while embracing it. Once, in New York, he showed me a printed card with a dirty poem on it that some union official was sending back with him for Jerry Cohen. Its last line was quite clever, and I laughed, thinking this line was the reason he had shown it, but glimpsing Chavez's face, I wished I hadn't. His expression was in no way disapproving—he thought the last line was clever too. But he hated the implied degradation of women, and was merely reflective, watching my reaction.

Chavez went up to the meeting again, and after a while Mack Lyons came down. He said he had come to pick up a briefcase, but he did not go back. Lyons is tall, thin and good-looking, with a mustache; cool as he seems his brow is almost always furrowed. Sitting down, glaring about him, he made it plain that he had felt superfluous in the motel room. "I felt I was cheating, being up there," he fumed; he did not elaborate. Lyons' brother had been killed in Vietnam, fighting a people, as the black saying goes, who "never called me 'nigger,' " and in some ultimate irony this black soldier died accidentally at the hands—white hands, presumably—of his own side, in a burst of what Lyons refers to acidly as "friendly fire."

Soon Chavez, Cohen and Mrs. Huerta reappeared; we sat around the poolside table, under the shade of its gay striped umbrella. They reported that Don Connors had not yet reached Robert Di Giorgio. It was a beautiful bright Saturday, and Di Giorgio's men meant to track him down and spoil his weekend. Cohen claimed that Connors was patronizing them: " 'You boys,' he keeps saying!" But Chavez had respect for Connors: "He fights a hard fight for them, but he's not sneaky." Cohen nodded, popping his hands. "We're going to hit 'em," he vowed a moment later. "All kinds of suits. I'm going to sue Di Giorgio for subverting the Union contract. I'm going to sue the growers for misrepresenting their product: to sell stuff that is non-Union-picked under a Union label is a transgression of truth-in-packaging laws." Cohen sprawled backwards in his chair, squinting as the sun struck his face. "Maybe I'll sue Jesse Marcus for assault with a deadly weapon."

We waited a long time. Dolores Huerta sat with her ankles in the swimming pool, cooling off. Nearby, on one knee, Mack Lyons was talking to her. At the suggestion that he cool his feet he looked angry and uneasy, as if he expected the manager to come running out, shaking a white finger, but finally he took off his shoes and socks, rolled up his pants, and stuck his legs into the bright blue pool.

"I still get that bad feeling in restaurants," Chavez says. "Just a little bit. The Mexicans, the green-carders, don't have it—my kids, neither. They aren't conditioned the way we were. If somebody called me 'spick' or 'greaser'!" He stopped, looking physically sick. "But the kids just laugh; they let 'em have it right back. I couldn't do it; I was hurt too much. For some it was better than others, but if you were darker, poorer . . .

"Getting rejected, you know, hurts very deep. Even today, something hits me for a second." He put his hand on his stomach. Talking about his early migrant days, he described how his family, wintering in Brawley, would leave every morning around three o'clock to work in Indio, two hours away. Cesar's father would never stop anywhere for coffee, but one morning he tried a broken-down place that looked as if it needed any trade it could get. Cesar went inside with his father. Mr. Chavez, who scarcely spoke English, stood there politely, holding his empty coffee jug.

The woman yelled, "We don't want Mexicans here! Get out!" To this day, Chavez remembers the look on his father's face.

We waited for a long time in the heat. Mrs. Huerta wondered aloud why Di Giorgio wasn't raising table grapes any more. She had heard that Di Giorgio had not resisted the government enforcement of the water quota because at Sierra Vista the grape vines, which may be productive for thirty years or more, were getting old and had to be replaced: the quality of their grapes was growing poor. The grapes—

"Dolores! Dolores! Can you see this?" Chavez gestured impatiently with a pencil. "Watch! Look, Dolores! The age of the vine has nothing to do with size or color or sugar content! These are things I know!"

Someone brought up the vandalism at the Forty Acres, and I made some careless reference to the threats on Chavez's life, which I was slow to learn should be taken seriously. Instead of commenting, Chavez left his chair. He would go and see how things were coming along, he said; however, he wandered off in the wrong direction. Soon he returned and was asked if he wished anything to eat. It was now past one o'clock. "No," he said, grinning. "I'll be eating my insides until this thing is over." But a little later he dozed off in his chair. "He can sleep anywhere," Helen Chavez assured me when I described this later. "That's how he keeps going." Chavez himself says, "I always get my sleep, no matter how bad things are. Of course, I never had a serious personal tragedy; I might not sleep then."

At two-thirty Don Connors, a big florid silver-headed man, went by on his way to the snack bar. He called out that he still had not talked to Di Giorgio but would reach him at three o'clock; he was going to grab something to eat. He was followed by Di Giorgio's Richard Meyer, who in 1966 had said, in discussing the Union during the Sierra Vista dispute, "As long as I'm working for Di Giorgio, we won't capitulate, and if we do, I'll quit."

Chavez suggested that we take advantage of the time to find some Diet-Rite. In the parking lot the car was very hot; entering, he astonished me by rolling up his window again. This time, however, he reached forward and turned on the air conditioner, which I had failed to notice; it was lost in the array of knobs and dials that gives the consumer a sense of living dangerously. On the ride south he had doubtless thought that I was some sort of masochist but was too polite to draw attention to it; this time, in a car like a hot popover, he did not bother to stand on ceremony.

The Miracle Market, a few miles away, had piped music and innumerable machines of chemical-colored bubble-gum balls and candies for the women in hair curlers who dominated the clientele; it also had Diet-Rite Cola. By the time we returned Connors was ready, and the Union negotiators trooped upstairs to the motel balcony.

A short time later they emerged; in the parking lot, Chavez did a little dance. "Cesar was extremely tough," Mrs. Huerta whispered. "Cool and tough. He was scared to death of starting the whole fight over again, but he didn't flinch. 'If you want to go to war,' he said, 'that's fine with me.'" Jerry Cohen, elated too, was repeating some of the great lines of the victory: "'We got a contract, and god-damn it, we're going to hold you to it!'" Di Giorgio had been told that in addition to the suit, a boycott of S & W products would begin on Monday unless the HI-COLOR label was withdrawn, and that the non-Union growers who had used that label (Dispoto, for one) might be sued in any case. Connors advised Di Giorgio to give in. "Jerry and I heard him say that on the phone," Chavez admitted. "We weren't eavesdropping; it was an accident, right?" He seemed genuinely worried, and Cohen laughed. "We were just going out, and we heard it," Chavez said. "It was an accident."

Mack Lyons, quieter than the other three, saw us to the car, and Chavez gave their parting full attention.

"Oh! I never asked you! How is your family, Mack?"

"Oh," Lyons said. "One has the measles."

Chavez nodded: measles could be serious. He patted Lyons on the shoulder as he said good-bye. "We'll be out of a job, Mack, one of these days, I hope."

On the way home everybody was exuberant. " 'No more guerrilla warfare'! They were *begging* us!" Cohen yelled. "The Vietcong, that's what they call us!" Chavez cried, raising a clenched revolutionary fist. "The Vietcong strikes again!" Though he took full part in the conversation, he was now noticing the passing scene. "Look at the toilets!" he called at one point, pointing to five brand-new field toilets lined up for the world to see in a ranch yard at Giumarra. "Next thing you know, they'll be putting them in the fields," somebody said. I wondered aloud if Connors would warn Dispoto of the impending suit. "Don't worry," Cohen said. "They're on the phone right now." He was lighting another cigarette, and Chavez, who is intolerant of smoking, made a few remarks. He himself has been giving up smoking for thirty years. The last time was a few years ago, and Mrs. Huerta remembered the exact date: January 1, 1966.

We discussed old Mexican Westerns: *Viva Zapata, The*

Magnificent Seven, The Treasure of the Sierra Madre, Vera Cruz. Everyone was happy, all talking at once. "Boy, did they kill those Mexicans!" Chavez laughed. "Forty-two got it in one scene—I counted them! There was this very smart white guy, and he just kept plugging those dumb Mexicans. I kept my eye on one of the Mexicans, you know, and he kept showing up again; that same guy got killed three or four times single-handed! Another time Fernando came running in; he was watching TV. 'Dad! Dad! You want to see a bunch of Mexicans killed on film?' " Chavez sighed. "He was very upset. 'Those stupid gringos,' Fernando said."

"Do you notice they don't kill Negroes in the films any more?" Cohen remarked.

"That's right," Mrs. Huerta said. "They kill them in the streets instead."

Everyone laughed briefly, without joy.

"He got into other scenes too, this guy," Chavez said after a while. "Altogether he got killed about ten times." He seemed subdued. In the silence, more than halfway home, he began to strap himself into his safety belt. "How fast are we going, Peter?" It was a comment, not a question, and it seemed odd, since on the way to Bakersfield I'd had to drive much faster. I offered to slow down, but Chavez said no, it was all right. Preoccupied, he could not work the belt; the strapping in went on and on. On the way south he had not bothered with the belt at all.

The glove compartment snapped open with a loud bang and Chavez jumped; his arms shot up to shield his head. He grinned cheerfully at his own nerves and clowned a little, pretending that the snap of the compartment door had been the snap of a six-gun leaving its holster. "*Zam!*"

he cried. "See that?" He dropped his hand to his side. "See how I went for my gun? The Diet-Rite Kid!" Again his mouth widened in a smile, and his dark eyes watched us laughing.

In Delano, Leroy Chatfield came outside to hear the news; he strolled beside Chavez around the corner toward the Pink Building. At this moment a big white station wagon passed me, going much too fast for this narrow street, and spun around the corner onto Asti, where it braked to a violent halt opposite Chatfield and Chavez. The driver of the car was Gilbert Rubio and his passenger was Joe Mendoza, who was pointing something at Chavez. "*Click!*" Mendoza said, working his camera. "*Click, click!*" Chavez walked toward the car, and Mendoza, for want of a better plan, kept clicking idiotically. "You look like someone roughed you up!" he jeered at Chavez. Chavez said, "What?" and Mendoza repeated his taunt. "You say you want to rough me up?" Chavez inquired. He kept on coming. Taken aback by his coolness, Rubio and Mendoza roared away. A little later a woman from a right-wing paper came around and was surprised to see Chavez intact. "You don't look so bad to me," she said. Apparently she had been told that Chavez had been beaten up. "She looked kind of disappointed," Chavez said.

I had not heard the exchange between Chavez and Mendoza, which was related to me by Leroy Chatfield when the car had gone. Like all of Chavez's people, Chatfield worries constantly about Chavez's safety. The Chavez house is continually threatened and broken into, and the strain on Helen and the children is considerable. Yet Chavez refused to have a bodyguard. In a rare reference to his own safety, he remarked to Chatfield that no meaningful protection can be bought. "No man," he said, "will jump in front of that bullet, not for money. For love, maybe, but not for money."

Like Dolores Huerta, Chatfield warned me that Chavez must never be left alone; he wanted to put a stop to Chavez's long walks from his house to his office. Since the next day was Sunday, Chavez would be sure to walk, and it was important that somebody accompany him. I volunteered.

6

BEFORE leaving for California I had expected that I would be impressed by Cesar Chavez, but I had not expected to be startled. It was not the "charisma" that is often ascribed to him; most charisma is in the eye of the beholder. The people who have known him longest agree that before the strike, Chavez's presence was so nondescript that he passed unnoticed; he is as unobtrusive as a rabbit, moving quietly wherever he finds himself as if he had always belonged there. The "charisma" is something that has been acquired, an intensification of natural grace which he uses, not always unconsciously, as an organizing tool, turning it on like a blowtorch as the job requires. Once somebody whom he had just enlisted expressed surprise that Chavez had spent so little time in proselytizing. "All he did for three whole days was make me laugh," the new convert said, still unaware that he'd been organized.

Since Chavez knows better than anyone else what his appeals to public sentiment have accomplished for *la causa*, I had no doubt that as a writer I would be skillfully organized myself; but warmth and intelligence and courage, even in combination, did not account for what I felt at the end of the four-hour walk on that first Sunday morning. Talking of leadership during the walk, Chavez said, "It is like taking a road over hills and down into the valley: you must stay with the people. If you go ahead too fast, then they lose sight of you and you lose sight of them." And at the church he was a man among his neighbors, kneeling among them, joining them to receive holy communion, conversing eagerly in the bright morning of the churchyard, by the white stucco wall. What welled out of him was a phenomenon much spoken of in a society afraid of its own hate, but one that I had never seen before—or not, at least, in anyone unswayed by drugs or aching youth: the simple love of man that accompanies some ultimate acceptance of oneself.

It is this love in Chavez that one sees and resists naming, because to name it is to cheapen it; not the addled love that hides self-pity but a love that does not distinguish between oneself and others, a love so clear in its intensity that it is monastic, even mystical. This intensity in Chavez has burned all his defenses away. Taking the workers' hands at church, his face was as fresh as the face of a man reborn. "These workers are really beautiful," he says, and when he says it he is beautiful himself. He is entirely with the people, open to them, one with them, and at the same time that he makes them laugh, his gaze sees beyond them to something else. "Without laying a cross on him," Jim Drake says, "Cesar is, in theological terms, as nearly 'a man for others' as you can find. In spite of all his personal problems—a very bad back, poverty, a large family—he does not allow his own life to get in the way."

We sat for an hour or more in the adobe shade outside the small room where he had spent his fast, and as he spoke of the old missions and his childhood and the fast, I grew conscious of the great Sunday silence and the serenity that flowed from the man beside me, gazing out with such equanimity upon the city dump. What emerges when Chavez talks seriously of his aim is simplicity, and what is striking in his gentle voice is its lack of mannerisms; it comes as naturally as bird song. For the same reason, it is a pleasure to watch him move. He has what the Japanese call *hara*, or "belly"—that is, he is centered in himself, he is not fragmented, he sits simply, like a Zen master.

For most of us, to quote Dostoevsky, "to love the universal man is to despise and at times to hate the real man standing at your side." This is not true of Chavez. But he is super human, not superhuman. He acknowledges that his reactions are not entirely unaffected by the humiliations and pain of his early life, so that even his commitment to nonviolence is stronger in his head than in his heart. And like many people who are totally dedicated, he is intolerant of those who are less so. I asked him once for the names of the best volunteers no longer with the Union, and he said flatly, "The best ones are still here." I dropped the subject. As his leadership inevitably extends to the more than four million Mexican-Americans in the Southwest, Cesar will necessarily become more lonely, more cut off in a symbolic destiny. Already, sensing this, he puts great emphasis on loyalty, as if to allay a nagging fear of being abandoned, and people who are not at the Union's disposal at almost any hour of the day or night do not stay close to him for very long. It has been said that he is suspicious of Anglos, but it would be more accurate to say that he is suspicious of everybody, in the way of people with a tendency to trust too much. He is swift and stubborn in his judgments, yet warm and confiding once he commits his faith, which he is apt to do intuitively, in a few moments. The very completeness of this trust, which makes him vulnerable, may also have made him wary of betrayal.

The closer people are to Chavez, the greater the dedication he expects. If they can't or won't perform effectively, he does their job himself ("It's a lot easier to do that than keep after them"), or if they are going about it the wrong way, he may let them persist in a mistake until failure teaches them a lesson. Some of these lessons seem more expensive to the Union than they are worth, but Chavez is determined that his people be self-sufficient—that they could, if need be, get along without him.

His staff has also learned to sacrifice ego to political expedience within the Union. Watching Chavez conduct a meeting, large or small, is fascinating: his sly humor and shy manner, his deceptive use of "we," leave his own position flexible; he directs with a sure hand, yet rarely is he caught in an embarrassing commitment. Most of his aides have had to take responsibility for unpolitic decisions initiated by Cesar himself, and may experience his apparent disfavor, and even banishment to the sidelines, for circumstances that were not their fault. The veterans do not take this personally. In private, Cesar will be as warm as ever, and they know that their banishment will last no longer than the internal crisis. They know, too, that he never uses people to dodge personal responsibility, but only to circumvent obstruction from the board or from the membership that would impede *la causa*'s progress; he is selfless, and expects them to be the same.

"Sometimes he seems so *damned* unfair, so stubborn, so irrational—oh, he can be a sonofabitch! But later on, maybe months later, we find ourselves remembering what he did,

and every damned time we have to say, 'You know something? He was right.' That edge of irrationality—that's his
greatness."

Because he is so human, Cesar's greatness is forgiven; he
is beloved, not merely adored. "Often he says, 'Have you
got a minute?' but what he means is, 'Talk to me,' and he
doesn't really mean *that*; he just has to have somebody
close to him all the time, it doesn't matter who, just someone who isn't a yes-man, who will bounce his ideas back at
him. We all take turns at it, and he knows we're always
there."

Jim Drake recalls a day sometime ago when he and Cesar
and Marshall Ganz drove north to a hospital in Kingsbury,
near Fresno, to visit Dave Fishlow, the editor of *El Malcriado*, who had been badly burned in a car accident. Although they had come one hundred and twenty miles, the
supervisor would not let them in because they arrived after
visiting hours. "Just a typical Valley cluck, you know. He
says, 'Now what's going *on* out here, don't you know you
can't break regulations? Absolutely not!' So I said, 'How
about letting me see him? I'm his minister.' So he agreed,
and then I said, 'Well, since you're letting somebody go in,
it might as well be Cesar, since he's the one that would do
your patient the most good.' But he said no, so I went in,
and Dave suggested to me that Cesar come around under
the window, just to say hello. But Cesar refused. You know
how he hates discrimination of any kind; well, he thought
he'd been discriminated against. I didn't but he did. He said
he had gone to the back door all his life, and he wasn't going
to do it any more. He was almost childish about it. That's
the only time I've ever seen him that mad—so stubborn, I

mean, that he wouldn't say hello to a friend. Most of the time that Cesar's mad, he's *acting* mad; he loves to act mad. But this time he was *really* mad."

On another occasion Drake himself got angry when Al Green, the AFL-CIO man, referred to Chavez as "that beady-eyed little Mex," and was astonished when Chavez, hearing this, burst out laughing. "He does very strange things; you can't anticipate him. When we had that conference at St. Anthony's Mission, he was very anxious at have everybody get to work and everything, and then he just disappeared. Later we found out that he and Richard and Manuel had been scooting around taking pictures of the nearby missions."

"In public, he's simple in his manner," Dolores Huerta says, "and when things are tense, he can make everyone relax by acting silly. When he used to drink a little, he was a real clown at parties; there were always games and dancing, and he would dance on the table." She laughed, remembering. "But I find him a very complicated person." In truth, Dolores finds Chavez difficult, but Dolores can be difficult herself, and anyway, her openness about him is a sign of faith, not disaffection.

One person in the Union with reservations about Chavez remarked to me of his own accord that in the creation of the United Farm Workers, Chavez had done something that "no one else has ever done. What can I say? I disagree with him on a lot of things, but I work for him for nothing."

This last sentence is eloquent because it says just what it means. Applied to the Chavez of *la causa*, ordinary judgments seem beside the point; a man with no interest in private gain who will starve himself for twenty-five days and expose his life daily to the threat of assassination, who takes serious risks, both spiritual and physical, for others, may be hated as well as adored, but he cannot be judged in the same terms as a man of ordinary ambitions.

The fast began on February 14, 1968, just after his return from a fund-raising journey around the country. Everywhere he went, the militant groups which supported him or sought his support were ranting about the violence planned for the summer of 1968. In the background, like a pall, was the destruction of Vietnam, which was still seen by its perpetrators as a tactical problem, not a moral one, and in the foreground, in Delano, his own people were rivaling the growers in loose talk of quick solutions. It was winter, in the hungry time between the pruning and girdling of vines, and the strike had drained the workers' nerves for two and a half years, and some were muttering that they had waited long enough. Many were still concerned with their *machismo*, or manliness, which sometimes emerges in oblique ways; as one worker says, "the women get afraid. The growers say they goin to call the law, and we don't know no law. So the women, they get afraid." They felt they were being cowardly in permitting the growers to continue exploiting them; anyway, wasn't violence traditional to labor movements? Hadn't violence gotten results in the ghetto riots of 1967? Perhaps a little burning in Delano, an explosion or two, might force the growers to negotiate. (Chavez doesn't deny this. "If we had used violence," he once told me, "we would have won contracts long ago, but they wouldn't be lasting, because we wouldn't have won respect.") Depressed, Chavez decided on the fast as a kind of penitence for the belligerence that had developed in his own union, and a commitment to nonviolence everywhere.

From every point of view, the twenty-five-day fast was the most serious risk that Chavez had ever taken, and it placed the hard work of six years in the balance. Chavez himself speaks mildly of the fast, but his people don't feel mild about it, even now; it split the Union down the middle. Helen, Richard and Manuel knew that Cesar had been fasting before he made it known, but they were stunned by his intention to prolong the fast indefinitely. So were Leroy Chatfield, who still speaks of Chavez's announcement speech with awe, and Marion Moses, a volunteer Union nurse now on the boycott in New York, who has lent me some notes that she set down at the time.

Chavez called a special meeting for twelve noon on Monday, February 19, assembling the strikers as well as the office staff and families, and talked for an hour and a half about nonviolence. He discussed Vietnam, wondering aloud how so many of his listeners could deplore the violence in Asia, yet promote it in the United States. He said that the Mexican tradition of *machismo*—of manliness proved through violence—was in error: *la causa* must not risk a single life on either side, because it was a cause, not just a union, dealing with people not as green cards or social security numbers but as human beings, one by one.

"Cesar took a very hard line," Leroy Chatfield says. "We were falling back on violence because we weren't creative enough or imaginative enough to find another solution, because we didn't *work* hard enough. One of the things that he said in the speech was that he felt we had lost our will to win, by which he meant that acting violently or advocating violence or even thinking that maybe violence wasn't such a bad thing—that is really losing your will to win, your commitment to win. A cop-out. This seems like a very idealistic position, but there's truth in it. Anarchy leads to chaos, and out of chaos rises the demagogue. That's one of the reasons he is so upset about *la raza*. The same Mexicans that ten years ago were talking about themselves as Spaniards are coming on real strong these days as Mexicans. Everyone should be proud of what they are, of course, but race is only skin-deep. It's phony, and it comes out of frustration; the *la raza* people are not secure. They look upon Cesar as their 'dumb Mexican' leader; he's become their saint. But he doesn't want any part of it. He said to me just the other day, 'Can't they understand that that's just the way Hitler started?' A few months ago the Ford Foundation funded a *la raza* group and Cesar really told them off. The foundation liked the outfit's sense of pride or something, and Cesar tried to explain to them what the origin of the word was, that it's related to Hitler's concept. He feels that *la raza* will destroy our union faster than anything else, that it plays right into the growers' hands; if they can keep the minorities fighting, pitting one race against another, one group against another . . . We needed that Ford money too, but he spoke right out. Ford had asked him if he wouldn't be part of that Southwest Council for *La Raza*, or whatever it is, and he flatly refused. I mean, where would Mack Lyons be if we had that kind of nonsense? Or where would *I* be? Or the Filipinos?"

In his speech on February 19, 1968, Chavez discussed the civil rights movement and how its recourse to violence had made black people suffer; black homes, not white, were being burned, and black sons killed. The Union, he said, had raised the hopes of many poor people; it had a responsibility to those people, whose hopes, along with all the

Union gains, would be destroyed after the first cheap victories of violence. Finally, he announced the fast. It was not a hunger strike, because its purpose was not strategic; it was an act of prayer and love for the Union members because as their leader he felt responsible for their acts as individuals. There would be no vote on the fast, which would continue for an indefinite period, and had in fact begun the week before. He was not going into seclusion, and would continue his work as best he could; he asked that his hearers keep the news entirely to themselves. Since it was difficult to fast at home, and since the Forty Acres was the spiritual home of the Union, he would walk there as soon as he had finished speaking, and remain there until the fast was done. Throughout the speech Chavez quoted Gandhi and the Epistles of St. Paul. "His act was intensely personal," Leroy recalls, "and the whole theme of his speech was love. In fact, his last words to us before he left the room and started that long walk to the Forty Acres were something like 'I am doing this because I love you.'"

Helen Chavez followed Cesar from the hall, and everyone sat for some time in stunned silence. After that, as Marion Moses notes, "A lot was said, most of which, as far as I am concerned, had little or nothing to do with what Cesar was really saying to us." The meeting was taken over by Larry Itliong, who said straight out that Brother Chavez should be persuaded to come off the fast. Manuel Chavez then declared that Cesar was an Indian and therefore stubborn, and that once he had made up his mind to do something, nothing anyone could say was going to stop him. In that case, Leroy Chatfield said, in the most impassioned speech of all, every precaution must be taken to guard Cesar's health—good bed, blankets, and so forth—and to insure quiet, no cars were to be permitted on the Forty Acres until the fast was over.

Tony Orendain said sourly that the meeting need not concern itself with Cesar's blankets; the brothers should get back to work. Other members made many other comments: Epifanio Camacho, for example, dismissed the whole business of striker violence as grower propaganda, and therefore saw no reason for the fast. Camacho, as well as other Protestants and agnostics, white and brown, still resented the Catholic aura of the Sacramento march and now felt offended all over again. They were supported by those Catholics who felt that the Church was being exploited, and also by most of the white volunteers, and the Jews especially, who disliked any religious overtone whatsoever.

For the first week after the announcement, before the press arrived, almost the whole board of directors, led by Orendain, were boycotting the fast and refused to attend mass at the Forty Acres. On the other hand, the membership, largely Catholic, accepted the fast in apprehensive faith. "If Cesar thought it was right," Richard says, "then they did too." Fred Ross, like Chatfield, was worried that Cesar might be damaging his health, but they soon realized that nothing was going to stop him.

The Franciscan priest, Mark Day, later announced that he would offer mass at the Forty Acres every night of the fast, and Marion Moses went there after the meeting to help clear out the storeroom for the service. "Nick and Virginia Jones," she wrote, "pitched a little pup tent and stayed there the first night, and gradually there were more and more tents at the Forty Acres. It looked like a mining settlement in the Old West. We built a fireplace and we had chocolate every night. The masses were beautiful. On the first night Leroy and Bonnie made an offering of a picture of JFK, and Tony Mendez gave a crucifix. About 100 people came to the first mass and probably 200 will come tonight. It really looks good—the huge banner of the Union is against the wall, and the offerings the people make are attached to the banner: pictures of Christ from Mexico, two crucifixes, a large picture of Our Lady of Guadalupe—the whole wall is covered with offerings. There is a permanent altar there (a card table) with votive lights, almost like a shrine. It's impossible to describe the spirit of what is happening."

The people obeyed Cesar's request that no one try a fast of sympathy on their own, but he learned later, from the open annoyance of their wives, that three young men had taken a vow of chastity for the duration of the fast, and held to it. He speaks of this sacrifice with regret, but it seemed to him a convincing proof of the farm workers' new spirit.

The resentment of the young wives was not the only obstacle Chavez had to deal with: many other people had serious doubts right to the end. "When we visited Cesar in his little room at the Forty Acres," Leroy says, "he would point at the wall and say, 'See that white wall? Well, imagine ten different-colored balls, all jumping up and down. One ball is called religion, another propaganda, another organizing, another law, and so forth. When people look at that wall and see those balls, different people look at different balls; each person keeps his eye on his own ball. For each person the balls mean many different things, but for everyone they can mean something!' My ball was propaganda, and I kept my eye on that; I could therefore be perfectly comfortable, and understand the fast completely in those terms, and not negate the other nine balls—organization, say. And as matter of fact, we never organized so many people in such a short time, before or since. The fast gave the lie to the growers' claim that we have no following. Some people came every night to that mass at the Forty Acres, came sixty-five, eighty-five miles every night. People stood in line for an hour, two hours, to talk to him. He saw it as a fantastic opportunity to talk to one man, one family at a time. When that person left he went away with something; he's no longer a member, he's an organizer. At the Sunday mass we had as many as two thousand people. That's what the growers don't understand; we're all over the state. In fact, there's nowhere in this state or anywhere in the Southwest where the people don't know about Cesar Chavez and the United Farm Workers. And they say, 'When is he coming? Are we next?' "

People close to Chavez like to envision a national farm workers union, but if Chavez has any such idea, he keeps it to himself. UFWOC now has offices in Texas, with sympathetic organizations in Arizona, Oregon, Washington, Ohio, New York, New Mexico, Wisconsin and Michigan. The Texas strikes, led by Gilbert Padilla, operate mostly in Starr County, which echoes Kern and Tulare counties in its cries of outraged patriotism. Although Texas can claim more paupers than any state in the nation, and although Starr County residents, mostly Mexican-Americans, had an average per capita income of $1,568 in 1966, a Starr County grand jury has called the strike effort "unlawful and un-American . . . abusive of rights and freedoms granted them as citizens . . . contrary to everything we know in our American and lawful way of life." It is just this spluttering hypocrisy, of course, in a country that is surely the most violent and unlawful on earth, that has alienated the best of the nation's young people and a growing minority of their parents. How much closer to what we were taught was the true spirit of America is the spirit of an elderly migrant, one of the objects of Starr County's righteous wrath: "I have lived in poverty and misery all my life and I live in poverty during the strike . . . but now I can walk with dignity."

The fast was also a warning to the growers that after a century of exploitation—the first anti-Mexican vigilantism occurred in 1859—the brown community was as explosive as the black, and that Chavez could not control his people indefinitely. If his nonviolent tactics failed, he would be replaced by more militant leaders, and there would be sabotage and bloodshed. Already minor violence had been committed by Union people or their sympathizers, and the threat of further violence was the main reason for the fast. Without question, the fast worked. It taught the farm workers that Chavez was serious about nonviolence, that it wasn't just a tactic to win public support; and it taught them what nonviolence meant.

Chavez spoke a lot about the fast during the Sunday walk. Although he had fasted twice before, for periods of four days and ten, he had had no idea, when he began, how long this one would last. "I told everybody that it should be kept as secret as possible, but that the people could come to see me day or night, and the strike should go on as usual. But it didn't; there was a lot of confusion.

"When I disappeared, there was a rumor that I had been shot, and then everybody said that I was very sick, and finally we had to tell the press the truth, but we still said we didn't want any interviews or pictures or anything. I didn't talk to the newsmen, didn't want to, I just wanted to continue working." He laughed. "I did more organizing out of this bed than I did anywhere. It was really a rest, though; to me, it was a vacation.

"As soon as the word got out, the members began to come. Just people! From all over the state! We estimated that ten thousand people came here during the fast—we never turned anybody away. Anyway, everything went beautifully. The Filipinos came and began to paint these windows, and all kinds of little things began to appear. They weren't artists, but the things looked *beautiful*"—he spoke this last word with real intensity, turning to look at me. "I think the fast was a sort of rest for the people, too. You know? Oh, I could go on for days about the things that happened in the fast that were really great! I guess one time I thought about becoming a priest, but I did this instead, and I'm happy to be a part of it. For me, this work is fun, it's really fun! It's so great when people participate. Mexico is such a poor country, and I could never understand how, after the Revolution, they could produce all that beautiful art. But now I see it in our own strike, it's only a very small revolution, but we see this art beginning to come forth. When people discover themselves like this, they begin to appreciate some of the other things in life. I didn't understand this at first, but now I see that art begins in a very simple way. It's very simple—they just go out and *do* things.

"Then they began to bring things. Offerings, you know, religious pictures, mostly. Some people brought a hundred-and-fifty-year-old Christ of the Miners, handmade out of silver down in Mexico, and there were some other real valuable pieces. We've got everything safe, and we'll put it on display one day here at the Forty Acres.

"Something else very beautiful happened. For years and years the Mexican Catholics have been very discriminatory against the minority Mexican Protestants. They didn't know anything about them, they were just against them. Well, we used to hold mass every day in the store across from my room, we made it into a kind of chapel. And about the fifth day a preacher came, he works out there at Schenley and he has a little church in Earlimart. And I said, 'How would you like to come and preach at our mass?' He said, 'Gee . . . no . . .'" Chavez shrank back, imitating his voice. "'Sure!' I said. I told him this was a wonderful time to begin to repair some of the damage that had been done, the bad feeling, but he said, 'I can't preach here, I'll get thrown out.' I said, 'No, if that happens, I'll go out with you.' So he said, 'All right, fine.' And when he came, I introduced him, gave the full name of his church and everything so there would be no room for doubt about where he came from. And he did it in great form, and the people accepted him. There was a great spirit; they just took him in. So three days later I asked another one to come, and he came, and he was also great, and then a Negro minister came—it was beautiful. So then the first one came again with his whole group, and they sang some real great Mexican Protestant music that we're not familiar with because of that prejudice. And now our Franciscan priest has gone and preached out there, in that little Protestant church in Earlimart!"

I asked him if his concept of the fast derived from Gandhi.

"Well, partly. In India, fasting is part of the tradition—there's an Indian engineer here who is a friend and comes to see us, and he says that in India almost everybody fasts. But Mexicans have the Catholic concept of sacrifice; the *penitencia* is part of our history. In Mexico, a lot of people will get on their knees and travel for five miles.

"I didn't know much about it, so I read everything I could get my hands on, Gandhi, and I read some of the things that he had read, and I read Thoreau, which I liked very much. But I couldn't really understand Gandhi until I was actually in the fast; then the book became much more clear. Things I understood but didn't feel—well, in the fast I *felt* them, and there were some real insights. There wasn't a day or a night that I lost. I slept in the day when I could, and at night, and I read. I slept on a very thin mattress, with a board—soft mattresses are no good. And I had the peace of mind that is so important; the fasting part is secondary."

During the fast Chavez subsisted on plain water, but his cousin Manuel, who often guarded him and helped him to the bathroom, was fond of responding to knocks on the door by crying out, "Go away, he's eating!" I asked if, in the fast, he had had any kind of hallucinations.

"No, I was wide awake. But there are certain things that happened, about the third or fourth day—and this has happened to me every time I've fasted—it's like all of a sudden when you're up at a high altitude, and you clear your ears; in the same way, my mind clears, it is open to everything. After a long conversation, for example, I could repeat word for word what had been said. That's one of the sensations of the fast; it's beautiful. And usually I can't concentrate on music very well, but in the fast, I could see the whole orchestra and everything, that music was so clear.

"That room, you know, is fireproof, and almost soundproof—not quite, but almost. It's a ten-inch wall, with six inches of poured concrete. There were some Mexican guitars around, this was about the nineteenth day, and I turned to Helen and my brother Richard and some of my kids, and said, 'I hear some singing.' So everybody stopped talking and looked around: 'We don't hear anything.' So I said, 'I'll bet you I hear singing!' This time they stopped for about forty seconds: 'But we don't hear anything!' 'Well,' I said, 'I still hear singing.' Then my sister-in-law glanced at Richard, her expression was kind of funny, so I said, 'We'd better investigate this right now, because either I'm hearing things or it's happening.' They said it was just my imagination, and I said, 'Richard, please investigate for me, right now, because I won't feel right if you don't.' So Richard went outside, and there were some guys there across the yard having a drink, and they were singing." He laughed. "Then, toward the end, I began to notice people eating. I'd never really noticed people *eat*. It was so . . . so . . ."— he struggled for words to express fascination and horror —"well, to use what we call in Spanish a *mala comparación,* like animals in a zoo! I couldn't take my eyes off them!"

I asked Chavez what had persuaded him to end the fast.

"Well, the pressure kept building, especially from the doctor. He was getting very concerned about the acids and things that I didn't know anything about—a kind of cannibalism occurs, you know, the acid begins to eat your fat, and you have to have a lot of water to clear your kidneys. First of all, I wouldn't let him test me. I said, 'If you declared me physically able to begin the fast, then it's not a sacrifice. If you find out that I'm ill, there will be too much pressure not to do it. So let me begin, and after I've started, *then* we'll worry about what's wrong with me.' But I forgot that the doctor was responsible for me, that if something went wrong with me, he would get it. So I argued, and he worried. Finally, after the twelfth day, I let him check my urine, and about the seventeenth day I let him check my heart, and he said, 'Well, you're fit.' And I said, 'I know I'm fit, I knew it when I got into this.' And after the fast they gave me a complete analysis, blood and all that stuff, and do you know something?" He smiled his wide-eyed smile, shaking his head. "I was perfect!"

On the twenty-first day of the fast, Dr. James McKnight had insisted that Chavez take medication, and also a few ounces of bouillon and unsweetened grapefruit juice. Dr. McKnight and many others felt that Chavez might be doing himself permanent harm, and subsequent events seem to bear them out; the worsening of what was thought to be a degenerative lumbar-disc condition that was to incapacitate him for three months in the fall of 1968 was generally attributed to protein deficiency, not only in the fast but in the ascetic diet that he has adopted since. Chavez himself does not agree. His bad back gave him less trouble during the fast than at any time since 1957, when it first began to bother him, and chronic headaches and sinusitis also disappeared; he never felt better.

Remembering something, Chavez began to smile. "Usually there was somebody around to guard me, give me water or help me out if I had to go to the rest room, but one time, about two o'clock in the morning, they were singing out there, and then they fell asleep, and the door was open. This worker came in who had come all the way from Merced, about fifty miles from here, and he'd been drinking. He represented some workers committee, and his job was to make me eat, and break my fast." He began to laugh. "And he had tacos, you know, with meat, and all kinds of tempting things. I tried to explain to him, but he opens up this lunch pail and gets out a taco, still warm, a big one, and tries to force me. And I don't want to have my lips touch the food—I mean, at that point, food is no temptation, I just thought that if it touched my lips, I was breaking the fast, you see, and I was too weak to fight him off. This guy was drunk, and he was pretty big, and so he sits on top of me, he's wrestling with me, and I'm going like this"—Chavez twisted and groaned with horror, rolling his eyes and screwing up his mouth in a perfect imitation of a man trying to avoid a big warm taco, crying "Oh! Ow!"—"like a girl who doesn't want to get kissed, you know. I began to shout for help, but this guy really meant business. He had told his committee, 'Look, you pay my gas and I'll go down there and make him eat; he'll eat because I'll *make* him eat, and I won't leave there *until* he eats.' So he didn't want to go back to Merced without results. First he gave me a lecture and that didn't work; then he played it tough and that didn't work. Then he cried and it didn't work, and then we prayed together, and that didn't work, either."

I asked if the man was still sitting on him while they prayed, and Chavez said that he was. By this time we were laughing so hard that we had to stop on the highway shoulder. Chavez's expression of wide-eyed wonderment at human behavior is truly comic; reliving the experience, he pantomimed both parts. "He got my arms, like this"—he gestured—"and then he got my hands like *this*"—he gestured again—"in a nice way, you know, but he's hurting me because he's so heavy. I'm screaming for help, and finally somebody, I think it was Manuel, opens the door and sees this guy on top of me; Manuel thinks he's killing me, but he's so surprised he doesn't know what to do, you know, so he stands there in the door for at least thirty seconds while I'm yelling, "Get him off me!' Then about fifty guys rush in and pull him out of there; I thought they were going to kill him because they thought he was attacking me. I can hardly speak, but I try to cry out, 'Don't do anything to him, bring him back!' 'No!' they yell. 'Bring him back!' 'No!' they yell. I'm shouting, you know. 'Bring him back, I have to talk to him, don't hurt him!' " Chavez's voice, describing this scene, was quavering piteously. "So finally they brought him back." He sighed with relief, quite out of breath. "He wasn't hurt, he was too drunk. So I said, 'Sit down, let me explain it,' and I explained it, step by step, and the guy's crying, he's feeling very dejected and hurt." Chavez laughed quietly at the memory, in genuine sympathy with the emissary from Merced.

On the seventeenth day, Chavez asked Richard to construct the cheap and simple cross that was later destroyed by vandals. The cross was the ultimate affront to at least two volunteers. One dismissed the entire fast as a "cheap publicity stunt"; the other, who had once been a priest, accused Chavez of having a messiah complex. Both soon quit the United Farm Workers for good. The messiah charge, which has been made before and since, does not ring true to my own experience of Chavez. His account of the taco man from Merced, to cite just one example, is not a parable constructed by a man who takes himself too seriously; perhaps what the ex-priest was threatened by was not an aspirant messiah but a truly religious man.

"Anyway, the kids began to feel the pressure, and my father and mother. My dad began to lose his sleep—he's fantastic, he'll never talk about himself—but he's over eighty, you know, so I got a little worried. He has fasted a couple of times himself. Once he had dysentery and he couldn't clear it up, and he was dying. And one of those hobos on his way through—this was in the Depression, and they were white Okies, mostly—learned about my father and said he could take care of it. He was an old guy with a beard, he had books in his bindle, you know, and my sister translated for him into Spanish, and he said, 'I'll either save you or I'll kill you, and I'll be back in three days, so you think it over.' Well, my dad had been to a specialist and everything, and nobody could help him, but he said, 'Hell, how can I stop eating, I can't stop eating for even half a day!' And the hoob said, 'No, you can go for twenty days, maybe thirty days.' Anyway, when the hobo came back, my dad said he would try it. So he stopped eating, and in three days he got rid of the dysentery, there was nothing to feed it. He went on for twenty days. I said to him, 'Dad, you fasted for twenty days,' and he said, 'Yes, but that was different.'

"I had no set date in mind, but a combination of things made me end it on March eleventh. I could have gone a few days more. I broke the fast on a Sunday, it must have been about one or two o'clock. I ate a small piece of bread, but actually, I kept on fasting for the next four days, because you can't eat right away. So really I felt weaker *after* the fast was over."

The fast continued four days longer than Gandhi's famous hunger strike in 1924 (or so I've read; Chavez would be the last to make this claim). As it wore on through February and into March, many of the farm workers became apprehensive, and a number of strikers came to

Manuel and swore that they would never be violent again if he could just persuade Cesar to quit; like the emissary from Merced with his bag of tacos, they were terrified that the leader of *la causa* would be harmed.

During the fast Chavez received a wire from Senator Robert Kennedy (I WANT YOU TO KNOW THAT I FULLY AND UNSWERVINGLY SUPPORT THE PRINCIPLES WHICH LED YOU TO UNDERTAKE YOUR FAST . . . YOUR WORK AND YOUR BELIEF HAVE ALWAYS BEEN BASED SOLELY UPON PRINCIPLES OF NON-VIOLENCE . . . YOU HAVE MY BEST WISHES AND MY DEEPEST CONCERN IN THESE DIFFICULT HOURS) and the senator, with a phalanx of the press, appeared in person on the epochal Sunday when the fast ended.

In early 1960, while in the CSO, Chavez had met Robert Kennedy in Los Angeles, in a brief early-morning meeting that concerned a voter-registration drive for John Kennedy's presidential campaign; when he saw him next, he was Senator Kennedy, attending the hearings of the Senate Subcommittee on Migratory Labor in 1966. Apparently Kennedy had seen no point in going to Delano, but was finally persuaded by an aide that endorsement of Chavez and the minority-group Mexican-American cause could not hurt him politically and might be a very good investment; the investment was to win him the California primary two years later. And Chavez took Kennedy's commitment at face value. "Even then, I had an idea he was going to be a candidate for the Presidency, and I was concerned for him because he endorsed us so straightforwardly, without straddling the line. This was a time when everybody was against us; the only people for us were ourselves. I was sitting next to Dolores Huerta, and we both had the same thought—that he didn't have to go that far. Instead of that

awful feeling against politicians who don't commit themselves, we felt protective. He said we had the right to form
a union and that he endorsed our right, and not only
endorsed us but joined us. I was amazed at how quickly he
grasped the whole picture. Then the hearings started and
they began to call the witnesses, and he immediately asked
very pointed questions of the growers; he had a way of
disintegrating their arguments by picking at the very
simple questions. He had to leave just before the hearings
ended, but he told the press that the workers were
eventually going to be organized, that the sooner the
employers recognized this, the sooner it was going to be
over. And when reporters asked him if we weren't Communists, he said, 'No, they are not Communists, they're
struggling for their rights.' So he really helped us, and
things began to change."

On March 11, 1968, while in Los Angeles, Kennedy was
notified that the fast was ending; he chartered a plane and
flew to Delano with the United Auto Workers' Paul
Schrade. At first, according to Chavez's aides, Kennedy
seemed rather cold. "He felt kind of uneasy," Chavez told
me, "and one of our people heard him ask Paul Schrade or
somebody, 'What do you say to a guy who's on a fast?' He
was only in the room with me about thirty seconds. He
looked at me"—Chavez grinned mischievously— "and he
says, 'How are you, Cé-zar?' I said, 'Very well, thank you.
And I thank you for coming.' He said, 'It's my pleasure,' or
something. So then we kind of changed the subject."
Chavez laughed. "I was very weak, and I did not know
what to say either; I think I introduced him to Paul Schrade.

"The TV people were there, and one poor cameraman

got blocked out, the monitors wouldn't let him by. I saw he was frantic, and I was too weak to shout, but finally I signaled Leroy Chatfield, and Leroy got him in. The poor guy was really pale. And he said, 'Senator, this is probably the most ridiculous request I ever made in my life, but would you mind giving him a piece of bread,' and the senator gave it to me, and the camera rolled, and the man said, 'Thank you very, very much.' "

Chavez, who used to be stocky, had dropped from one hundred and seventy-five pounds to one hundred and forty during the fast; bundled up in a dark-checked hooded parka against the March cold, he was half carried to the Mass of Thanksgiving held in a Delano park where an altar had been set up on the flatbed of a truck.

The mass began with a prayer in Hebrew: the sermon was Protestant, and Catholic ritual preceded the breaking of the poor man's bread, *semita*. After Chavez and Kennedy had shared bread, priests passed through the thousands of witnesses, distributing the loaves. Because Chavez was too weak—he could scarcely keep his head erect during the ceremony—others read his speech for him, both in English and Spanish. In it, he told the gathering that his body was too weak and his heart too full for him to speak. He thanked everyone for being there, then told them that the strict water fast had been broken with liquids on the twenty-first day. He touched on the purpose of the fast, and concluded as follows: "When we are really honest with ourselves, we must admit that our lives are all that really belong to us. So it is how we use our lives that determines what kind of men we are. It is my deepest belief that only by giving our lives do we find life. I am convinced that the truest act of courage, the strongest act of manliness, is to sacrifice ourselves for others in a totally nonviolent struggle for justice. To be a man is to suffer for others. God help us be men."

Chavez's concept of the meaning of life being based in service to mankind is like that of Tolstoi and Hesse; his love is philosophical, not just religious. "How many people do you know," Dolores Ruerta inquired one day, "who *really* love people, good and bad, enough to lay down their lives for them?" She meant that last part literally.

Robert Kennedy, who recognized Chavez's uncommon qualities, declared that he was present out of respect "for one of the heroic figures of our time—Cesar Chavez!" After taking communion with Chavez, he began his speech in a Spanish so awful that he stopped with good grace to laugh at himself. "Am I murdering the language?" he inquired, and was wildly cheered. "*Hool*-ga!" he cried, in an effort to pronounce the strike slogan. "*Hool*-ga!" During the offertory, on behalf of his auto workers, Paul Schrade presented the Union with $50,000 for the construction of the new headquarters at the Forty Acres. After a feast of thanksgiving contributed by numerous families and committees, the meeting concluded with a fiery speech by Reies Lopez Tijerina, the leader of New Mexico's Mexican-Americans, who was later mentioned as a possible Vice-Presidential candidate for the Peace and Freedom party. Tijerina is an old-style Latin demagogue, full of shout and menace, but he failed to excite the *campesinos* of Delano. "The trouble is," one staff member says, "that you get spoiled working for Cesar. When I see a person ranting and raving, I don't feel there's much substance there. It turns me off."

. . .

The mass was attended by from four to ten thousand
people, depending on the source of the estimate: about
eight thousand is probably right. "I told the senator that
we could do most everything in Delano except control
crowds, and he said that that didn't matter so long as the
crowds were there. But he had a heck of a time getting
from where we were sitting to the car. The crowd was
pushing and surging, and when he got there, he didn't get
in; the way the people were reacting, he wanted to stand
there and shake their hands and talk to them. Everybody
was afraid of so many people pushing like that, and when
Jim Drake got him inside, the people were saying through
the windows, 'Aren't you going to run?' 'Why don't you
run?' 'Please run!' Then Jim got the car moving, and Kennedy turned to the people in the car and said, 'Maybe I
will. Yes, I think I will.' So when he announced his candidacy a week later, it was no surprise to us. Everybody
had suggested that I leave Delano for a little while after
the fast, to rest, so Helen and I were on the coast near the
Santa Ynez Mission. Helen got a paper and brought it
back to the farm where we were staying, and I was excited,
but I knew he was going to do it all along.

"On March 19, when Paul Schrade called to ask if I
would endorse him and be a delegate, I knew it would not
be honorable to ask for something in return. With most
politicians, this would have been all right, but not with
this man, who had already helped us so much. After a
three-hour discussion, our members voted unanimously
that I should be a delegate, and we immediately began a
voter-registration drive.

"We worked right up to the last minute, we had a

beautiful time, and the drive was a tremendous success. Some precincts went out one hundred percent for Kennedy! But I was very tired, and I felt embarrassed when my name was called at the rally at the Ambassador, and so I left early, before the senator came downstairs. The last time I ever talked to him was when he gave me that piece of bread."

In the voter-registration drive for Kennedy, Chavez's CSO experience, combined with his great gifts as an organizer, were very effective; the Mexican-American vote in June was virtually unanimous, and few people doubt that it was Chavez who won for Kennedy the primary that Kennedy had to win in order to be nominated. Possibly the task was made more urgent by the murder of Martin Luther King, soon after the voter-registration drive began; there was a growing fear among the poor that all their champions were to be assassinated. Although King and Chavez had never met, only corresponded, the loss of King was personal for Chavez. "That was one time I came very close to losing my cool. I was at a rally in Sacramento, and I really resented the press, you know, resented their questions." Still, he had not lost hope. In a telegram to Mrs. King he said: "DESPITE THE TRAGIC VIOLENCE THAT TOOK YOUR HUSBAND, THERE IS MUCH THAT IS GOOD ABOUT OUR NATION. IT WAS TO THAT GOODNESS THAT YOUR HUSBAND APPEALED . . ." In his opinon, King's kind of nonviolence, like Gandhi's, was the practicing of what Christ preached, but generated violence on the other side because it wasn't passive. Since Chavez's nonviolence is also of this kind, he has had to live with the possibility of his own assassination; fear of death was one of the problems that he dealt with in the fast.

"No one accepts death, I think," he has said, "but what is the alternative? If you lock yourself in or give up, it's a living death; that's no alternative. Death is not enough to stop you. You're really too busy to think of it. Unimportant, day-to-day things get your attention, which is just as well."

Between the King and Kennedy assassinations, the following document was widely circulated in the Valley:

BAKERSFIELD, CALIFORNIA

THE NEW CATHOLIC CHURCH "APOSTLES CREED"

I believe in CESAR CHAVEZ, creator of all the TROUBB-BBLE, and HELL, and the "UNITED FARMERS ORGANI-ZATION COMMITTEE." I believe in SAINT MARK DAY (the 2 bit politician priest of Delano) that "FOXXES" THE POOR FARMERS THE "CATHOLIC WAY" . . . I believe [Chavez] is the NEW POPE HOLY . . . I believe that he is SAINT CESAR CHAVEZ . . . I believe in WALTER REU-THER, HIS MENTOR. I believe in the $$$$$50,000 FIFTY GRAND CHECK donated by Walter Reuther to Chavez so Saint Cesar could HARRASS THE POOR FARMERS AND NON UNION WORKERS IN POOR CALIFORNIA . . . I believe HE will be SHOT "a la KENNEDY STYLE" (oh happy day) . . .

I believe LBJ-HHH-and MACNAMARA, did all their best to give all us poor Americans a GOOD FOXXING with VIETNAM, NORTH KOREA, LA FRANCE, THE ARABS, THE JEWS, THE CUBANS, THE NEEGAHS AND THE CIVIL RIGHTERS. I believe that ALL THE CATHOLIC BISHOPS in HEAH-U.S.A. are for CESAR CHAVEZ, CIVIL RIGHTERS, CARD BURNERS, DRAFT DODGERS, RAPERS, THIEVES, MURDERERS AND THE NIGGERS.

I believe BISHOP TIMOTHY MANNING OF FRESNO will "RENOUNCE" HIS IRISH BLOOD AND ANCESTOR-SHIP and will claim to be (like Chavez) a real COOL MEX-ICAN and half NEGRO. (He is a NIGGERS LOVER).

... I believe GEORGE C. WALLACE WILL SCARE THE
SHEETS OUT OF ALL THE NEEGAHS (neeegers to you)
by being ELECTED PRESIDENT OF THE U.S.A. I believe
FATHER GROPPIE THE S.O.B. OF MILWAUKEE WILL
REST IN HELL NEXT TO A BELOVED FRIEND OF HIS,
(REV.) M.L.K. (Beautiful News.)

I believe that MARTIN LUCIFER KING is also resting in
... HE ... (how do you spell it?) we got it; in he/// hea///
ven; their NEW BLACKIE SAINT (whose dead MARTYR-
DOM) Oh yeah? the Catholic Church BLAMES ON US
POOR CATHOLICS ... I believe that VERY SOON WE
(You and I) WILL ATTEND A JOYFUL FUNERAL FOR
OUR HONORABLE GUEST??????? AND NEW SAINT.
(Can you name him?) GLORY BE, GLORY BE, AMEN,
AMEN, amen, ALELUYA, ALELUYA; Pax bobis. PAXXX
BOBIS? Pax bobis my eye. PAXXXXXX FOXXXIS US ALL.

7

ON Monday morning I drove out to the Schenley ranch to ask the workers about pesticides. Like the rest of us, farm workers are slowly being poisoned by the pesticide residues that we take in with our food at every meal; in addition, they suffer from direct exposure that has often been fatal. According to the Union, the California Public Health Department has many documented cases of pesticide poisoning among farm workers, including mass blindness and the death of children, but it doesn't act on them.

"You can smell the poison sometimes in Delano," Chavez says. "It's very very strong. Workers can't begin to comprehend the dangers of these sprays; most of them look so innocent. I'm determined to do battle against the growers on this, and I think the best way is to put it in the contract. The workers have to be educated. These sprays are creepers. If they knocked you out immediately, it would be a lot easier to educate the people and to make our point. But a guy might go out and spray for a week, and that's the end of the job with that grower, and then he may take a job with another grower doing something else, and maybe several jobs later he begins to have trouble with his eyes, can't focus and comes in to see a doctor. Well, that's an industrial-accident case, but it's hell to prove it, since the damage was done so long before. The insurance company won't honor it. I think the whole industrial insurance thing has to be changed; even the payments are very discriminatory and unjust to farm workers.

"The ones that are most innocent are the ones that are most often hurt, especially if they don't read English. I've gone out personally and had it out with them. The guy says, 'Well, it's *my* life, ain't it?' And I say, 'No, it's not your life, it's everybody's life, and we got to start some place, so we're starting with you. What do you think would happen if you died of poisoning? And you had a union? Who do you think would be blamed? The employer? Hell, no. *We*'d be blamed, for not protecting you.'"

The road to Schenley passes its wine-processing plant, a dark, looming industrial building which is less incongruous than one might imagine in this flat, manipulated landscape. Arriving at the ranch offices, I asked to see P. L. Vargas, head of the workers' ranch committee, and was rudely informed by the red-haired ranch superintendent, E. L. Redger, that I would have to see Vargas at his own house after working hours. Even before he learned my mission, Redger's face revealed anger, and I got the impression that this anger was a part of him, like his thin mouth; he looked like a man who has waited for George Wallace all his life. As I left he offered the tight-faced opinion that Paul Vargas had invited me as an excuse to avoid work.

I had hardly reached the public road when I overtook a yellow spray buggy, and I shouted to its driver, asking for P. L. Though the sprayer was shut down, there was so much white poison powder blowing loose in the machinery that the driver was wearing gloves and goggles and a snoutlike mask of the sort worn a few weeks later by Mayor Daley's goon squads in Chicago; he yanked his mask down long enough to cry out, "*Peek*opp, *peek*opp!," pointing at a pickup truck down the road. Catching up with the pickup, I yelled to Mr. Vargas that Redger had forbidden me to enter the ranch, at which Vargas yelled back, "Follow me!" and led me straight into the vineyards. We passed down miles of monotonous green walls, arriving at a point where some dusting rigs were waiting for more bags of pesticide. "You ask these guys anything you want!" P. L. Vargas shouted. "I going to call Dolores!" He drove off in a fury.

One of the spray men told me that Dolores Huerta had had trouble before with Redger, whose low opinion of his workers is reciprocated. "I know this guy for nine, ten year," one told me, "and he never once say hi—he walk right by you. Against the Union, against *every* poor people; he just don't like Mexicans, I guess." The man laughed, perplexed. "Maybe this kind of man, he don't like nothin."

There were three Mexican-Americans on the dusting rigs, and none of them wore gloves; they explained that the company issued gloves for the wet spraying of parathion and other chemicals but not for dusting with dry sulphur. One of the three men was still feeling sick from the last wet spraying, and all three were anxious to talk about it.

"Before the Union come, we didn't get no gloves, no anything, and we got the itch"—he pronounced it "eetch" —"oh, some guys got it bad! That wet spray in the wind, it bring them little eggs—how you call them? Blisters? Blisters. The dry sulphur ain't so bad until you sweat; then it get under your skin and the itch begin. You have to use soap and water right away, and before the Union, they never give these things. And some the people get sick from eatin without washin their hands—oh, that stuff is bad! Got to keep the children away from that! My eyes get red and they sting, you know, but I ain't like P. L. I still see pretty good."

"That wet spray!" another said. "Every time the wind blow in the wrong direction we used to get wet, and then we get a rash, start scratching, everything get worse. Between my legs, under my arms. My stomach. Our eyes used to burn."

"We still don't have no spray suits, but they say they goin to buy some. Maybe next year. We got masks and gloves. A lot of ranches, they don't even got no gloves yet."

"Sometimes at night, the wind change and you don't notice it; you dust the wrong direction and you got trouble. We try to tell the new people to watch the wind and everything, tell them to wear a mask, but they don't know anything. One guy never listen, and he sniff that stuff, and in five second"—he snapped his fingers—"the blood start coming up. He didn't die but he was very very sick for three weeks there. And some of the sick ones, they won't go to the doctor—they just don't believe in doctors."

A man in a sombrero with a small bell dangling from the rim grunted disgustedly. "Them ones that come up from Mexico," he said. "They so damn ignorant, you know." In the same context, Chavez had said "innocent." I asked the men what they thought of Chavez. "Cesar?" They looked at the man in the belled sombrero, who spoke up for the others. "Cesar's a pretty good man," he assured me solemnly. "A pretty good man."

The three chattered resentfully about Rubio and Mendoza.

"He t'rowin around a lot of money—where he get that?"

A foreman, Danny Sanchez, came along on his tractor, dragging more sacks of sulphur powder on a wagon. While the drivers loaded up their hoppers he paused to listen, nodding his head. "This guy Joe Mendoza, and Gilbert Rubio," he said, "they got a bunch of people wit them, but that is a labor contractor's organization. Before the Union, I work pretty close to the big trucks on the ranch, you know, and I hear what they tell on the radios, and one day I hear one of the labor contractors askin for a raise, he wanted eleven dollars a ton. So I get back to work, and I ask the pickers how much they gettin paid for a tank of grapes, and they say, 'Eleven dollars.' 'Eleven dollars?' 'Yah, they payin eleven dollars.' Well, in a tank they two and a half tons, so the contractors, they receivin all the money for the peoples, and they takin more than half of it for themselves!" Sanchez laughed. "That's why the crew pusher don't want no Union, he wants to keep everyting the way it is, so he goin along wit Rubio and Mendoza!"

A man finished loading and drove off down the lane. Before entering the rows, he got off his tractor and started up the blower that discharged sulphur from the hopper, then darted back like a shadow through the white cloud to throw the tractor into gear and escape the poison that he had let loose.

P. L. Vargas returned with permission for me to be where I already was. "Anybody want to come to see P. L.," he muttered, angry still, "they come to see me."

I talked with him and Sanchez for a little while. Both men were unabashed admirers of Cesar Chavez, and ir-revocably pro-Union; in talking to me about it, they interrupted each other out of pure enthusiasm. They agreed that if a secret ballot could be taken, 95 percent of the workers on most ranches would be pro-Union, but that the workers were uneducated people who did not speak English very well, and were afraid. "They scared if they do anything, the boss just kick them out," P. L. Vargas said. "And if you got kids, you got to work, you know. If you got kids, you got to work every day." Vargas is a very big man, with heavy eyebrows and small steel glasses; at the very mention of children he looked worried. "Yah!" Danny said. "We know we livin in a free country, but the growers don't know it yet! When the picket line came to Di Giorgio, they had *everyting* out there to drown them out." At the memory, Danny giggled with delight. "Man, they had radios, they had loudspeakers, car horns, bells! Why they don't want a secret ballot? Because they afraid!"

Now they were not only paid a decent wage but the wage was guaranteed. Dispoto, P. L. said, was paying $1.60 per hour at the moment because he needed people for the harvest, but later he could drop the wage to $1.40, and anybody who didn't like it was out of a job. He and Danny had a two-year contract for $1.90 an hour; it would automatically be raised 10 cents next year. Not only that, but the work hours were regulated now, with time and a half for overtime. "Before we used to work like a mule," P. L. said. "Now we just do our day's work."

Danny said, "Before, man, I work on the dustin rig from six o'clock in the evenin to eight, nine o'clock the next mornin. Dustin all night long. Sometimes we work fourteen to sixteen hours a day."

P. L. Vargas still looked worried. "Sometimes they want you to prune two rows a day, and if you don't do that, they fire you. You say, 'Look, you go too fast, you hurt the vines.' Sometimes they forty cuts to a vine, but they don't care!"

"And not all the people work the same—not all guys work the same like us," Danny said. "Some guys fast, some guys not so fast, and then they are older guys, and ones that ain't had the experience. They *try* to work fast, but they just can't. They very poor people, so they sweat, you know, they get nervous cause they so afraid, so they work like animals. They *run!*" Danny laughed. Like P. L., he is a broad, strong man, and his wide, open face has a mustache on it. He laughed not because he was too callous to see the pathos of the people, but because the pathos made him nervous. "They *run.* And when they see the boss, they take their hats off"—he tugged his forelock—"and keep runnin. If they don't, they get fired right away." He acted out the dialogue: " 'We got no more work for you.' 'Why?' 'We got no more work for you, I said.' "

Vargas' big face curled up in pain and distaste. "Before Cesar was here, everybody was afraid." He doffed his hat in a slow, obsequious gesture. "Now we not afraid no more. We goin to say the truth, and we goin fight for the right."

"We learnin," Danny said. "I tryin to learn a little bit every day now, because I never go to school, and my father never had no chance to go, so this is what I wantin for my kids."

"We got paid vacations now," P. L. Vargas said, in a voice suggesting that he could still scarcely believe it. "We got seniority."

"Yah!" Danny said. "You know Henry?" he asked P. L., who did not bother to answer. "Well, we got this colored fella, Henry, that was out here eleven years and never got no seniority on the best jobs. Now he's drivin a tractor, and he don't believe it!" Danny squealed delightedly. "He just don't believe it!" Danny was silent for a little while, rolling his sombrero in his hands. "I want the same thing for everybody," he said. "I want the Union for every poor people in this country. I win more money, then they must win it too, because they live in the same country where I live and they buy the same thing what I buy." He nodded his head. "If you got a big family, one-forty an hour is not much—you got to work twelve to sixteen hours every day. This is the way they killin the peoples. A man workin seven days a week for twenty, thirty years—I don't think that man is livin."

Wondering if Danny Sanchez was the "Danny" Chavez had spoken of who had been converted, I asked him if he had not been against the Union in the beginning. Danny looked sheepish, but he didn't bluster. "Yah," he said. "People like me, they never heard nothing about a union, we never know nothing what's happen in the world. So I was really against the Union, because I was afraid about my job. I'm wrong, I know it, I *know* I'm wrong, but anyway, after two, three month, I change!" Beaming, he spread his arms out wide, inviting me to look at a changed man. "I change!" he repeated gleefully, as if this were magic. "And now I the Union man!"

"These people from Mexico, they very ignorant," the man in the belled hat repeated. He spoke mildly, and Danny Sanchez took no visible offense; on the contrary, he nodded cheerfully, as if what his friend had said was a well-known fact. "They're makin thirty dollars a day," the man continued, "and they don't care about the people who have to stay here. They go back to Mexico and live like kings over there, but the people that have to stay, the Americans, we're the ones in trouble."

Paul Vargas wanted me to talk to some more people, and at one of the labor camps, now closed down, we listened for a while to Henry Thomas, a dignified black man with a gray mustache. Mr. Thomas discussed the difference that the Union had made there at the ranch. "A lot of discrimination in jobs they had that they don't have it now—I mean, they still a *little* in here, but it ain't nothin like it was." He glanced at P. L. Vargas, who was leaning against the car. It was noon now, and the fields were quiet. Around us, in a grove of trees, stood the small boarded-up cabins that had sheltered the wetbacks and *braceros* of other years. Like the mockingbird hidden somewhere in the grove, the sweet-voiced old man spoke quietly, so as not to stir up the heat. "Conditions of work, they *much* better. It changed so much, just like daylight and dark. I been here a long time, and for my race of people it's been pretty tough. You had some was able to stay, and some wasn't. Some people can take more. The reason I'm here is because I guess I can take more than a whole lot of other people can." His voice was bitter, rueful, but there was a stubborn pride in it. "I been *done* enough to go, but I won't go. But since the Union, it been lightenin up a whole lot; I don't know anything would have helped it any better than the Union, and I wish everybody in the whole country would see it that way, but they some over where I live, they don't want to work on the Union, but it the best thing *I* know of. And I think it's goin to get better, and I got somebody in front of me if anything go *too* far wrong; it ain't like it used to be. I got a chance to explain, and maybe they do something about it." He paused. "I mean, sometime it still seem when they got nobody for a certain job, they just grab me, and I'm willin to go along with all that, to help; I don't want to be complainin all the time, because I know the Union, it's a lot to get started in a place, and *somebody* got to take something, y'know. I willin to go along with it." Again he was looking at P. L., who was looking at the ground. "Sometime it do seem like they pass me over for the good job, and I know how to do every job they is here. But I'm an old man, and I realize *that* too, y'know. . . . And I gettin a dollar-ninety here bein the yardman; I can remember when I were gettin ninety . . . Me and another colored boy that were workin here, they told us they weren't gone to give out no more vacations, but they had some mens in here was gettin vacation and I was entitled to it long ago. I been here steady since 1955, and I started in '52. Well, the year that the Union came, they give me a two-week vacation, and I don't believe I would *ever* got a vacation in my life if it hadn't been for the Union. Might be it *could* have happened, but that is my belief about it." He shook his head. "Oh, Chavez is a fine man: if it wouldn't been for him, I don't know *where* we would have been. Nobody else stood up for us. This boy"—he pointed at P. L.—"they tried to strike in '52, and they didn't get *nowhere—everybody* against 'em."

At the mention of the old strike, one of so many that had been put down, P. L. Vargas raised his head. "They broke that one. Policemen, they were beginning to break the heads. They done ever'ting. Put me in jail. We kept them closed for one month, and then they got in the police."

"I had a chance to come in here to work that year," Henry Thomas said, "but I an old union man all my life, and I don't work where they got a strike. I don't do that. I know better, see. The union where I was, down in Galveston, Texas, longshoremen, y'know, you could get killed." He gazed around him. "It's so different here now, it's a pity. I couldn't think of all the things, how much different it is. Before, it was always they hire you temporarily, and then good-bye. Now it seem like things are steady, so I don't worry. Man! Ninety cents an hour, and that hour weren't anything like the hour we got now! You had to cut grapes four rows a day, rows like them ones here"—he pointed at the fields—"two in the mornin and two in the afternoon." He laughed uneasily at this recollection. "And if you didn't, you was out, 'cause the man had a timecard and he fire you."

"One fella were only t'ree, four vines short," P. L. said, "and he got fired."

"And some of these vines is really hard to cut. You got to make a good cut. When you cuttin too fast, in the prunin, you just butcherin up stuff. 'Course they *want* that, want one man to rush the other fellas, get more done. Just like slaves. It was a shame the way we used to do. And no ice water, no toilet, nothin like we got now. And you have to keep the toilets clean now, 'cause I had that job of keepin 'em clean, had to check the towels and toilet paper every mornin. But I get along pretty good; I can't grumble about it. If they tell me to do too many jobs, it ain't none of my fault. I just do what they tell me, that's the way I figure it."

Again he seemed proud of his stubborn endurance in the face of discrimination, an endurance that today would earn him the contempt of most young blacks, and the name "Tom." I asked him how he happened to leave a shipyard job in Ventura that he had mentioned earlier.

"Well, I tell you the truth, it's a silly thing for me to say, but I come over into farm work because at that time they was takin out all your income tax and social security out of your check each week, and I say, 'I'll go work on the farm where I get all my money.' Now I know better, and I wish I had stayed with it, because I right at the age where I be gettin my money back. I'll be sixty-two pretty soon. But anyway, it was 1948 when I started roamin up and down the highways, pickin peaches and cuttin grapes, pickin cotton, just roamin from place to place. Seem like that was the right thing to do."

Mr. Thomas fell silent, and P. L. Vargas said that this labor camp had been used mostly for wetbacks and *braceros;* the several labor camps on the 3,200-acre ranch had been segregated to prevent fighting between the races. Mr. Thomas remarked that Negroes had never liked living on the ranch, preferring their own community over near Pixley. "The most of the colored in this country come from the South, and they don't want to stay on no white man's place, because they had enough of that back there. I'm tellin you just like it is." From an old country Negro this mild criticism of the white man to a white man's face required courage which young city blacks, spoiled by the white man's guilt, would never understand. "All 'ceptin the winos, they don't care. I seen them winos go and leave their time, three, four days' pay. Wine-drinkin people, a man lookin for *them* now, gone find them drifted all over the country."

P. L. Vargas nodded. "One year we have colored and the next year they don't come, because they the first ones laid off. They run them off the ranches and they don't come back no more."

"Now, Martin Luther King," Henry Thomas said, "he wanted to help the people and he got killed. He the only one that stood up for the colored people, and they couldn't buy him, that's why he got killed. There's been Negroes started out all right, but they get to livin good themself, so they throw the rest of us away." Slowly, the old man shook his head. "Martin Luther King didn't do that. He stood up so strong and so good, and he didn't cause none of that trouble like they said he did."

The road back to Delano passed groves of olive and pomegranate trees. It crossed the Friant-Kern irrigation canal, a rigid, endless trench of bare cement with a string of water at the bottom, then skirted the Sierra Vista Ranch, where I left it. The appearance of Sierra Vista is not improved by octagonal sentry towers, left over from its days as a relocation camp for the uprooted Japanese of World War II. One tower, high, dark-green and weathered, was circled by a pigeon, which cracked the blue silence with a sharp snap of its wings.

Sierra Vista has been sold off to a number of local growers, but the vineyards I passed looked unweeded or abandoned. The rank greenness of hot-summer weeds contrasted strangely with the bony sentry towers and the barren sheds along the rail spur. The screen doors were warped and rusty, the signs faded; the open sheds looked windgutted. Yet the stillness hanging over the place, the effect of airlessness and desolation, was offset by something that nagged at me for several minutes before I perceived what it was. For the first time since my arrival in Delano I saw birds—not many birds, it is true, but more than one bird at a time. Besides one mockingbird and a gang of English sparrows, a few swallows were coursing back and forth over the weed-thickened vineyards. A house finch was singing on a shed, and a kestrel hovered on quick wings in the field corner. Where there are swallows and kestrels, there are insects and possibly mice; where there are mice and finches, the seeds have not all been treated with alkyl mercury preservatives or fungicides like hexachlorobenzene. At Sierra Vista, named at a time when mountains were still visible through the haze of progress, nature was fighting to regain a foothold, and what made this possible was the reduction of pesticide and herbicide application due to man's departure.

With the world population out of control, the use of pesticides has become necessary for efficient food production. But as currently managed in American agriculture, the broadcasting of these deadly and long-lived poisons ranks with the mass production of cars and highways as an ultimate expression of free enterprise run amok. It is now well known that the proliferating organophosphates are a family of chemicals related closely to the nerve gases developed during World War II; what people may not know is that after the war, the wholesale distribution of these poisons was encouraged by the Department of Agriculture, which in turn was encouraged by the same firms that produced the nerve gas: Dow Chemical, whose stockholders also enjoy the profits made on napalm, is one of the companies that benefited most from the department's indulgent attitude.

In agriculture, the chlorinated hydrocarbons such as DDT are being replaced by these organophosphates, among which the cheapest and most effective is parathion. This poison is so powerful that less than one fifth of the amount used annually in California's fields would enable everybody in the world to commit suicide. Parathion has brought death to farm workers with such frequency in America and abroad that a symposium, convened by the World Health Organization in Milan, Italy, in 1964, considered the suggestion that parathion be outlawed as a pesticide. In the end, financial considerations prevailed; poor countries threatened with famine cannot worry about a few farm workers if parathion is cheap. (The world's apathy toward the misery in Biafra may be no more than a first symptom of the world callousness that will develop in the face of the great famine predicted widely for the next decades.) Meanwhile the insects, notoriously tolerant of poisons, continue to prosper, and the manufacturers continue to build up the volume and toxicity of their products. The United States government, ever responsive to business lobbies, appears willing to risk the nation's health before it risks the profits of the chemical industry by enforcing strict controls on the use of pesticides. On the state level, the same ethics apply; out of deference to its biggest business, California has left protection of the workers to the people who care least about it.

Cesar Chavez is reluctant to raise the issue of poison spray because he knows that any honest investigation will reveal a danger to the public, not to mention the worker, which might wreck an industry on which his own people depend (the public is also threatened by the absence of field toilets, since many serious diseases, including polio and hepatitis, may be transmitted by human feces in the fields). In recent years, infestations of canned tuna fish by the algae *Salmonella,* and one bad lot of cranberries, almost put both industries out of business. What would happen to

Delano if a child ate a bunch of unwashed grapes and died of parathion poisoning?

Evidently the growers recognize their vulnerability on this issue, to judge from the fact that Kern county's agricultural commissioner has twice refused the Union access to the public records on pesticide use within the county, and in 1968 was supported in this decision by a restraining order issued by the Kern County superior court. The growers keep saying that they have nothing to hide, but their own actions refute them. "Between 1950 and 1961," according to Truman Moore's *The Slaves We Rent*, "3,040 farm workers were poisoned in California by pesticides and other farm chemicals. Twenty-two workers and sixty-three children died."

8

AT the Union offices on Monday afternoon, the air was full of the talky enthusiasm of an amateur operation, though these people are amateurs only in the sense that most of them are not paid. (The law office is supported by the AFL-CIO and the Roger Baldwin Foundation of the American Civil Liberties Union; Jim Drake is paid by the Migrant Ministry; Leroy Chatfield is supported by the UAW.) The night before, Jerry Cohen had gone up to San Francisco, and this morning there had been a press conference at which Cohen announced the filing of a $50-million suit against Dispoto Brothers, Sabovich and Sons, John J. Kovacevich, and any other grower using Di Giorgio's HI-COLOR label. Cohen had also told reporters about the violence used against the pickets in the Coachella Valley, but the press was greedy for "hard" news. "These days," Cohen said later, "you got to get someone killed before they're interested."

By late afternoon a report had come in from New York that Waldbaum's chain stores had canceled a previous order of seven thousand boxes, or approximately six boxcars, of California grapes; this may have been the order Mr. Dispoto had received while I was sitting in his office. Dispoto's attorney had already called to say he would receive Dispoto's copy of the suit, which his client had heard about on his car radio.

Chavez came in, saying, "Yup, yup, yup!"; he had just talked to Connors on the phone. " 'That fifty million is a dirty trick!' Yup! 'You never told me!' Nope!" He carried a bottle of Diet-Rite, and opening a bottom drawer of his desk, he took out a package of matzos crackers to go with it. He held the matzos high between two fingers. "It's a raid!" he cried. "They're raiding my matzos!" He handed some around. "That's not *all* I've got in there, you know," he said. With much ceremony, he reached slowly into the drawer and drew out some dried apricots and prunes.

Chavez has dispensed with breakfast and is careless about lunch; in Delano, he sometimes eats one modest meal a day. On the other hand, he will accept both lunch and supper so long as the Union does not have to pay for him, and as he is fond of Chinese food, we drove down to Bakersfield in the late twilight to eat dinner in a "beautiful" Chinese restaurant. Ann Israel took Helen Chavez, four Chavez daughters and a friend; the youngest Chavez girl, Elizabeth, went with Cesar and me and his two youngest sons, Birdie (Anthony) and Babo (Paul), in Leroy Chatfield's Volvo. The only child missing was Fernando, now nineteen, who was living with his grandparents in San Jose.

All eight Chavez children have nicknames. Elizabeth is called "Titibet," her own pronunciation of her name; due to early rotundity, Paul was known as "Bubble," since modified to "Babo"; "Birdie" is so called because of a putative resemblance to a bird. "My own name was 'Manzi,' " Cesar says. "As a small child, I was supposed to have liked *man-zanilla*—you know, camomile tea? So the family always called me 'Manzi.' I forbade this when I began courting, but some of them still use it, the ones in San Jose."

The memory of "Manzi" made him smile, and he talked cheerfully for a little while about his childhood. Chavez's grandfather, also a Cesar Chavez, had been a peon in Mexico. As a homesteader, he acquired some 160 acres of sage and mesquite desert in the North Gila River Valley about twenty miles northeast of Yuma, part of which he built carefully into a farm. He also became a U.S. citizen, Cesar says, with the help of a politician who needed his vote. Cesar's parents, Librado and Juana Chavez, had been born in Mexico but Librado came to the United States as a small child, and Cesar Estrada Chavez entered the world on March 31, 1927, as an American.

According to Cesar, his grandfather admired the big Mexican haciendas, and since he had nine sons and six daughters to help out, he designed his house accordingly. It lasted a half-century and might have lasted indefinitely in that dry climate had the roof been of tile instead of adobe, because the walls were twenty-four inches thick. The farm was cool in summer, warm in winter, with wide barn areas for livestock food and farm equipment; it stood on a slope against the hills, with a laundry-and-wood shed on one side and a garden on the other. Right in front of the house was an irrigation canal into which Richard was always falling.

"When we were very small, Richard and I and my mother and my grandmother would plant a row of vegetables." The truck farm had cotton and lettuce, carrots, watermelon and other crops, with maize, grain and alfalfa for the animals, and it fed not only their own families but the numerous hobos who wandered up and down the land in the Depression years. "At that time my mother's patron saint was St. Eduvigis. I think she was an Egyptian queen who gave everything to the poor, and my mother had made a pledge never to turn away anyone who came for food, and so, you know, ordinary people would come and have the food, and there were a lot of hobos that used to come at any time of day or night. Most of them were white. We lived in my aunt's house in Yuma for a while, and my mother sent Richard and me out into the street sometimes to look for *trampitas*—that was our affectionate way of calling the hobos. I remember the first one. We found him sitting under a retaining wall, right around the corner, and we wanted this one bad, so we could quit looking and go out to play. But when we told him all about the free food just waiting for him around the corner, that tramp couldn't believe it. 'What for?' he said. 'What are you doing it for?' 'For nothing,' we said. 'You just come with us.' We hustled him around the corner and he ate the food, but he still didn't believe it. She'd just give them very simple things—beans and tortillas and hot coffee—but it was a meal, and soon all the hobos knew about her, because word spreads. She would not let them do anything in return—chop wood or offer pencils. So they were very kind about coming at the right hours, and even the ones that talked rough outside took their hats off when they came in, and were very respectful. We didn't have much, and sometimes there was enough for everybody and sometimes there wasn't."

His grandfather died when Chavez was very young, and his grandmother became the head of the farm household. At that time she was the only literate member of the family. The children, all about two years apart, were Rita, then

Cesar, then Richard, then Eduvigis, called "Vicki," then Librado, Jr., called "Lennie"; another baby sister, Helen, died on the farm. Richard, or "Rukie," named for a lullaby word, recalls that their grandmother was "about ninety-eight years old and blind," but nevertheless, she was a person to be reckoned with. Rukie and Manzi, who tended to her needs, would tease her by keeping her food just out of reach—"Here it is! Here it is!"—and sometimes Manzi, on the way to the outhouse, would lead the old lady all over the farm. For deeds like these, they were sometimes caught and clouted by the adults.

"We were very mischievous," Richard recalls with pleasure. According to Dolores Huerta, they still are—Manuel, too. "There were times when the whole Union was collapsing around our ears, and those three could always make a joke of it."

Cesar's cousin Manuel came to live on the farm when he was small, and has been so close to Cesar ever since that each refers to the other as "my brother." For a time, in fact, because Manuel claimed it, it was assumed by people that they *were* brothers, and the story goes that one time someone came to Cesar and begged him for enlightenment: Was Manuel his brother or was he not? In this period Manuel's volatile nature was a constant threat to Cesar's program of nonviolence, and Cesar had to consider the question a few seconds before he answered it. "Sometimes," Cesar said.

Manuel Chavez does not look like Cesar and Richard: his head is not rounded but angular, and he has a watchful eye and a hard, high cheekbone. Apart from his work as an organizer, Manuel is a troubleshooter for the Union, and the Union wit; his celebrated sense of humor works beautifully with that of Cesar, who seems almost relieved when Manuel teases him about his nonviolence and even his faith. One day Manuel did a deadly imitation of Cesar's response to a hostile priest who forbade him the use of a parish hall— "Oh, Father, *why!*" Manuel cried in a sweet piteous voice, raising his hands, palms together, like a supplicant, and rolling his eyes toward heaven. Cesar laughed, delighted. Much as Cesar respects and likes his staff, Dolores says, it is Manuel and Richard whom he turns to in bad times or in crises.

The farm in the Gila River Valley represents a lost home to all three men, and perhaps because he came there late, and though of the three he describes the farm with the least joy, Manuel seems the most bitter about the loss. By the end of the Depression, the family's money was all gone, and the farm was seized by the county to pay off the local taxes and the water bill. "It was peanuts!" Manuel told me, pounding his fist into his palm. "Maybe a thousand dollars! And a friend offered to pay it or something, and they refused! Because it was good land by then, and the bank wanted it, this rich banker. So there was a tax sale and it went to him. It's the old story: they let us work that rough, dirty land, and then they grab it!" Manuel's eyes squinted. "When we get through in California, that's the next place we're going to go to! Arizona!" While in the Coachella Valley the previous June, Manuel and Richard drove over to see the homestead, now a ruin of fallen adobe on another man's farm. Manuel took photographs of the ruined farm, which looks much smaller than the farm of Cesar's memory. Richard thought that it had kind of shrunk a little.

"I missed that house," Cesar says. "And I was so sorry when I heard later they were using it for animals. When I was living there we had all kinds of space; it seemed like the whole world belonged to us. In the cities, I couldn't get used to the fences. I missed our house all the more. We couldn't play like we used to. On the farm we had a little place where we played, and a tree in there was ours and we played there. We built bridges and we left everything there and when we came back the next day it was still there. You see, we never knew what stealing was, or to be stolen from. Then we went to the city and we left a ball outside just for a second and *boom!*—it was gone. And, oh, it was so hard to get a new one. We left it out there and we came back and it was stolen. And I couldn't understand how it could be stolen—why? To us it was a real tragedy. And then my shoes were stolen; that's a big joke in the family, it always has been. We were living in Oxnard. We were playing handball and I had shoes with leather soles, so I took them off and played barefoot, and I looked around and the shoes were gone. And I had to walk—I was about twelve then—I had to walk home barefoot all the way across town."

Chavez was quiet for a while, then said, "In Brawley, we used to shine shoes, and we really hustled. The cops wouldn't let us into Anglo Town, but there was a diner right on the line, and everybody talked about how it was supposed to have beautiful hamburgers. It also had a sign reading WHITE TRADE ONLY, but we had just come from the country, from Arizona, from a community that was mostly Mexican or whites too poor to bother about us. So we didn't understand yet, and we got up our nerve and went in. The counter girl was at the far end with her boy friend, and we were looking at them over the end of the counter." For a moment, as he spoke, Chavez looked exactly like a wide-eyed boy in search of a beautiful hamburger:

"Two hamburgers, please!" He shook his head. "The girl said, 'What's the matter, you can't read? Goddamn dumb Mex!' She and her boy friend laughed, and we ran out. Richard was cursing them, but I was the one who had spoken to them, and I was crying. That laugh rang in my ears for twenty years—it seemed to cut us out of the human race."

A few years later the Chavez family, still migrating, entered a run-down diner and were seated by the waitress before the boss came in and told her, in their hearing, to throw them out. When she protested, he threatened to fire her. She came to the table in tears.

The Chavezes were getting up to go; they called to Cesar who hung back. "No," he answered. "I have to speak up someday, and it's going to be today." He went over to the boss and said, "Why do you have to treat people like that? A man who behaves like you do is not even a human being!"

"Aw, don't give me that shit," the man said. "G'wan, get outta here!"

Cesar went. He was then fourteen or fifteen, he recalls, but it was not his age that made the difference between this story and so many others in his life. He spoke up for the first time because the waitress, by treating him as a person, gave him the sense of identity that he has since given to the Mexican farm workers.

"Another thing that we learned—my dad especially—was that people would lie to you—lie without batting an eye. For instance, they'd say, 'If you go to such and such a place, they have a job for you at a very high wage.' And we always went for it hook, line and sinker. They'd get you to go because you were competition. And we'd get there and we'd find there was no housing. The wages weren't what they'd said and in many cases there wasn't even a job. We'd have to wait around a week or so for a job to start. I remember now that my dad and my brother had a heck of a time trying to understand why anyone would really—you know—just *lie*. So many things we couldn't understand. See, we were really poor, but on the farm we had all the milk we wanted, all the eggs we wanted and all the chicken we wanted, and all the vegetables during the summer, and some fruit that we raised ourselves. And suddenly we had to pay for everything. We didn't have electricity or gas, of course, or running water. We had a well, and used the kerosene lamps and cooked with wood. We came to town and my mother couldn't get used to cooking with gas; she was afraid of it. We had to buy wood. Well, wood was fast disappearing and was very expensive. It was so strange. We had all we wanted over there on the farm. Cottonwood and mesquite and paloverde—that's ironwood. You get one of those started and it'll burn all night. Oh! And we had umbrella trees!"

With the loss of their land in 1937, the Chavez family began the long grim period that Manuel calls "our migrating years." Up and down the byways of California, with the armies of the dispossessed, they followed the crops. Like all the rest, the Chavezes were true paupers; their struggle was for shelter, clothing, food. In this period John Steinbeck, outraged by a lettuce strike in Salinas, was writing articles that would evolve into *The Grapes of Wrath*.

No one complains at the necessity of feeding a horse while he is not working. But we complain about feeding the men and women who work our lands. Is it possible that this state is so stupid, so vicious, and so greedy that it cannot clothe and feed the men and women who help to make it the richest area in the world? Must the hunger become anger and the anger fury before anything will be done?

Some of the migrants had cars; others traveled in rickety old buses. On the sides of the buses were scrawled names like "To the Four Winds" and "I Am Going—Who Cares? Who Cares?" For many, including the Chavezes, the car often served as a home. One long rainy winter in Oxnard, the whole family lived in a small tent.

When the trek began, Manuel was twelve, Cesar ten, and Richard eight; their childhood was already over. Rita and the boys worked with the parents in the fields, picking prunes and figs and apricots, turning grapes for raisins, hunching and stooping down row upon row, from the Imperial Valley north to Marysville, a small part of the tattered army that Woody Guthrie sang of in "Pastures of Plenty":

> At the edge of your city you will find us
> and then
> We come with the dust and we've gone with
> the wind.

In November they would come back south again, taking such poor segregated schooling as they could find in the brief winter season between pruning and girdling: Chavez still recalls the battered books and pencil stubs that young second-class citizens were issued. Although the family were U.S. citizens, they were in constant peril of deportation: the Border Patrol, known as *la Migra*, rarely concerned itself with the difference between Mexicans and Mexican-Americans. "My mother was so frightened of *la Migra*," Cesar says, "that she would be trembling whenever we were near the border."

To this day, the journey from the farm on the Gila River to the slums of Sal Si Puedes, in San Jose, is the archetypal journey which hundreds of thousands of dispossessed rural Americans are still making, and which millions of poor people are making all over the world; one day the *barrio* will extend from San Jose to Buenos Aires. But the Chavezes' journey was a long one, and there were no real homes along the way. The family paused in Brawley, Oxnard and Delano, then went on again. Cesar alone attended more than thirty schools without ever reaching high school. Sometimes the family lived in tents or under bridges, eking out a meager diet with fish and greens culled from roadside ditches. "Mexicans like hog weed," Cesar says enigmatically. He and Richard collected tinfoil from old cigarette packs found on the highway; for an enormous ball weighing eighteen pounds, they got enough money to buy two sweatshirts and one pair of tennis shoes.

In 1939, in San Jose, Cesar's father joined a CIO union that was organizing workers in dried fruit; like all the rest, this union was broken as soon as it went out on strike. During World War II Mr. Chavez joined another short-lived union. "He had to join to get a job, that's all," Richard says. "He never could understand union ways. He was a big man, very strong, and when they told him to load three sacks of apricots on a cart when five was easy for him, it bothered him; he was getting good pay, he thought, so why not do the best he could? Manuel's dad, too. They weren't real union men. My father is a very sweet person, but he never wanted to get involved; he was content with life the way it was."

Cesar remembers it differently. He describes his father as a true unionist who would join any workers organization that might help: "We were involved in more plain walk-outs than any other family."

Cesar stopped talking to point at freight cars on a rail-road siding; the cars, softened by the twilight, were heaped with huge coarse sugar beets. "That is one crop I'm glad is automated. That was work for an animal, not a man. Stooping and digging all day, and the beets are *heavy*—oh, that's brutal work. And then to go home to some little place, with all those kids, and hot and dirty—*that* is how a man is crucified. *Cru*-cified," he repeated, with a very low, intense burst of real anger. He gazed back at the silent cars of beets as they dropped behind. "The growers don't care about people and they never will. Their improvements, their labor-saving devices, are all for their own benefit, not for ours. But once we get a union, we'll be protected."

But automation threatens to remove the jobs before the Union can get decent job conditions; wage increases and other benefits will only hasten the process. The growers all talk of a machine that will automate the table-grape industry within five years, and although this seems un-likely—individual grapes infected with mildew must be cut out of each bunch or the grapes will rot in shipment—the fact remains that crop after crop is being automated. Reading my thoughts, Chavez said, "We're not afraid of automation. We'll split the profits of progress with them fifty-fifty."

Two thirds of the way to Bakersfield, Cesar strapped himself into his safety belt. In the back of the car, the three children were singing:

> "If I had a hammer, I'd hammer in the morning
> "I'd hammer in the evening, all over this land

"I'd hammer out mercy, I'd hammer out justice
"I'd hammer out love between the sisters and
    the brothers
"All over this land . . ."

The children said they had learned the song from the radio. Cesar did not know it. He said he liked music but could not sing a note. "First I liked Mexican music—you know, *mariachi*. Then I went through the stage as a teenager when I rejected Mexican music; I thought it was silly. I liked Glenn Miller and Benny Goodman, Woody Herman. All the big bands had one-night stands around here, and we saw most of them. But then I began to go back to Mexican music. I think *mariachi* is beautiful; it gives me a real beautiful feeling." He sighed. "But I cannot sing. I used to like to dance, but I cannot sing. *'Todo está en el hombre menos al cantar bien.'* That was one of my mother's *dichos:* 'Everything is given to man except the ability to sing.'"

At Bill Lee's Chopsticks we sat at a big table in the corner. Sylvia, Linda, Elouise, Anna and their friend Obdulia wished the combination shrimp plate; the rest of us left the ordering to Cesar. Because the table was split into two camps, there were lots of jokes between Cesar and his children about shrimp strikes and hungry strikebreakers who might cross the picket line in the middle of the table. In the excitement Cesar repeatedly confused the names of Sylvia and Linda, his very pretty eldest daughters, until Linda cried cheerfully, "He doesn't know us apart!" Cesar shook his head ruefully; he gazed at her until she looked at him and smiled. "Do you remember when I had you numbered? Number Five!" He saluted. "'Yes, Father!' Number Eight!" He saluted. "'Yes, Father!'" But when he called Linda "Sylvia" again, his wife hissed at him with real ve-

hemence. She had been reserved and very quiet all evening; he looked at her with genuine concern.

"There was a Colonel Somebody at Schenley," Helen
Chavez said, in an attempt to ease matters. Cesar called
him 'Major.'"

"Sometimes I called him '*Mayor*,'" Cesar said, feigning
terror. Helen, who has fierce Spanish eyebrows, was still
looking cross; her father was a colonel under Pancho Villa
in the Revolution, and Chavez teases her about her hot
blood. He began to tease her now about their courtship.
They had met in Delano during World War II when Chavez, then fifteen and still migrating, had found himself
stranded there, out of a job. At that time Helen Fabela, a
pretty Delano girl, worked in the People's Market at Garces
and Glenwood. "She used to give me gas coupons, I think,"
Cesar told the children. "Then she asked me to a show. How
could I say no?" In spite of herself, Helen Chavez began to
smile.

"Who paid?" Sylvia asked.

"She did, of course. And once I was sitting in the Pagoda
restaurant with Roberto Jimenez. We had ordered a *big*
bowl of rice"—with his usual optimism about the past,
Cesar spread his hands apart to show the great size of the
bowl, but his wife shook her head;"Twenty cents' worth,"
she said, trying not to laugh—"and your mother came in
with her girl friend and asked if they could join us, and I
said, 'Of course.'" He chuckled and looked contentedly
at his wife. "She had a job and I did not—what could I
do? The little money I could make I sent to my mother."

"I give all my money to my mother too," Babo announced, and Birdie snorted.

"*What* money?"

"Oh, I got a few pennies," Babo said.

Cesar did not mention the time, in 1945, when he and Helen were arrested in Delano for sitting on the wrong side of the segregated movie theater and refusing to move. He gazed appreciatively at his children as he chewed.

"Were you a lover in your days?" Linda inquired.

"Love 'em and leave 'em, I bet," another daughter said, and the shrimp eaters giggled in unison. The children are all salty and affectionate with their father without being impolite.

"Well, I was very friendly, you know; a lot of girls were my friends, but I was not a lover." Chavez said this simply, without coyness. He has no *machismo*, but on the other hand, he much prefers domesticated, motherly women: if Cesar woke up thirsty in the night, he would expect Helen to fetch him a glass of water. Once an aggrieved female aide accused him angrily of being a phony: "You're just as *macho* as all the rest; you think women are different!" "That's right!" Cesar retorted. "They're all crazy!"

Babo was trying to extract his fortune without breaking his cookie, but the rest of us read our fates aloud to the whole company. Birdie, who is the youngest child, read out the following in a slow and serious voice: "You will be able to encourage a younger person."

Cesar was called to the telephone, and we waited for him in the street. The only bookstore for fifty miles in any direction was across the street from the restaurant, and Helen said, "I hope it isn't open. Books and camera stores —he'll be in there all night." Helen's shyness made me feel shy myself. She mistrusts reporters and had no real reason to make an exception in my case; doubtless she felt that in making friends with me, Cesar and Ann Israel had made a great mistake. The reporters that flock around the Union are only another burden in a life of unbroken toil and insecurity; apart from that, Helen is very shy by nature, and determined that the outside world shall not invade her private life. "Her sense of privacy is what I like about her," her husband says. "I mean, I like *everything* about her, but I really like that a lot." In the Sacramento march, Helen refused to walk in the front ranks with the leaders but remained well behind, out of range of the TV cameras and microphones.

I said I supposed she would be very glad when the strike was over. Her smile, when it appears, is a beautiful surprise. "Yes," she said, with all her heart. She paid no attention to the fatuity of my remark; standing there on the sidewalk, considering life without the strike, she didn't even know that I was there.

Over the radio, on the way home, came a gust of windy platitudes out of Miami; the Republican National Convention had begun. I turned off the radio, and Cesar and I reminisced about our service days. We are the same age, and we were both Navy enlisted men in the Pacific at the end of World War II, so that our points of reference, at age nineteen, were much the same. We both liked Benny Goodman and Sugar Ray, and remembered the better fights of Rocky Graziano and Tony Zale.

Cesar first became interested in photography while in the Navy. "I got in this poker game," he said. "I think it was the first and last time I ever gambled. And I won and I won—I could not stop winning; there was more money lying there than I had ever seen before. And I couldn't quit; the guy who gets that far ahead, he can never quit." He shook his head. "I'd gotten myself in a terrible fix by winning all that money, you see." Finally a loser begged Chavez to buy his camera so that he could keep on losing. Chavez forgets what happened to the money, but he kept the camera and started taking a few pictures. He dislikes the tourist feeling that he gets from having it strapped around his neck, but he still uses it occasionally and looks forward to a life in which he might have time to be a professional photographer.

After joining the Navy in 1944, Cesar served for two years on a destroyer escort on weather patrol out of Saipan. He had never been on a ship before, and at first he was very seasick and frightened of the sea. The ocean still disturbs him. "I like the sea, but I don't rest there. I think. The waves coming in, you know—they make me think. I love the woods," he says. "Big trees. That's where I rest."

In 1948 Chavez and Helen Fabela got married; Richard married Sally Gerola a few months later.

"We went to live on a farm near San Jose, and there was a little tiny house for me and my family. I was married, and then my mother and my dad, my sister and brother. We worked the strawberries, sharecropping—it was horrible. We worked there for two and a half years and never made any money: we figured later that the whole family was making twenty-three cents an hour. At the end of every month we just didn't have anything left over. We worked for two and a half years every day—every single day—and I couldn't get my dad to leave. I didn't want to leave him there, yet I couldn't get him to leave because he'd made a commitment, you know. His word! There were hundreds of people caught in this exploitation. Finally, *finally* we got him to admit that we were being taken and that the best thing was just to leave the whole damn thing."

While still childless, Richard and Cesar shared a house in Sal Si Puedes, and often the same tree in the apricot groves. Cesar talked continually about the exploitation of farm workers, but could think of no way out. Toward 1950, hearing of well-paid work in the lumber camps of northern California, the brothers migrated to the Smith River, just south of the Oregon border. It was summer, and they slept in the big woods along the river. One day they asked the foreman if they could build a cabin in the woods, and because they were both good, dependable workers, the permission was granted. In their spare time they built a serviceable cabin, and in the process learned basic carpentry. For Richard, this was a turning point; three years later he became an apprentice carpenter. And for a time Cesar himself worked in a cabinet shop, as a "putty man and glazing expert," Richard says. "He has small hands, you know, and was very good at it."

The brothers loved the cool forest and the river, they were proud of their fine cabin, and they made good money. Nevertheless, though both had steady work and could have brought their wives there, they returned that same year to San Jose. As Richard says, "We'd left something behind, I guess, that we didn't want to leave."

By 1951, Richard had already moved into the trade of carpentry, and by 1952, Cesar found a union job in a local yard as a lumber handler. In this period he made friends with the parish priest, Father Donald McDonnell, who taught him a good deal about the labor movement. "I would do anything to get Father to tell me about labor

history," he has said. "I began going to the *bracero* camps
with him to help with mass, to the city jail with him to talk
with the prisoners—anything to be with him so that he
could tell me more about the farm labor movement."

But Chavez still smoldered about his inability to improve
his own plight and that of farm workers; like the rest, he
was penniless and uneducated, and his first child, Fernando, had already been born. Embittered, he fought off
Fred Ross when Ross first appeared in Sal Si Puedes. But
within a few days, in Ross's words, the greatest potential
grass-roots leader that Ross had ever seen "burst into
flame."

Jim Drake, Leroy Chatfield and Dave Averbuck were
already at Jerry Cohen's house when we arrived. Like Cohen, Averbuck went to law school at Berkeley, where both
were sympathetic to, though not a part of, the Free Speech
Movement that began the modern rampage of student protest. Though he had worked with Cohen only a few months,
he had quickly learned about the perils of his job. Ten
days before my arrival, while working late, they were surprised by an intruder who entered the law office through
a window. Pointing a gun at the young lawyers, the man
said, "I'm going to get you bastards," then retreated the
way he had come.

The group chattered for a while about Cohen's press
conference in San Francisco, then discussed the possibility
of a meeting with Senator McCarthy. "The Democrats
should run *you*, Cesar!" Cohen called. "You'd *really* stink
things up, back in Chicago!" Chavez peered at him, dis-
ingenuous. "You mean stink bombs?"

"No, I'm serious. You could really raise the issues!"

"Oh," Chavez said. "The issues." He marched up and down the living room, waving a Diet-Rite at the multitudes. "The Leader of the People!" he cried, jutting his jaw. "Down with the Grape Society!"

The talk shifted to the June strike in the Coachella Valley, where the first grapes of the season are harvested. Immediately the voices became excited, recalling the atmosphere of violence.

"Dolores has stopped more violence than anybody," Cesar said. He jumped up and down, waving his arms like semaphores, to show how Dolores put a stop to violence. "She gets right *in* there!"

"Oh, man," someone said. "The Tigress!"

"Dolores stops it, and Manuel—"

"Yah." Cesar nodded, then smiled affectionately. "Manuel."

"Remember that time we were in arbitration?" Cohen said. He turned to Ann Israel and myself and started to laugh. "Manuel keeps arguing, see, and he's pronouncing the arbitrator's name wrong—the guy's named Kagel and Manuel keeps saying 'Bagel'—and finally Kagel says, 'Sit down, you jerk!'" Jerry stopped for a moment, awed. "Imagine saying *that?*" he whispered. "To *Manuel?*"

Cesar was imitating Manuel; he bobbed and weaved and shadow-boxed. "'You say that again, I pop you in the nose!'"

"And we got a lousy decision, too, remember?"

Cesar dropped his hands. "Yup. After all the preparation." The arbitrator had denied them a successor clause in the Di Giorgio contract, which meant that a buyer could not be held to the Union contract in case of a property sale. He sat down, in a different mood. "Well, we were damn lucky in Coachella. Damn lucky." He raised his fingers to his eyes. "All those strikers. Twenty people trying to control five hundred." He looked around the room. "Man, *anything* could have happened," he said worriedly, as if none of them had realized it before now. "In those last three days, after they screwed us with that injunction, a lot of our guys went crazy. They get that kind of look in their eye and nothing can stop them. Manuel!" He was on his feet again, crouched like someone trying to corner a ram, then grabbed and missed. "Every time I turned my head, Manuel got away. And one guy had a chain wrapped around his fist—" Chavez stopped, shaking his head.

"When Manuel hits someone," Jim Drake said, "they don't get up."

"Oh Lord! Somebody hit that one guy who ran our pickets down, and I saw the blood jump right out of the guy's face. We were really *lucky* down there. We were lucky!"

9

BY Tuesday morning the victory of Monday had been offset by bad news from Marion Moses in New York: threatened with a $25-million suit by the chain stores on the grounds of secondary boycott and restraint of trade, the AFL-CIO unions supporting the grape strike had withdrawn active support. Already the Grand Union stores were selling grapes, and the other chains were beginning to break ranks: the New York boycott, almost totally effective in June and July, had been broken. Miss Moses, whom I got to know in New York, is one of the most dedicated and effective people in the Union, but today she was very upset, and so was Fran Ryan, another volunteer in the New York office; their voices could both be heard at once over the loudspeaker phone in Chavez's office. Now and again Chavez would caution them to speak more carefully; the Union assumes that its telephones have been bugged by the opposition. As the girls clamored on, he sat back, sighing. "It's good for them; this is their baptism under fire and they'll come out stronger. They thought they had all the grapes off the stands, and now a few have come back on and they see defeat. Dolores and some of the men, they'd never get upset like that. Dolores gets *better* under pressure; she thrives on it."

Chavez put his hands behind his head and leaned back, staring at the ceiling. "Sometimes he gets that faraway look in his eye," Drake says, "and we know he's cooking up something big: he's going to change the whole direction of the Union. I don't know anybody who is so willing to change direction. We keep poking along in a kind of a broken-down fashion—cars break down, people get tired —and it takes a lot to change the direction of even a small bureaucracy like this one. But not Cesar: he thinks nothing of shifting the whole business in a new direction, and it always works out fine. Like the other night, he solved all that talk of arms by saying he'd guard the Forty Acres, and he meant it, but he also knew that the workers would back down."

"If anybody says, 'Let's do something,' " Chavez says, "and they're sincere, that interests me. I say, 'Okay, let's do it.' What I can't stand is somebody finding all the reasons they *can't* do something."

After a while Chavez intruded quietly on the four-way conversation. "Marion? Marion, we're sending everybody over there to help you. My brother Richard, my brother Manuel, my wife, my kids. Everybody." He grinned at the people in the office. "And they'll all be equipped with Diet-Rite!"

"Helen?" Marion's voice said. A second later she recognized the put-on and began to laugh, which was what Chavez wanted. She teased him about the dangers of Diet-Rite; she had read somewhere that something in Diet-Rite "potentiated" with the liver enzymes . . . Chavez clapped his hands over his ears, hunched up on his seat like the hear-no-evil monkey. "I don't want to hear it!" he cried. But seconds later, having dealt with the emergency, he moved firmly back to business. He told Marion that the pesticide campaign—he referred to it as the "fishing project," to circumvent the wiretappers—had been deferred, and his own trip to New York postponed; he had to go to Cleveland and San Francisco. "Marion? What is the price break on those new HUELGA buttons that we ordered?" Though it exhausts him, the strike is fun for Chavez, not a burden, and he has energy for its smallest aspects, in part because he avoids paper work and administrative detail of all kinds. As Cohen says, "Cesar couldn't bear to sit in an office and administer contracts. If he got the grape industry signed up, he'd take on the Jolly Green Giant."

"In the left-hand corner, Marion—these are the bumper stickers now—we have about a two-and-a-half-inch circle, which will be red with a black eagle on it. Then, next to that, in large squat bold letters, we have BOYCOTT on top, and GRAPES on the bottom. *Nothing* else."

Chavez's aversion to paper work is fortunate, since his office, which he shares with Jim Drake, is barely large enough to contain their two desks, and the cramped effect is much increased by the dark windows, which are permanently shrouded by red HUELGA curtains with black eagles. On the wall to Chavez's left is a map of the United States with flags showing the locations of the boycotts, and on the opposite wall, by the door, is a photograph of a picket line silhouetted against the dawn, and another of George Meany with Larry Itliong. Behind Drake's desk, where Chavez can see it, is a simple Mexican straw crucifix, and behind his own desk is a "martyr's shelf," with photographs of Gandhi, Martin Luther King, and Robert Kennedy, and busts of John Kennedy and Lincoln. The Kennedy photograph also contains Dolores Huerta, and in the corner of the Gandhi frame is a small image of the Virgin of Guadalupe.

"Marion? When the boycott is over and we all come home, we'll have a real big celebration! We'll take over Delano!" He listened a moment, grinning. "Good-bye. My brothers will be seeing you pretty soon, I guess."

When the conference with New York was finished, Jim Drake went over the day's mail. *Barron's,* a "national business and financial weekly," had come out on August 5 with a wild attack on the "disgraceful" boycott, repeating most of the half-truths of the growers: "Mr. Chavez, who never soiled his hands with such toil himself . . ." Everyone laughed. A letter from a Kennedy sister requested Chavez to write his impressions of Robert Kennedy for inclusion in a memorial publication; because the Kennedys were in a hurry, he was instructed to "set pen to paper" within the month. Chavez, accepting the obligation, let his head sink into his hands. "Ow!" he said. "When will I find time for *that?*"

Since Chavez's voter-registration drive had won the California primary for Kennedy, the surviving Democrats continued to agitate for his support. Vice-President Humphrey, whom he had met with secretly in Los Angeles the week before ("That was one meeting too many," he remarked) was now seeking his endorsement, and so was Senator McCarthy, who wanted to share a platform with him in Cleveland the next evening. Chavez had declined. He had a prior obligation to address the Typographical union, which he admires because, unlike most trade unions, it fights race discrimination.

Chavez admired McCarthy's initiative in regard to Vietnam, and his own avoidance of the Vietnam issue has nothing to do with apathy or disinterest. "Cesar is very concerned about Vietnam," Leroy says. "He hasn't had a chance to follow it carefully or read much about it, but he constantly questions me about it, and draws parallels between Vietnam and our situation here. And of course, they call us the Vietcong." Chatfield laughed. "And we *do* use guerrilla tactics. We're flexible, highly mobile: Cesar talks about striking at a big target that is too cumbersome to strike back. Anyway, he really understands about Vietnam, not all the battles but the *core* of the situation. He's interested, too, in how the Vietcong mobilize and how they move, and why they seem to be so effective, when the Americans have been so ineffective. For example, when the Vietcong invaded Saigon, he questioned me about it over and over. And he was fascinated when I told him that at Khesanh the Vietcong figured out that it took five seconds to get a response to their own fire, so they planned their strategy on being able to shoot and move on within four seconds, so that when the response came they were not there. The idea of mobility is very appealing to him. Once he divided our whole striking army into groups of three, which he called *racimos*—that's a little bunch of grapes— that could be deployed or redeployed or put together into larger groups, which broke down again into groups of three.

"All the same, he doesn't let Vietnam get between him and what he's doing. He's been asked countless times to speak at a Vietnam rally or something, and he won't let himself be sidetracked. During the Poor People's Campaign, he was getting two telegrams a day from people who wanted him to come there and lend his name, and finally he said, 'It's not that we're not sympathetic or don't endorse you, but what you're asking me to do is exactly the same thing as asking the Memphis garbage men to put aside their strike and come to Delano to help the farm workers.' "

Chavez acknowledged that Humphrey's role in Vietnam had been "very bad," but he hadn't forgotten the Vice-President's early fights for civil rights, and he was rightly put off by McCarthy's inability or even indifference to establishing a relationship with the poor. As Dolores says, "McCarthy feels uncomfortable with poor people, and so we feel uncomfortable with him." To offset this impression, McCarthy needed Chavez worse than Chavez needed him: before a secret meeting with McCarthy that took place at the Bel Air Hotel in West Los Angeles on Sunday, August 11, a McCarthy aide confessed as much, and told me further that the senator had set the whole next day aside in case Chavez should invite him to Delano. Chavez *did* invite him to Delano but did not promise to endorse his candidacy, and McCarthy decided, after an hour's conference with his staff—Chavez was cooling his heels down in the lobby—that he would not meet with the farm workers after all. He sent down word that the Secret Service had canceled the Delano visit for security reasons. Chavez, who could have lived cheerfully with the truth—that without a Chavez endorsement, McCarthy felt that his dwindling time might be put to better use elsewhere—shrugged his shoulders and got up to leave. "The senator was very moved and very impressed by the whole experience with you," the aide said, trailing Chavez to the door. Chavez, whose back was to the aide, smiled at his friends. "Well, we were, too. We will tell the press"—he winked at me—"that we were charmed."

McCarthy's understandable reluctance to retread old

RFK ground without a payoff led him to make what seemed to me a bad mistake, because a Delano visit could not have hurt him, and although, as things turned out, it could not have helped him very much, he did not know this at the time. Chavez *had* been impressed: "He seemed very humane, a good guy." Jim Drake said, "I understand now why the kids like him; he's the kind you would like to have for a father." Tony Orendain found him pleasant enough, and so did Dolores, though she was more taken with the salmon-colored carnations in his room than with his candidacy. Unlike Humphrey, McCarthy had not bothered to inform himself about their problems, and she was also disappointed by his seeming indifference toward the subject of police brutality, an indifference that he was forced to abandon two weeks later when the police invaded his Chicago headquarters and beat up some of his own supporters.

10

O N Wednesday, August 7, Chavez left for Cleveland. I was to meet him on Friday morning in San Francisco, where he had an appointment with Mayor Joseph Alioto; in the days between, I talked to more workers and growers, and went back south to the Arvin-Lamont vineyards to join the picket lines.

Between five and six each morning the strikers got breakfast in Filipino Hall, in a small mustard-colored mess hall furnished with red-checked oilcloth tables; each table had its own sugar and salt shakers and chili peppers. The morning I ate there I sat beside Mrs. Zapata and Señorita Magdalena, the swinging beautician from Mexico City who got knocked cold by chemical spray, but usually I went to the Carousel, on the north edge of Delano, where the growers convened at the same hour. Many of these men were from out of town, supervising the harvest of their properties in the Delano area, but they were uniformly sympathetic with the "boys in Delano. Some of your biggest and toughest growers in California are right here in your Delano area," one man told me.

Out-of-town growers are less guarded with reporters than those of Delano, and like the growers of Lamont, they admitted readily that the boycott had hurt them badly.

"They sent him to school in Chicago, you know, to learn all that." I inquired about "they" and "that," and the man squinted at me over his stalled coffee cup. "Well, all those angles—they're kind of Communist, right? One of the top Commies in the country was his teacher." He referred to that savage old radical, Saul Alinsky, head of the CSO, and the source of his misinformation was a John Birch Society publication called *The Grapes: Communist Wrath in Delano,* which reads, in part: "Cesar Chavez spent six years in Chicago studying at the 'Alinsky School of Revolution' before his 'teachers' thought he was ready to return to California . . ." (Chavez scarcely knows Alinsky, and he first went to Chicago in 1966, remaining there only a few days.) *The Grapes* also refers to the Reverend Chris Hartmire as a "former convict" (he was once arrested in a civil rights march), and calls the UFWOC banner "the flag of the Trotskyite revolution in Mexico"; its author expresses the fear that the federal government will lend money to the "unions" to purchase Di Giorgio's excess land in order to set up "co-operatives."

The growers, mostly Catholics themselves, were especially upset by the Church, which was still in the process of an official shift to a position in support of Chavez. From the beginning the growers had reviled the few priests who had spoken out or picketed in Chavez's cause; they were called "false priests" so that they could be shoved and spat on in good conscience, and were treated worse than the Protestant clergy or even the volunteers from the New Left, who were dismissed as "outside agitators." The growers refused to see what religion had to do with farm problems; as it happens, Alinsky agreed with them. Like all old-line labor people, Alinsky was suspicious of a union for which people worked for nothing. "This isn't a union," Alinsky has said, with some justification. "It's a civil rights movement." And now the Church itself, led by Bishop Timothy Manning of Fresno, had reiterated its support of the farm workers' right to bargain collectively in their own behalf, and denounced the stubborn refusal of the growers to recognize that right, much less negotiate it.

As a result, Martin Zaninovich and other Delano growers had publicly withdrawn their financial support of the Catholic Church, and during lunch at the Delano Kiwanis Club, on Friday, August 2, Jack Pandol had told his fellow boosters that "We have documentary proof there are Catholic priests involved who have only one purpose—to destroy the big farms and establish communes . . . These are not priests, they are revolutionaries!" According to a man at the Carousel, one grower in Fresno had given his church "all these new apostle statues—cost fifteen, twenty thousand dollars—and now he's trying to get his apostles back!" I suggested that the Church was only coming, a bit late, to a recognition of its responsibilities to those members of its flock who could not afford to buy it new apostles. The man threw down his toast. "Yeah? Well, we're in the flock too! They shouldn't try to segregate us!"

The growers had told me that every year on August 7, a hard rain is expected in the Valley. But this day would be desert dry, like all the rest; already, to the east, the brown dust fog of the atmosphere was reddening, like a new bruise. Coming onto U.S. 99, I passed a migrant car headed north. The car had broken down, and its numerous occupants stood miserable in the dawn mist staring at it; though empty, the vehicle was settled on its springs as if it would never rise again.

The migrants would not wave to an Anglo for help, and because I was late I did not stop to offer it. There was a garage at this highway approach, and anyway, there was nothing I could do. I drove on in guilt. It is not racists or rednecks or right-wingers who are the most formidable enemy of the poor, but "responsible" people who back away at the first threat to their own convenience.

In the Lamont-Arvin fields, the grape harvest was in its final week. The last vines to be picked were the ones nearest the public road, and Bianco was harvesting right on Main Street, just beyond the north end of Lamont. All of the ranches had certified strikes, but the Union, anxious to encourage slowdowns which might offset the faltering New York boycott, was maintaining pressure. The strike lines had been swelled by office staff and children, and Union picketers had come from as far away as the Christian Brothers ranch at Sanger, sixty-five miles north. Anna Chavez and Abel Orendain, both about twelve, were there ("I'll be sorry when the strike is over," said Abel, who collects fossils. "It's fun, and I get to meet a lot of people"), and so was at least one Mr. Bianco, walking up and down on the road shoulder over the few feet of no man's land between the workers and the pickets. A round-faced man in a yellow polo shirt, Bianco was aggressively friendly to the pickets and even permitted them to pass out propaganda to the workers ("It's a free country we're living in, right?"), but he was harried by the Reverend Nick Jones, who had worked on a Bianco ranch, and by Dave Fishlow, who jeered at Bianco's claim that growers could not afford to raise grapes under the restrictions of the Union. On a bull horn, Fishlow related how his grandmother had been paid 36 cents apiece for sewing dresses, and was lucky to make three of them a day. "So they organized the International Ladies' Garment Workers Union, and they were called 'Commies,' 'Jewish troublemakers'! And the owners, the fat cats like you, Bianco, claimed that the ILGWU would put them out of business! The U.S.A. wasn't going to have any more dresses! Just like what *you* say—right, Bianco? But they signed a contract with the workers, just like *you*'re going to sign, Bianco, and now the garment workers get a decent wage!"

Between bouts on the bull horn, Fishlow told me how Dolores Huerta, on the picket line, had once asked for a glass of water from a woman in the field. The woman had fetched a glass from the pickup truck and was carrying it across the line to Dolores when a foreman caught up with her and kicked the glass out of her hand. "So the girl started to cry, and Dolores started to cry, and the whole crew of women started to cry, and before you know it, a crew of thirty had walked out, just because a foreman had lost his temper and made a stupid mistake. So we keep the heat on them."

Joseph Brosmer, big arms folded, was there to see that Bianco did not lose control, and Bianco checked in with him every few minutes ("How much you pay your nursemaid, Bianco? He get the minimum wage?"). Bianco had made the mistake of debating publicly with Jones and Fishlow, and now they were getting to him. Bianco declared that he talked to his workers and ate with them, and when Jones asked why he didn't negotiate with them instead, Bianco cried out that these people knew nothing about business. ("Lucky for you, Bianco!") He was trying hard to smile, to shrug off his tormentors in a playful manner, but a tic was working at the right corner of his mouth, and at one point he wheeled like a badgered animal. "Don't you call me 'brother'!" he yelled at Nick Jones. "I'm not your brother!"

"Okay," Nick said. "Brother."

On Brosmer's advice, Bianco had asked me not to tape his arguments, and I complied without regret, since they were identical to those of all the other growers. "There's just one worker at Sierra Vista now," Mr. Bianco said. "A guard." Like all the rest, he was sincere in his profession of good will toward his men, and like the rest, he refused to see that these people had been exploited, because to acknowledge this not only would be expensive but would unravel a whole carefully constructed legend about free enterprise and the American Way of Life.

> We can't afford to lose our jobs, so we keep quiet and don't complain and the farmers think we are happy.
> You whistle in the fields and you go out and get drunk on Saturday night because you just can't face the truth—that you are so damned poor, that the kids are sick and that your life is depressing.
> In the fields the bosses shout at us in front of our wives and families. They insult our womenfolk and bully our children. And because we are so poor, we cannot afford to lose the job. We take it. This destroys the family. And it destroys the men as individuals.
> When the men get home, their authority is gone. Their wives say, "Yes, you tell us what to do, but you didn't say anything to that little guy in the fields."
> When we tried to fight back in the past, we found the grower was too strong, too rich, and we had to give up.
> Cesar Chavez has shown us we can fight back. We are trying to build a political power base and trying to keep it

nonviolent, but we have a hell of a time controlling the militancy of the young people.*

"Agricultural employers are opposed to bargaining with their employees in a way that will require a real sharing of power," the Reverend Chris Hartmire has said. "Bargaining with labor contractors, talking with crews, discussing wages with groups of workers—all this is appropriate and desirable in the view of agricultural employers because final decisions, final power, continue to rest with them. But when facing independently organized farm workers who make demands instead of asking favors, who threaten economic pressure and who ask to be treated as men in a community of men, then growers are adamant in their resistance. There are a number of ways employers camouflage this basic resistance to genuine collective bargaining; the most obvious is to claim that the workers are happy and not really on strike. Strikebreakers have been used for decades by employers to fool the public into thinking that work continues and all is well—except for a few 'outside agitators.'

"The fact that farm workers are willing to cross picket lines and be strikebreakers does not prove that workers are happy and 'all is well.' Anyone with eyes to see knows that this is not true. What it does prove is that there are many men and women and children in our society who are so economically insecure and so afraid of their employers and so despairing about the future that they are willing to betray their own brothers and their own children to gain a day's wages."

. . .

* Ernesto Laredo, Los Angeles *Times*, November 17, 1968.

: 2 5 1

The next day the strikers moved on to Sabovich and Sons, one of the farms that was being sued for $50 million. If Sabovich was uneasy about the suit, there was no sign of it; HI-COLOR boxes were lying around like litter. The ubiquitous Brosmer said that the suit had been filed mostly in the newspapers; he had just talked to one of the three defendants, who as yet had received no legal notice of it. I guessed that he meant John J. Kovacevich, whose offices are in Arvin, and decided to call on him as soon as the picketing was finished for the day.

Across the road, the remorseless Jones was shouting into his bullhorn, "Where is Sabovich today? He's not working in this hot sun, not Mister Sabovich!" (The heat in these fields often exceeds 100 degrees, and Chavez says that heat prostration is second only to pesticides as a cause of worker illness.) The Filipino strikers were gabbling in Tagalog to their countrymen in the work crews, and in their innocence they railed at "Sonobitch," which was what they thought Nick Jones was saying. Greatly amused, the Mexican-Americans took up the cry.

"Where is Sonobeetch today? Hey? Sonobeetch!"

Down the rows the *campesinos* squatted under the low vines. Grape workers pick and pack in teams; ordinarily the team is a family group, and some of the children in the field are no more than eight years old. California law forbids the hiring of minors under eighteen, but there is no law to prevent young children from accompanying their parents into the field. Since the workers are paid piece-rate, by the box, in addition to the hourly wage, the system is very precious to the grower, who may have a piece-rate work force of five or six while paying wages to just two. Like the rest of California's commendable labor legislation, the child labor laws are not enforced except under duress, and enforcement, in this case, would be resisted by the workers themselves, who expect the children to help out. "We have accepted child labor," Chavez has said, "because otherwise our families couldn't survive." But the "helping out" is not restricted to light work; the older the worker, the more skilled he is apt to be at cutting and packing, so that the heavy labor of lugging grapes often falls upon the youngest children.

The disadvantages of migrant children are not limited to heavy work. With a seventh-grade education, Chavez went three grades further than the average; educationally, as in all other ways, migrant children are the poorest in America. A medical survey made a few years ago in California showed that two thirds of the migrant children under three years of age had never been inoculated against diphtheria, whooping cough and smallpox—diseases which in the rest of America have virtually died out. In addition, over five hundred minors in this state suffer serious agricultural accidents every year. Chavez speaks of the Isaac Chapa family, which lost a four-year-old boy in Wasco, in July 1965, when the child, crossing a potato field to go to his parents, tripped on a furrow and could not get up in time to avoid the digging machine; two or three years earlier, while the Chapas were working, their young daughter drowned in the Friant-Kern Canal, near Earlimart.

Directly in front of me, two thin small boys were working. One child, obviously under ten, was struggling to lift a box of grapes onto a stack six boxes high; at this sight the whole picket line began to whistle and boo. Then Nick Jones was bellowing for us all.

"Hey! Hey, what do you think that weight does to that

child's bones? Who's the father of that little boy? Eight or nine years old, carrying twenty-six-pound boxes—are you proud of that? Do you want to bend his bones before they can get hard? Who's the father of that little boy? Let 'em pack grapes, but for God's sake don't make them lift boxes! Isn't it time those kids stayed home so they could play baseball and go fishing? Isn't it time you made enough money to afford that for them? DON'T YOU KNOW THAT BENDS HIS BONES? Do you want to work under these conditions, where they bring kids out into the fields and ruin their bodies? WHO'S THE PROUD FATHER OF THOSE BOYS?"

Finally a man straightened up from his work and waved both arms violently at the harsh metallic voice as if to fight it off. "YOU! YOU IN THE WHITE SHIRT! ARE YOU THE PROUD FATHER?"—and a minute later a blaring pickup truck careened along the picket line, making it scramble, and wheeled on spitting tires into the mouth of a service road that paralleled the row of vines, slamming to a halt by an irrigation tank. A close-cropped Marine-style American in boots jumped out of the cab and rigged an amplifier to the tailgate. He gave the picket line the benefit of a big contemptuous smile before sauntering back to the truck controls and turning on the radio. Nick Jones recognized this newcomer as a Giumarra foreman who had threatened him on the main street of Lamont. "We're going to get you down one of these days," the foreman had said, "and you're not going to get up." Death threats have been common enough since the strike began, and few of them are taken seriously, but at least one of Chavez's staff thinks that violent death, on one side or the other, is inevitable.

"A couple of people are going to end up in concrete before this is over," he says, "and it might be us."

Apparently Nick Jones had taken the threat seriously enough to be made angry by it, because now he lashed the foreman with real ferocity.

"WHERE ARE *YOUR* KIDS, GROWER? HOW ABOUT THOSE LITTLE KIDS YOU'VE GOT WORKING OUT THERE—YOU PROUD OF THAT? HEY, BIG MAN! YOU PROUD OF KILLING THOSE KIDS?"

The foreman, yanking at his wires, was wearing a bad smile, but his whole body was as stiff as kindling. Over the pandemonium of his machine, I yelled for permission to cross the line and talk to him. His taut face neither gave permission nor denied it, so I crossed the line. He waited for me by the truck, fists on hips, boots spread; he had mixed two stations, and the scramble of scratchy voices and tin music scoured the ears.

"HEY, BIG MAN! HOW ABOUT THOSE KIDS, MAN? YOU PROUD OF THAT? COME ON OUT OF THERE, KILLER! BE A MAN!"

"Hey, can I talk to you a minute?" I tried to get his attention, but he would not take his eyes off Jones. I'm going to fix that guy, his mouth said, as if he was making himself a promise.

"Listen," I tried again, "the growers say they have nothing to hide, that their workers don't want a union, so why do you do this?"

"HEY, GROWER! YOU AFRAID?"

"I like to entertain them," he said viciously, enunciating. He shouldered past me, headed for the road, and it looked very much as if Jones had provoked the incident that he had been working toward for the past two days. Jones was directly in his path, jumping around like someone inciting a bull, and directly behind Jones was Brosmer. I thought the foreman would dismantle Jones right on the spot, but he had seen Brosmer and continued across the road. The two of them talked head to head for a long time, and then the foreman went back into the field. Soon Brosmer was beside me. "These people can become very adept at inflaming other people; this is what I want to prevent." He was still a little tense; it had been close. "I don't think any useful service is performed by violence," Brosmer said, folding his arms again.

"That's another mistake," Jones told me, jerking his thumb at the truck amplifier. He was tense too. "Growers can't help making those mistakes, because they're stupid. They have no respect for people; people are objects. They don't think they can offend their happy workers by blaring loud noises into their ears, but they're wrong. Those people are pissed off."

The amplifier had effectively drowned out the shouting from the picket line. "They give them music but they don't give them toilets," Ann Israel remarked, and it was true; there were no field toilets anywhere in sight at any of the vineyards we visited in this area. The solitary toilet I had seen out in the field was at the vineyard of Bruno Dispoto, who'd had a day's notice of our coming.

The red flags were rolled up, and the strikers crowded into their old cars; they were told to go to the Giumarra property beyond Weed Patch. As the caravan headed south, an ancient biplane, dusting, banked as slowly as a kite over the sky webs of utility wires; the poison settled in a fine pale mist. Along the road a Mexican boy half turned, still walking, saw white faces in my car and turned away. In the rear-view mirror I watched his hand come up as a strikers' car, full of Filipino faces, came along, but the Filipinos did not give the boy a lift, perhaps because their old car was too full.

Together with another family corporation, the Joseph Giumarra Vineyards, Inc., is a $25-million operation which owns more than 12,000 acres, or 19 square miles, in Kern and Tulare counties; Giumarra is the primary target of the UFWOC boycott, as well as the main reason that the boycott is now directed against all the growers. Giumarra was first struck in September 1965, and most of its workers walked out; some went back eventually, and others were replaced with scabs. In July 1967, when UFWOC renewed its pressure, the great majority of Giumarra workers signed cards in favor of UFWOC representation, and on August 3, because the company refused to hold a representation election, much less negotiate, the great majority of its workers—estimates vary from 75 to 95 percent—once again went out on strike. Despite this, Giumarra's counsel claimed that this "socialist–civil rights movement" of "do-gooder elements, beatniks and socialist-type groups" did not really represent its workers. With negligible interference from the U.S. Immigration Service or the Justice Department, Giumarra proceeded with the illegal recruitment of Mexican strikebreakers, and obtained from the state judiciary an injunction against strike lines which to this day forbids picketers to demonstrate at less than fifty feet from one another. Barred from picketing effectively, the Union began a boycott of Giumarra labels (Arra, Big G, Grape King, GVC, Honeybunch and Uptown), at which point Giumarra began shipping its products with the labels of other companies. The Food and Drug Administration is as attuned to special interests as other government agencies, and by the time it got around to requesting Giumarra not to continue breaking the law (by December, Giumarra grapes were going out under more than a hundred different labels) almost all of the company's crop had been picked and sold. In January 1968, since so many other growers had participated in the fraud, the Union began the current boycott against all growers of California table grapes not picked on a Union farm. At this point the growers put "Arizona" labels on their grapes, and the boycott was extended to table grapes grown anywhere in the United States.

Meanwhile, Union pressure had obtained the federal conviction of a Giumarra labor contractor for illegal recruitment of Mexican citizens, and state convictions against Giumarra on twenty-three counts of unfair labor practices (mostly the absence of sanitary facilities) and violations of child labor laws, none of which, thanks to the deference that this huge company receives in California courts, has impaired its usual practices in the least. (Giumarra pleaded guilty to all twenty-three counts, for which it was sentenced on March 11 to pay $1,495; the sentence was then suspended.) Since Giumarra makes an estimated $875 profit on a boxcar of grapes, and may send out two thousand boxcars in a year, these practices are very profitable. The profits are increased by huge subsidies from the Department of Agriculture; in 1966 Giumarra received approximately a quarter of a million dollars of the taxpayers' money for *not* growing cotton, and in 1967, received still more. These subsidy programs, strongly supported by the old growers on the Senate Agriculture Committee (Eastland, Talmadge, and the like; Senator Eastland's own plantation in Doddsville, Mississippi, receives enormous subsidies), have reduced field employment already deflated by automation, and increased the migration off the land into the big-city slums that is defeating urban employment programs before they can begin.

"I wonder sometimes," Governor Reagan told the California Farm Bureau Federation in April 1968, "at your determination and ability to stick it out in the face of so many adverse factors . . . You know that you are not going to get a break from the federal government, but you keep hoping that you might get a break from the weather." This self-serving speech is not astonishing from a politician who still had reason to believe that a staunch defense of the haves against the have-nots might win him the Republican presidential nomination; what is astonishing is that the growers, as talks with them make plain, sincerely believe it. They believe it because they have recited it so often. But the truth is that in order to avoid the union protection for its employees which was granted years ago by every other large industry in America, the factory farms are hiding behind the honest plight of the small farmer, who is paying a fatal penalty for their selfishness.

On February 7, not long after the conviction of the labor contractor, UFWOC volunteer Fred Hirsch was so badly beaten by Giumarra men that he required hospitalization for three days; on February 14 Chavez and Epifanio Camacho, representing the Union pickets, were served with subpoenas for alleged violations of the picketing injunctions obtained by Giumarra the summer before, and for throwing dirt clods at a Giumarra foreman who had been charged—as usual, to no avail—with obscenely propositioning a twelve-year-old girl on the picket line; as a basis for a possible future arson suit, the suggestion was also made that UFWOC might be responsible for the burning of a Giumarra packing shed, despite the published statement of Mr. Joseph Giumarra (the eldest of many Giumarras, and the one least violent about the Union) that the Union had nothing to do with it. In this period Giumarra foremen were driving up and down the picket lines with rifles mounted on their trucks, and the violent atmosphere hastened Chavez's decision to undertake the fast, which began on February 14. He had been fasting for thirteen days when he and Camacho were haled into the Kern County Courthouse in Bakersfield, where more than a thousand workers set up a silent vigil around the building. Perhaps this ominous, silent gathering of the dispossessed was a factor in the court's decision to postpone the hearing until April 22; later the charges against Chavez were dropped entirely. When Chavez returned to the Forty Acres, he was visited by William Kircher of the AFL-CIO and by Walter Reuther, who endorsed the fast with a UAW present of $7,500. Reuther has been a good friend to the farm workers from the beginning, and Bill Kircher, in the opinion of Jerry Cohen, "has done more for the Union than any single labor leader in the country." (A long-time rivalry between Reuther and Kircher became formal in the spring of 1969, when the UAW joined forces with the Teamsters. UFWOC, a virtually autonomous "organizing committee" of the AFL-CIO, was seemingly caught in the middle; few thought that the Teamsters would resist any opportunity to grab America's farm workers for themselves. But his people feel Chavez is deft enough to avoid any threat.)

In the summer of 1968, a year after the mass walkout, Giumarra's work crews had been replaced by people whose indoctrination against the Union is so thorough that UFWOC would lose an election held there today. A worker at Schenley told me that his old friends at Giumarra will no longer talk to him for fear of getting into trouble.

At the Weed Patch vineyards, anti-Union prejudice could not help but be enforced by the contrast between the old cars of the strikers and the new cars of the strike-breakers, lined up on opposite sides of the road. "Takes the whole family to make payments on new cars like that," Jones commented. "These folks live in a dump somewhere so they can have that car." (The big fat cars of small thin people are a pathetic symptom of the culture's emphasis on the symbols of success, but at least these workers had safe transportation; while I was in Delano, the news came that four more migrants had been killed in New York State when the unlicensed bus transporting them, lacking brakes, was destroyed at a railroad crossing by a train. Such accidents are common in California; in 1953 alone, 28 workers died in four transportation accidents, with 341 injured.

Soon after the appearance of the pickets, the field work was curtailed, and a few workers leaving the vineyards passed the picket line on the way to their cars. Most of them dodged the pickets, but one or two were caught in brief, uneasy conversations. "They say they makin more money than us," a striker told me, "but they don't. They workin seven days a week and I only workin six, and I makin more.

But they afraid, and they don't want to know nothin; they just workin for that new car to show the people back in Mexico."

As the picket line disbanded, a Giumarra foreman came out to the end of a row. Looking over the motley picketers and their old cars, he forced a loud laugh of derision. Somebody jeered back at him about the repeated infractions of child labor laws. "Yah?" the man bawled. "Well, at least we don't have liberals around!"

From Giumarra, the strikers' caravan went cruising, looking for grape pickers near the road. To the north, the vineyards were interspersed with fields of cotton and potatoes, as well as sections of unreclaimed near-desert where brown Herefords lay in the thin shadows of the billboards. Many of them advertised pesticides: EPTAM (SELECTIVE HERBICIDE FOR POTATOES. CONTROLS GRASSES AND WEEDS). AZODRIN (KILLS MITES, LYGUS, WORMS, PINK BOLL-WORMS). The slogan of one pesticide company is WE KILL TO LIVE.

At midmorning, there was very little shadow; already the sky looked dead. Because the low Tehachapis of the Sierra Nevada are visible to the east, the atmosphere here is less surreal than in Delano, where the mountains rarely loom out of the haze. Still, the regimented crops were squat and monotonous, and as in Delano, there are few birds; the few escapees from Eptam which held out in the low ditches were the only signs that nature was permitted here at all. In every distance in these fields, irrigation pumps seesaw slowly. Some of the pumps stand over fifteen feet high, poised over the azodrined earth like big black mosquitoes, proboscis probing, to suck up the poisoned water from dying acquifers below.

: 262

We struck next at Cal-Fame, a vineyard farmed co-operatively by small growers, where we were joined by Mack Lyons and some workers from Di Giorgio. Under Brosmer's guidance the small growers were jovial with the pickets, who waved flags, shouted cheerily, and in the absence of Mrs. Zapata, played Union songs and *mariachi* music. "You fellas ain't botherin us one li'l ole bit," one Okie foreman called. "We *like* music." Soon fraternization became so general that workers came wandering out across the property line, and I got talking to a young black guy in a new sombrero with wild-colored band, worn rakishly over his face. He had a goatee and tight stud clothes that were not meant for picking grapes and somewhere, groov- ing away, there had to be a cool stud car to match. I asked this resplendent person what he thought about the Union and Chavez, and he said, "Not so much, man. I guess he's made a big improvement around here, but I don't fool much with them *chicanos*." His smile was supercool—good- natured and self-inclusively contemptuous. After a soft pause he whispered, "Why?" I explained a little about what Cesar Chavez hoped to do, and all the time he watched me with that soft cool knowing smile, but at least he was listening. Finally, not smiling, he said he had noth- ing against the Union, but that he was doing all right on his own. "In the wintertime I'm out of luck, man, but I can make up to five thousand dollars a year."

Three black pickets from Christian Brothers now came over and added some gentle arguments to my own. They told him about disability insurance, workmen's compensa- tion, and how in the Union the work went at a certain speed: a man worked like a man, not like an animal. The owners couldn't force the men to rush one another, and the older guys weren't fearful that they would lose their jobs to the first kids that could move faster. "When we gets laid off," one said, "we can go right on over there and collect our unemployment; when *you* gets laid off, you starve." The three pickets were older men in age-softened shirts and sky-blue coveralls, and they were using the wrong approach: the young cat had never been disabled in his life and knew he never would be, and anyway, he was not some old cotton-picking Tom but a beautiful spade making good bread while he waited for Black Power, and if he could turn the heat on and make $40 a day doing piece work, no old shuffler was going to hold him back. These three Toms were Negroes, he was black—that's what his smile said. Too politely, he inquired about the minimum wage; though they recognized the put-on, they talked past it, and after a while the young man became serious too. "What it cost to join up in the Union? Three-fifty? When a man join up, do he pick a certain job, or do they pick it for him?" He was inquiring about discrimination. "Anything a man know to do, he do!" a picket said. "Truck driver—"

"Let's stop this hangin around!" a foreman yelled. "The trucks ain't movin!"

The picker was cool enough not to turn his head; as he gravitated backward toward his row he acted more casual than ever. "How about a non-Union job?" He winked at me, to show he was having fun with them. "Sure," a picket called. "If they ain't enough Union to go around, they *tell* you to work non-Union! They *tell* you that!"

Slowly the picker resumed work, but his heart wasn't in it. When he finished the vine closest to the road, he stayed there, fiddling, squatting on his heels in the hard shadows as he watched white, black and brown Americans in the ultimate democracy of a picket line. Watching him watching, I felt certain that today or tomorrow this man would come over to the Union. Catching me observing him, he nodded sardonically. Hey, man, his nod said; it committed him to nothing. I had seen this look before: Maybe we can work together, Whitey, but trust and friendship are going to have to wait.

A blue pickup truck came bouncing through. In the front seat with the white driver was a black worker with an Afro haircut who took me for a picket. As he passed I heard his voice: "Go, man!" With his fingers he was making a V-sign beside his head, where the driver could not see it.

The pickup stopped just down the way, and the grower joined a mixed crowd of farmers and pickets exchanging ritual unpleasantries among the trucks. A Mexican-American striker, challenging a grower, was pointing at the old Okie foreman who liked music. "Anglo get the good job, right? Because I a Mexican? What the difference between him and me?"

"You think about it," the white man said. "Let me know what you come up with."

"I think about it already!" The Mexican pointed fiercely at his own face. "Is because I got brown eyes!"

The grower from the blue pickup asked me where I stood, and I said I thought the day was past when people had to work without the protection of a union.

"You unionize farm labor and they'll be just what you might call dictators," he burst out. "Just tell the farmer what to do!" I said that a no-strike-in-harvest-time clause was included in all the Union contracts; he changed the subject. "These Mexicans aren't even good workers," he complained. "They gripe about minimum wage, minimum wage, but they don't want to work. I've worked with every type of people since I was sixteen, and I'm twenty-six now, and these are the laziest goddamn—why, they're lazier than Negroes! The Filipinos are the best workers in California—hard, fast workers, no complaints. It's Filipinos, then whites, then Negroes, then Mexicans!" I said I had heard from other growers that Mexicans were pretty good. He glared at me; I was a hard man to get along with. "Well, some of them nationals from Texas work all right," he said, "but they quit on me, so that's why I had to get these colored boys."

I asked if he had ever met Chavez, and he said he hadn't and didn't care to. "Why? Because he's a Communist! You go down to L.A. and go to the newsstand and he's in every Communist brochure down there! Cesar Chavez!" He declaimed the name with immense bitterness. "Every damn newsstand, there's Cesar Chavez in the Communist papers! . . . Huh? You don't believe that? Probably you didn't think Castro was a Communist either! Wait and see. If they unionize us it'll be Chavez and the Communists, and they'll do it with the help of people like you!"

The growers' efforts to dismiss Chavez as a Communist have been given respectability of sorts by the 1967 Report of Un-American Activities in California, which devotes over sixty pages to proving a fact so obvious and inevitable that nobody has ever bothered to deny it: the Communist party, at least in the beginning, was sympathetic to the grape strike. (Recently the party has attacked Chavez for religious tendencies and counterrevolutionary tactics.) In addition, the report does its ambiguous best to pin a subversive tag on individuals associated with *la causa*, making much of the information that the first NFWA attorney, Alex Hoffman, was formerly a member of the Student Progressive Association, which lobbied in Sacramento against the Loyalty Oath Bill; that Wendy Goepel, one of the first volunteers, had attended the "Communist-controlled" 1962 World Youth Festival in Helsinki; that Luis Valdez had accompanied a group of students to Cuba in 1964; that Chavez himself had made clear to Ben Gines, the AWOC organizer who defected to the Teamsters during the Di Giorgio fight, and to Al Espinosa, the Delano police chief who is a labor contractor on the side, that he wished "to change the whole social system." Most if not all of these charges are perfectly true; in fact, Chavez has said in a *Ramparts* interview that "if this spirit grows within the farm labor movement, one day we can use the force that we have to help correct a lot of things that are wrong with this society." But it is not Chavez's unrevolutionary reforms, it is plain materialism that is the true betrayal of the Constitution and the Bill of Rights, encouraging the richest land in history to abandon thirty-five million of her people to poverty or worse, to pollute and scar an entire continent for private gain, to crush modern equivalents of the American Revolution in other countries, and to force a "democracy" that is rotting at home upon weaker nations of the hemisphere where U.S. economic interests are imperiled—all this in the name of an anti-Communism which is not only irrelevant but fraudulent, and which has led America into more dishonor than any phenomenon in her history. These crusades for big business, tricked out in patriotic colors, go down the consumer's throat like so much jello; signs like AMERICA: LOVE IT OR LEAVE IT, which are very popular in the Valley, bully the citizen who has enough pride in his country to be ashamed of it, and enough spine to stand up and say so.

As a survivor of McCarthyism, Chavez is used to being Red-baited; he is not so much distressed by it as wearied. "I'm not interested in the past. I don't ask a man his politics or his religion when he comes to work with us. We do warn everyone who comes to help us that we do not want them coming with political hang-ups or hidden agendas. We can't guarantee that Communists or anyone else won't try to infiltrate our union, but this accusation makes one think that the accusers seem to feel only the Communists are interested in serving the poor and oppressed. . . . If our work is considered Communistic by some, there's nothing we can do about it, but I'm not willing to admit that we Christians are not more willing to fight for social justice. Another problem is that anyone who is for the Union is labeled a Communist because to some growers all unions are Communist-inspired. We don't intend to let it deter us from the job at hand."

Nearby, Joe Brosmer was standing beside Ann Israel; he offered me his camera. "How about taking our picture for a souvenir?" he asked. I doubted out loud that he wanted the picture for a souvenir, and he shrugged. "I'll get it anyway," he said. "I just wanted to be frank about it." When I told Mack Lyons this, he took Ann's camera and walked straight up to Brosmer and snapped it contemptuously in his face. Brosmer folded his big white arms on his white shirt, eyes half closed, rocking a little on his heels. Clearly, my own picture had already been taken, it occurred to me on the way to Arvin, and I wondered what idiot Red file I was in.

. . .

On the way to Arvin we passed a camp behind a farm where women living in shacks in a near-junkyard were hanging out wash among the derelict cars: the tableau of waste and squalor seemed to typify the illness of America. According to the Kern County Housing Authority's own 1968 survey, over three fourths of the farm-worker housing in the Lamont–Weed Patch area is inadequate—that is, dilapidated, without foundations and often without plumbing. Because they are charged as much as $75 a month for hovels of this description, people pack into them like animals; inevitably, under such conditions, their health is very poor, and because of low morale and resources they do little or nothing about it. (A doctor in Fresno has noted a lack of identity in migrant farm workers, who have been treated like subhumans for so long that they have come to accept the verdict and sometimes act accordingly.)

Officials of the Farm Bureau Federation in Bakersfield admitted to the Housing Authority that the housing was kept miserable because they wanted the migrants to work, then leave the area; good housing might encourage them to stay and become a burden on the schools and facilities of the community. Instead, farm workers pile up in the urban slums, where they go on welfare and become dependents of municipalities with grim problems of their own; in effect, the cities pay for the selfishness of the rural communities. This situation will worsen as automation continues and populations grow, since the great majority of farm workers are untrained in any other work. "One of the most ominous developments is the appeal for law and order by many politicians," Ernesto Galarza, author of *Merchants of Labor* and a veteran defender of the farm workers, has

: *2 6 9*

said. "They are lining up on one side the Negro and the Mexican, who are dependent and who know it, and who feel the humiliations and frustrations of this dependence, and on the other side the middle-class taxpayers, who are hard pressed by the growing tax burden. This is the confrontation of the future. The anger it will generate will make the Black Panther movement look trivial."

The town of Arvin, a small outgrowth on Di Giorgio Road, was named for a grower named Arvin Missakian; otherwise, it is too nebulous to be described. On the far side of its railroad spur, toward the mountains, are the packing house, sheds and offices of John J. Kovacevich, whose views I sought on the subject of the $50-million suit. Ann Israel came with me, and as we drove across the tracks into the shed area, we saw grapes coming off a belt and dropping into a gondola, to be pressed for wine, an almost certain sign that Mr. Kovacevich had more table grapes than unfilled orders. (The alternative to wine is raisins, a product in chronic surplus.) The day before, Julio Hernandez had reported from Cincinnati that the price of Kovacevich grapes had dropped from 49 cents to 29 cents a pound.

At the office I asked to see the boss, and the secretary said she thought this could be arranged. But just at this moment a door opened and out came Joseph Brosmer. We gazed at each other in mutual consternation, and then he said, "I'll pave the way for you," and went back into the office, closing the door behind him.

A few minutes later Mr. Kovacevich came out. He is a tall, balding man in his late fifties, with fierce eyebrows pinching in on a big hawk nose. Making no effort to be hospitable, he demanded to know what we wanted, then told us to follow him into his office, where he slammed the door. I took a seat beside the desk, and Mrs. Israel sat down beside Joseph Brosmer on a couch against the wall. As usual Mr. Brosmer, though indoors and seated, had his arms folded on his chest.

Kovacevich, who was breathing hard, glared at me expectantly, and I said straight off that I was partisan to the Union, as no doubt Mr. Brosmer had told him, but that I was anxious to talk to as many growers as I could, to make certain that their side got a fair hearing. In the interests of accuracy, I continued, I would like permission to use a tape recorder, and I was in the process of unlimbering my small machine when Kovacevich snatched a copy of the San Francisco *Chronicle* from his desk and flung it against my chest.

"Are you silly or something?" he shouted. "Do you know how it feels to get sued for fifty million dollars?" In the bad silence that ensued, I glanced at Brosmer; he was staring like a corpse at his maddened client, as if seeking to subdue him by hypnosis. Kovacevich, declaring his innocence in no uncertain terms, swore that he would file a countersuit for libel; what the hell did I think this did to his good name? This seemed an implied acknowledgment that wrongdoing had been done, but having no wish to elicit extreme statements, I did not point it out. As a group the growers are so defensive that one must bend over backward to keep them from presenting themselves unfairly; the unprovoked opinions that they offer seem damaging enough.

Over Mr. Kovacevich's head were the Kovacevich labels, which include ROYAL K and K & K, and on a table to his right were photographs of his sons; I recognized one as an intelligent-looking boy of college age who had been sitting on the office porch when we came in. There was a certain resemblance to the father, though not just at this moment; in profile, calming himself, Kovacevich reminded one of a beaky bird whose crest, raised high in outrage or alarm, moves up and down as it settles back again. He was reeling off the usual arguments against Chavez, which once again were so uniform in their clichés that I wondered if they had not been memorized by all the growers up and down the Valley. Already that day, in the New York *Daily News,* the same arguments had been made in a full-page ad taken out by the California Grape and Tree Fruit League: once again, the consumer was informed that California farm workers enjoyed higher wages and more protective laws than any in the nation, and therefore wanted no part of a union: "They have *not* walked off the job! THEY ARE NOT ON STRIKE!" The ad concluded with an appeal to the consumer: "As a consumer you have the inalienable right to demand free access to any product. . . . Protect your pocketbook from chaos in the food stores! . . . Demand that your local food store carry California Table Grapes!" The growers ceaselessly suggest that wage increases will put their product out of reach of the consumer, but according to figures issued by the U.S. Department of Labor, the workers are paid but 2 to 5 cents out of each dollar invested, so that even a very large increase in pay could not increase the retail price by more than a few pennies.

Kovacevich also related the sad plight of the grower, crying out at one point that he could not buy a car; he had to rent one. (Perhaps he assumed that a left-wing reporter would be ignorant of corporation tax devices, and as a matter of fact, he was right; it was Mrs. Israel who smartened me up when we got outside.) In the course of this speech he let it be known that he was a friend of former Governor Pat Brown and Hubert Humphrey as well as of the workingman; Humphrey had been his guest at the Bakersfield Country Club, of which Mr. Kovacevich is a past president, and also at his house.

In effect, what we were hearing was a sincere and impassioned speech of self-justification by a man fighting angrily to banish a painful truth, and losing inch by inch to his own honesty. "Don't tell *me* about social consciousness!" he exclaimed to Mrs. Israel, who had been talking to him rather bluntly about just that. "I've got a boy who is study-ing sociology at Notre Dame, and I know all about it!" He indicated the picture on the table. "Sometimes a young man can be too social-conscious for his own good," he added somberly. He looked haggard and upset, and I wondered about that boy out on the porch, and about what he thought of the fight for a new order that was taking place in his generation.

Mr. Kovacevich says "Don't tell *me!*" a lot, and clearly he is a man who has not been told things very often. Like all of the growers that I talked to except Bruno Dispoto, he is sincerely sorry for himself, yet he seemed more reason-able than all the rest. He pointedly dissociated himself from the position of Jack Pandol, and he admitted that small "shotgun" labor camps still existed. He spoke of Leroy Chatfield, who had taught his sons at Garces High School in Bakersfield, as "one of the brightest people I ever met," and when I asked how he accounted for the fact that this bright person so fervently endorsed Cesar Chavez, he did not tighten up but said quite simply, "He must be an idealist, I guess." Saul Alinsky, whom he had once seen on

TV, was "brilliant"—an extraordinary statement in a community which had made Alinsky the Bolshevik evil genius behind Chavez—and alone among all the growers that I talked to, he made no attempt to identify Chavez with Communism. On the contrary, he spoke of Chavez as a human being, not some nightmare figure waving the bloody flag of revolution.

In consequence, the case Kovacevich made for the real problems of the American farmer in America, which are considerable, was much more effective for being free of slicked-over racism and self-serving patriotism, and as I sat there listening it struck me how sad it was that a man as otherwise intelligent and articulate as this one could not or would not meet with Cesar Chavez. I said as much, and to my sorrow John Kovacevich retreated, saying that Chavez was vengeful and could not be reasoned with: hadn't he sworn that before he was through he would stamp the damned growers right into the mud? I asked where he had heard that story, and he said, "At the Delano Kiwanis."

I wondered if John Kovacevich believed what he was told about Chavez because as a big grower in the Valley, it would take such courage not to; among the producers of table grapes, the first to acknowledge right on the side of Chavez will not be invited to the Delano Kiwanis or any place else.

Still, John Kovacevich is a natural leader and a highly respected farmer. A grower from Fresno, who told me that this man raises the best grapes in California and therefore America, refers to him as "Mister Grape." One of the reasons why Mister Grape is so respected, said my informant, is because of his willingness to experiment, to break new ground. Apparently Kovacevich has long since conceded that a farm workers union is inevitable: the question is whether he will follow the retreat of the right-wing growers to a "sweetheart" contract with the Teamsters, or follow his own conscience.

My impressions of Kovacevich were affirmed later by Leroy Chatfield, who said that the man was not only a Democrat—and therefore a near-radical by grower standards—but someone genuinely concerned about social issues. He had been a member of the State Labor Committee, and once told Leroy that he had refused to join the California Farm Bureau because it was so hopelessly right-wing. "He wants to do right," Leroy said, "he really does. And I admire him because as a parent he never gave me any problems. All the other growers did—Giumarra and the potato people, all of them. They thought their children were being poisoned by reading books on civil rights, the Peace Corps, and everything, but not Kovacevich. I was challenging his kids to read and to think and to discuss, and he genuinely seemed to appreciate it. When Mike changed from a business major to sociology or something, he went along with it, and as for the kids, they're fine. They had new cars and lots of money, but they weren't spoiled; in fact, they were sometimes worried about the workers." Leroy sighed. "You know something? I've always had a funny idea that John J. would call me up before this is over and say, 'Okay, let's talk.' "

Kovacevich had cited to me the case of Lionel Steinberg, a Coachella grower who treated his workers better than average, and who had bitched hard when his ranch was one of the first to be picketed. "Why him?" Kovacevich demanded. "He's been more liberal than anybody!"

Chatfield nodded when I told him about it. "Of course,"

he said. "That's exactly why we picked on him. He understands more, so he's more responsible."

Late in the day at the motel pool I scraped acquaintance with two growers who would not reveal their names: they lay on lounge chairs, white as potato except for their faces and arms. They were Italo-Americans and brothers, and they told me about the old Italian gardeners on their farm who were now dying out; with these old men, the old standards would disappear. "Everybody in this country is cutting corners on quality these days," one said; it was all the same to him. "Your quality product is a thing of the past," he added, dismissing my regrets, as well as quality itself, with one aw-get-outta-here wave of his hand.

These two men assured me that no outsider—they meant myself and said so—could understand the situation in the Valley, where even doctors and lawyers had worked as children "in the grape"; this was why all that trouble at Giumarra's over child labor laws was a bunch of baloney. The Giumarras had been poor fruit peddlers in L.A., for Chrissake, and they had worked *hard*, we *all* did, to make that money, and what was being done to them was a crying shame.

My bathing companions took the official Valley line that there was no labor problem and therefore no strike; that the growers would let their grapes rot before they let Chavez near them; that in any case, automation of wine- and raisin-grape harvesting had already begun, and automation of the table-grape industry would be under way within five years. (The five-year figure is as invariable as it is wrong: even if the machine is perfected and produced in that space of time, there will be a hiatus while the old vines are uprooted and replaced by new ones trained in a different way to accommodate mechanical harvesting. Either the defeat of Chavez or his victory could delay this problematical machine indefinitely.) "If that guy hasn't signed up the table-grape boys by this October," one brother said, "he's finished." This time the same hand motion dismissed myself and Chavez. "But he's making a lot of money, that's for sure." I shook my head. One brother actually sat up at that, cocking his head to look at me. "If he isn't," he said, "he's stupid. Or a Communist." I said he was neither. "Do you mean to tell me that's not a Commie flag, that one with the sickle on it?"

"That's not a sickle," I said, wishing Manuel were present. "That's an eagle."

"An *eagle*?" He didn't say "What's the difference?" but his shrug did.

Outside my motel room when I returned was an old blue station wagon belonging to Gilbert Rubio of the Agricultural Workers Freedom to Work Association. I invited him inside and gave him a drink, which he scarcely touched; he sat stiffly in the chair nearest the door and said that he wished to talk to me, but did not wish to talk to me in the absence of "Mister Joe Mendoza," with whom he would return later in the evening. Since I was in a hurry, I said fine, but Rubio kept talking, and as he never returned later, or ever again, I am sorry now that I was not more hospitable. Not that what he said was interesting, because it wasn't; it was the way he said it. Invariably, he said "Mister" Mendoza, "Mister" Chavez, even when complaining in intense yet monotonous tones of how Mister Chavez had wrongfully accused him of "embezzlement."

Almost everything he said was already written in the same words on a green AWFWA leaflet that he handed me, and most of it was directed against Chavez. I suggested that AWFWA was merely a mouthpiece for anti-Chavez propaganda that would fold up if Chavez were defeated, and Rubio said eagerly that this was true.

AWFWA, which calls UFWOC a Communist conspiracy, is often cited by conservative magazines (*Nation's Business* for October 1968 is one recent example) as evidence of the growers' contention that "real" farm workers resist Chavez, but having read its publications and talked to its co-director, I would have found it difficult to take them seriously even if I were against Chavez. Gilbert Rubio, who had been arrested a month earlier for threatening the pickets at Giumarra with a rifle, was so taut with frustration that I felt he might snap at any moment. He is an unprepossessing boy not yet in his twenties, with thick glasses and thick-looking skin from which small, frightened eyes peer out, as through a mask; there was no way to reach him, and I saw immediately why Cesar felt so sorry for him.

Rubio and I gazed at each other, mutually perplexed, and then he went away in his blue car. A few days later I watched him circle the Union offices, rounding the block again and again, horn blaring senselessly, before he took off across the vineyards, howling south toward McFarland; the sound of Gilbert's horn came trailing back long after the roof of his blue car had sunk into the green.

II

O N Friday, August 9, at eleven in the morning, I met Chavez at the Civic Center in San Francisco. I was wandering the marble caverns of the second floor, in search of the mayor's office, when I heard my name called in a voice with a soft ring that pierced the flat nasal clangor of the corridor. Chavez, waving, was penned in a circle of seven heavy men, perhaps fifty feet away. He had already met with Mayor Alioto, who said that if the growers would not negotiate, he would support the boycott. Now Chavez was dealing with lesser dignitaries, who were scraping an acquaintance that might prove useful to them later on: they were bunched like flies. "I wantcha to shake the hand of Seezer Sha-vez!" they hailed one another, anxious to be seen with him. Cesar stood quietly among them, hands in pockets, looking pleasant, gazing past the big avid faces with dark innocent eyes. In the cool air of San Francisco, he wore a dark-blue windbreaker over his plaid shirt.

The previous day Chavez had met with Carl Stokes, the first black mayor of Cleveland, and had gotten the impression from people there that the Cleveland police were working actively to depose Stokes and would probably succeed. He feels strongly that police chiefs should be elected. "It's becoming apparent to me now," he said as we left City Hall, "that the real problem we have in America is whether or not we are becoming a police state. And if we do, the Negroes will get it first." He was already worried about Nixon's nomination, feeling as I did that the exhumed Nixon was only the same old article in a new plastic bag. The day before, Hubert Humphrey had destroyed whatever faint hope one could have in him with his jingo cry "No sell-out in Vietnam!" We sadly agreed that the hope of a new America that had begun with McCarthy's wan revolution had probably been illusory.

Outside, on a rare day for San Francisco, a bright sun shone on the false gold leaf of the municipal façade, and far above, rippling nobly against the blue, American and Californian nylon flags flew in honor of the old imperial glories. Chavez talked more about Stokes, who apparently is a quiet man, much more to Cesar's taste than most politicians. "He's a real human being. And he's got a *lot* of black people in city government, not just one showcase Negro like they have here; his offices are crawling with them." Like Chavez, Stokes has been disappointed by the liberals, who cry out continually about principles but do nothing; a leader in office who was serious about reforms could not afford high principles that stood in the way of results. In Chavez's opinion, liberals were rarely as helpful to the poor as old-style local politicians, who were corrupt and didn't care who knew it, but worked hard for the poor because the poor got them elected.

Though they seem slightly incongruous in his soft speech, Chavez often resorts to athletic terms like "crack their line" or "plenty of muscle" or "throw him a curve." He is a realist, not an intellectual, and his realism has been fortified by extensive acquaintance with political treatises, from

St. Paul to Churchill, and from Jefferson to "all the dictators"; his self-education, in the CSO years, included readings in Goebbels and Machiavelli and Lord Acton. In *The Prince*, he was taught the folly of pure principles and of trying to please both sides. And yet, discussing this, Chavez looks wistful, as if he still hoped for a better world in which pure principles applied.

From City Hall we went to the Catholic archdiocese at Sixteenth and Church streets, where Chavez and *La Causa* received the official blessing of Archbishop Joseph T. Mc-Gucken. From here, we proceeded to the Federal Building for a lunch meeting with Democratic Congressman Phillip Burton, chairman of the House Education and Labor Committee. Mr. Burton has known Chavez since the CSO days, when Chavez was fighting the exclusion from old-age benefits of poor people who were not citizens. A big politician with big cuff links, Burton has two worry lines as sharp as scars between his brows; he said that he could eat a horse and ordered ham and eggs. Chavez had spaghetti. I ordered a beer, at which Chavez interrupted the congressman in order to warn me, very seriously, against the consumption of Coors, Colt 45 or Falstaff brands, which were all being struck by the Teamsters.

Burton recalled his first meeting with Dolores Huerta, and how she had cried on a visit to his office. "I didn't even know what she was crying about, but I would have signed anything. I felt like a monster."

Cesar laughed. "Lola," he said affectionately. "Later she called up and I asked her how she was making out with you, and she said, 'Everything worked out fine; I just sat in his office and cried.'"

Mr. Burton talked intelligently about the rural mentality of the United States Congress, which has caused it to favor the farmers' needs over those of the urban citizens, and the big farmer over the small—so much so, in fact, that the much-vaunted program of subsidies which was supposed to benefit the small farmer has done a good deal to put him out of business.

On a yellow legal pad, the congressman was taking notes on the indulgences that the growers receive from the many government agencies with which they deal: Chavez told him about the Border Patrol and the Immigration Service of the Justice Department, which had done next to nothing to defend domestic workers against the use of imported strikebreakers. He also spoke about illegal use of public water by the growers, and of the undermining of the boycott by the Defense Department, which in 1967, when the troop build-up had already slackened, bought 107 tons of table grapes for shipment to Vietnam, or more than six times as much as it had bought in the year that the strike began.

Mr. Burton feels that the federal government, and particularly the Defense Department, is so attuned to the interests of big business that it constitutes "the greatest anti-organized labor establishment in the country." Putting his notes away at last, he made that corridor gesture of politicians, a confidential summoning with all four fingers that precedes the elbow grip and the patronizing "Lemme tell ya what I'm gonna do."

It was midafternoon before lunch ended. Cesar still planned to reach Delano in time for the Friday night meeting, but he has very little sense of time, and he lingered with Lupe and Kathy Murguia for an hour or more in the small boycott office before he announced that he must stop off in Oakland on the way home. The boycott office in the Mission district is lodged between a small art gallery and a small psychedelic shop, and the people who drifted in and out were hung up somewhere between hip and YIP. "The fuzz, man," one guy said, shaking his locks. This was the whole speech. Later he said, "Underground, man. Got to go underground." He was the first Mexican-American hippie I had ever seen. When we drove away I wondered aloud why the man had felt the need to go underground, and Chavez, in deadly innocence, said, "Maybe it's cool down there."

On the way to Oakland we got into a discussion about drugs. Chavez mentioned that Pancho Villa's revolutionary army had made heavy use of marijuana, but that it was not really much of a problem among Mexicans or Mexican-Americans. Even so, the few drug users among them were hounded by the police, for whom narcotics have become a handy tool.

Dolores Huerta had worked hard on the drug issue in the CSO days. "We used CSO for a home base," Chavez said, "and went after anything we thought was wrong. We worked on the drug thing, and the old people, and we plotted against capital punishment—everything you can think of. Whenever we weren't fighting, we were plotting." He sighed regretfully. "Dolores is the only one I fight with, the only one who makes me lose my temper." He shrugged. "I guess that's because I like her so much. That girl is really something, really great. She's absolutely fearless, physically as well as psychologically, and she just can't stand to see people pushed around." I was sorry that Dolores was not hidden in the car. "I know I'm silly to get upset when he gets mad at me," she says, "but I just do."

While we drove through the dense traffic, Chavez talked about organizing; as always when on this favorite subject, he spoke with a quiet passion. He sees himself not as a union leader but as an organizer, and he told me once with cheerful fatalism that when his union is established and his own people, aspiring to consumer status, find him too thorny for their liking and kick him out, he may go and organize somewhere else, perhaps in the *chicano* slums of East Los Angeles. Asked if he would ever consider finishing his education, he said no. "If I had had half a chance, I would have gone to school, and at the time I resented it very much that I could not. But now I don't. I've had a wonderful education, the best kind, with some very good teachers: I wrote my term papers in meetings, and talking to people, and making mistakes. Anyway, poor people have to struggle so hard for an education that the investment becomes too big; there is no time left for living, because the person has to justify the awful expense to himself and others of that education. No." He shook his head.

For Chavez and all his people, organizing the poor is a high calling. "I kind of think of organizing as sacred work," Dolores says, "because it's a big responsibility, you know, getting people's hopes up, and then if you abandon them, and they get fired, maybe—well, you've ruined their aspirations, and you've spoiled the faith they have to have in anybody else who tries to help them." On the other hand, Chavez does not romanticize his work. "There's no trick to organizing, there's no shortcut: a good organizer is someone willing to work long and hard. Just keep talking to people and they will respond. People can be organized for the most ridiculous things; they can be organized for bad as well as good. Look at the John Birch Society. Look at Hitler. The reactionaries are always better organizers. The right has a lot of discipline that the left lacks; the left always dilutes itself. Instead of merging to go after the common enemy, the left splinters, and the splinters go after one another. Meanwhile, the right keeps after its objective, pounding away, pounding away."

Crossing the Bay Bridge to Oakland, we passed over Treasure Island, the navy depot from where both of us had sailed on the way to the Pacific. On this bridge there is a sign (perhaps it's been taken down; I didn't notice it) that celebrates the population race between New York and California, which California, with an increase of 600,000 mouths per year, is winning handily. Peering out through the fumes and girders at the conglomerate called the Bay Area, which spreads like a rust across the ruined hills, Californians must wonder at the optimism of their poet, Robinson Jeffers, who wrote that when man had at last burned himself out, the earth would heal itself from the awful ravages of the disease.

Chavez gazed out at the Oakland streets while I stopped to ask directions. The Bay Area is one huge classless slum, sprawling outward without aim or plan in response to economic tides and municipal expedience, the kind of suburb that will soon extend in an unbroken wasteland from Boston to Washington. Oakland's streets, grim and rundown, pour off into the bay below, which has turned from sea-blue to a dirty unnatural stain, like the River Styx. In the wilderness of semi-city, the elevated freeways run forever over the human labyrinths. Bright chemical pastels of industrial globes and tanks and towers lend a false color to the cheeks of the poisoned city: the sky sucked up thick columns of chemical smoke into the dense unnatural clouds. Blue was visible in the sky straight overhead, but the streets were hazed by a drifting ash of waste and gases. In the distance, rising out of the strange smokes like a bird straining on a string, was a green kite, seemingly the only green for miles around, and I wondered at the hope in the human being at the bottom of that string, following his kite skyward through the sunny gloom.

The Oakland boycott office, where Chavez stopped to speak briefly with a striker, was located in an old house, gray and famished at the dead end of a street; papers were blowing down the street into an empty lot of hard-caked ground which sloped down to the dark understructures of an elevated highway. In this no man's land, two black men leaned on the grimy concrete wall that raised the arteries of progress into the sky; the two stood opposite, like sentinels at the mouth of the dark entrance, too far from each other to make themselves heard over the howl of commerce overhead. Both gazed without interest at the waiting car in the dead-end street; they were waiting, too.

Going south through Oakland toward the freeway, Cesar pointed out St. Mary's Church, in the hall of which he had held his first big meeting for the CSO. "I was green, you know, but we brought in over four hundred people. Oh, I was so happy! I was *happy!* And Fred was happy, too." He berated himself for not having called Fred Ross, who retired to San Francisco in 1967 to write a book about organizers. "I wanted you and Fred to meet," he said. "To this day, he has never once been phony—he's a true friend.

Through bad periods, and from the very beginning, he never, never once forgot us."

By the time we reached the freeway it was nearly five o'clock and an hour later we were still caught on this belt of noise and ugliness that bored through the dirty reds and mustards of cheap outskirts construction. The outskirts went on and on and on into the shattered countryside. The rush-hour traffic was stifling the last chance of reaching Delano in time for the meeting, but Cesar said, "Maybe I could stop in San Jose and just say hello to my mother and my dad."

All of the Chavez family except Cesar and Richard live in San Jose. One sister is married to a carpenter, the other to a plasterer. "They're pretty good guys when they're not drunk," Cesar said. "But they're not interested in what we're doing. I don't see too much of them." He scarcely mentioned his sister Vicki and his brother Lennie, and I got the feeling that he rarely sees them, that they have been relegated to a beloved but somehow unsatisfactory side of the family that has not come heart and soul into *La Causa*.

"Lennie's a carpenter, too." Richard says. "He's a very, very fine person, but he's like I used to be: I believed, but I believed that the farm workers should do it for themselves."

Chavez talked a lot about his sister Rita, who became president of the San Jose CSO. In a fight to get blacks into her chapter, she had beaten down the savage prejudice against them among the *la raza* Mexicans, but not before she had been badly slandered in a hate campaign. "I was very glad about what Rita did—I was very proud of her. Oh, Rita's great! If she had a choice, she'd be swinging with us right now, down in Delano.

"When I got the CSO job, you know, it became a whole-family kind of thing. Everybody got involved in making decisions; my mother and my dad and my married sisters and Richard all got into it. Oh, I sort of *got* them into it, and of course we really didn't understand everything we were doing, we just knew that something had to be done. We had a very unsophisticated point of view, I know; we were kind of grass-roots." He winced like a man sucking an aching tooth. "All this language about poor people has developed since then, you know. We *were* the poor people, and we knew what we wanted without having it explained to us.

"Organizing has to begin at home. It's important to make people feel a part of things, to let them know they are making a contribution. Of course, I'm lucky to have an exceptional woman." Without Helen's support, Chavez said, he couldn't operate—not that she gave him a lot of advice, but she was always there as a kind of sounding board. "Even if I come home at four in the morning, I give her a full report on what has happened, and to this day—well, most of the time—she still wants me to do this."

Chavez recalled one Sunday when Helen succeeded in getting him to accompany his family on a picnic. There were so many workers coming to see him on their day off that he had planned to leave very early in the morning to avoid refusing them. But a few arrived before he could get away and had to be left untended to, and Chavez felt so miserable all day that he ruined the whole picnic. That evening he told Helen that he was being pulled apart, that he had to give his full time to the people and just do the best he could with his own family. She understood this, or at least tried to, and has dealt with it bravely ever since.

"It's lucky I have Helen there," he concluded, "because I'm never really home. I was home when two of the children were born and away for all the rest." He massaged his closed eyes with the fingers of one hand, a characteristic gesture of distress. "You know, I always felt that because I really wanted to do something for people, this would be all right. But we talk about sacrificing ourselves, and often we are sacrificing others. By the time Birdie came, Helen was pretty much used to it, I guess, but . . ." He was silent for a minute, then opened his eyes, and when he spoke again, his voice was harsher. "You cannot have it both ways. Either you concentrate your attention on the people who have claims on you, or you say, 'No, I have to help many more at their expense.' You don't exclude them totally, and they get more attention than anybody else, but they aren't going to get enough. You can't have it both ways. You cannot! Anybody who uses the family as an excuse not to do what he has to do . . ." He stopped again, then resumed in another voice. "I haven't been home in four nights. Sometimes I'm away for ten nights, maybe more. It hurts me not to be home with my family, you know, I feel it. I'd like to be home every night! But what about the work that has to be done?"

He was looking at me, but he didn't expect an answer and I didn't offer one. "It's rough on the children, I know that," he went on, as if I had suggested this. All of his four eldest children have worked in the fields. "They don't like living in poverty, especially when they know that it's intentional on my part. And things get harder as they get older; it's harder to get nice hand-me-down clothes and everything. But they are great, they are just great!" He smiled. "I told them that they were better off than the migrants, that at

: 289

least they had a purpose in their lives, and they understood this, they really did." He paused, subdued again. "They think I'm pretty old-fashioned. I tease Sylvia about always fixing her hair, the waste of time, you know; I told her that women are prettier the way they are made, that they should leave their hair the way it came. And I make a lot of fun of people who give their spare time to mowing the lawn, or washing their cars, or playing golf. To me, it's such a waste of time. How can you justify doing that sort of thing as long as all these other things are going on, the suffering?"

A moment later, very quietly, he resumed. "There's a saying in Spanish, '*Lo que no puedes ver en la casa, lo has de tener*'— 'That which you don't like you must have at home.' Sylvia finished high school, and I've asked her several times about registering for college, but she won't go. And Fernando." He nodded his head. "My son is a good golfer. He is a *real* Mexican-American." Chavez said this softly, slowly, but with honest bitterness; it was the first truly bitter remark I had ever heard him make. He caught himself immediately. "Well, that isn't fair," he said. "By 'real Mexican-American,' I meant he is just interested in material things. But Fernando isn't that way at all. He had a hell of a time in school, you know; we finally had to take him out. One fight after another. There was one grower's son who was really out to get him, they even fought after Fernando left school and came home on vacation. Here I was, dedicated to nonviolence, and my son fighting right and left." He managed a smile; Fernando had had no choice. "He always won. I think they finally had a great big fight that was supposed to settle things once and for all, and Fernando knocked him out." Cesar frowned a little, to repress a small note of pride. "By that time, anyway," he said, "he had already lost interest in the strike."

I said that it was probably a mistake to bring pressure on a son to share your own passionate interests; I spoke with the authority of failure, having made the same mistake myself. Cesar nodded. "I never once took him fishing or to a ball game or even to the movies." His tone judged himself with the same somber harshness that he had levied on his son. "I only took him to the office or out on the picket line. He'd be interested at first, but after a while he lost interest." He rubbed his eyes again. "He still doesn't know what he wants to do. He's out of a job, and he's not really in school, and he's liable to the draft; he's already passed his examination. He discussed with me the possibility of avoiding the draft." Cesar gazed at me again, and this time I thought there was a plea for a response. I said that my own son was only fifteen, but that I had told him that I would encourage him in any resistance to the Vietnam war; I hoped that he would not evade the draft but declare his refusal to serve and stand by that, in an act of civil disobedience. Cesar nodded. He paused again. "I told Fernando that he could not honestly qualify as a conscientious objector." If Fernando acted in civil disobedience, he should go all the way, Chavez felt, and announce that he was willing to take full punishment. "Perhaps he should even *ask* for the maximum penalty. I'm not trying to moralize for others, but that's what I would do. Otherwise, it is not real civil disobedience. If anybody takes a position and then uses the courts to get him out of it, that's not real civil disobedience. In the Union, we don't encourage people to avoid the draft, but we support them if they do, so long as they are willing to take full responsibility under the law." He mentioned Gandhi as an example of a man accepting penalties intentionally in a good cause. "If all the young men did this," he said, "there wouldn't be room for all of them in jail." What the young men needed, it was clear, was a good organizer. "We're deprived," he said flatly, after a time. "And we're going to stay deprived until we can get an education. I can't get my children to read. If I could just get *one*—maybe Birdie." He nodded. "Maybe Birdie."

Between the Oakland suburbs and San Jose lies a shrinking countryside of small truck farms and farmhouses; here, as elsewhere in America, asphalt and concrete are sealing over a rich farmland that will eventually be replaced by the multibillion-dollar development of deserts. Cesar remarked on how pretty these small farms were by comparison to the huge food factories of Delano. "They have life in them"— he pointed out the car window—"people still live here." Seeing people stooping in the rows, he talked about the short-handled hoe, which he sees as a symbol of man's exploitation of man. "You have to caress a plant tenderly to make it grow," he said, "and the short hoe makes you bend over and work closer to the plant. But a good man can work just as well with a long hoe, without the exhaustion." Stoop labor with the short hoe is so painful that an attack on the short hoe in a speech to workers brings a wild cheer of anger and approval every time he uses it.

We came off the freeway, turning left on the main avenue of San Jose; as we made the turn Cesar pointed out a small building, now a real estate office, that had been the first CSO chapter in San Jose. We went on east up the gleaming glass-plastic neon boulevard which has submerged Main Street all across America and infected the whole highway system of Florida and California; at the end of the avenue, low bare ridges of the Santa Clara Mountains eased the eye. Toward the eastern edge of town was the *barrio* called Sal Si Puedes.

Of the many communities he has known since leaving the Gila River Valley, Chavez identifies most strongly with Sal Si Puedes, where he lived for long periods both before and after he was married; he pointed out a wooden church that he had helped to build, though he admits he was not much of a carpenter. Apart from his personal life, it was the first community that he organized for the CSO, and there is scarcely a house in these small streets that he hasn't been in.

That part of the *barrio* where his parents live has a few trees and lawn patches among the bungalows. We stopped at the mailbox of L. E. CHAVEZ, and Cesar went into the yellow stucco house to see if his parents were at home. He came out again, laughing, tailed by two toddling nephews. "I asked these guys if they knew who I was, and one said yes, and I said, 'Who?' and he said, 'A man.' Then I said, 'No, I am your *tío* Cesar,' and he said, 'No! You are a man!'"

Cesar's father, in a clean white shirt half tucked into gray pants, was sitting in the sunlight by the door, and Mrs. Chavez awaited us in the doorway. They are eighty-four and eighty-two, respectively, and both have spectacles and snowy hair, but Mr. Chavez, who obviously had been a very strong, good-looking man, is troubled now with age and weight and deafness. Apparently, he has only grown old in the last five years; his wife is still alert and active. Mrs. Chavez wore a neat gray-checked gingham dress and bronze half-moon earrings, and her small house was tidy and cheerful. Inside were Lennie's daughter Rachel, a pretty girl of about fifteen, and Cesar's son Fernando, a tall, strong-looking boy with a generous, open face and manner; Fernando held a golf iron in his hand.

Cesar asked Rachel if she was coming to Delano the next summer to help in the strike, and she said enthusiastically that she would like that; I had the feeling he was talking to his son and apparently Fernando thought so too, because he murmured mildly that he had meant to accompany Manuel to New York to help with the boycott, and wondered why Manuel had not let him know that he was leaving. Chavez looked at him. "I guess you know we don't pay people to strike," he said in a flat voice, and the boy said easily, "I know. I wanted to go, anyway." He met his father's gaze. "Well, it's never too late, I guess," Cesar said; he turned back to his mother, with whom he was sitting on the couch. Fernando glanced at me and smiled; the smile made no comment, but he looked flushed. I asked him about his golf, and he told me that he shared a bag of clubs with a friend and had once broken seventy for eighteen holes.

Cesar spoke with his mother for all but a few minutes of the hour or so we spent in his parents' house. The pleasure he took in her company was a pleasure to see, and I doubt that Mrs. Chavez's eyes left him once during the visit. He paid small attention to his father, who sat quietly on a chair by the door.

Cesar speaks warmly of his father, from whom he learned his contempt of *machismo:* unlike most Mexican-Americans, and most Anglos, for that matter, Mr. Chavez never considered it unmanly to bathe his children or take them to the toilet or do small menial jobs around the house.

But it is his mother whom Cesar credits with his feeling of responsibility toward his people, and hers was also the original influence toward nonviolence. Richard agrees: "My mother is an illiterate, but she's an extraordinary person; I think she is the reason that we're doing what we're doing."

Before he left, his mother led Cesar into the bedroom, where he took her fragile hands in his and greeted her all over again, and said good-bye. He had not been there in a long time, and who knew when he would come again. She gave him a statuette of St. Martin de Porras, a black lay saint of Peru who is revered by Mexicans. The next morning Cesar placed St. Martin's statuette on the shelf of martyrs behind his desk.

On the way to the car Cesar knelt to talk to his small nephews, giving them 10 cents each from the $3.50 left over from the $5 expense money given to him by Jim Drake when he left for Cleveland. He asked the older child his name, and the boy said he was Aguilar Chavez Junior, the Third. This was impossible for so many reasons that everybody burst out laughing except for Aguilar the Third, who merely looked pleased. The boys said good-bye to "tío Cesar," and he left them, grinning broadly. "You see?" he said to me. "Money talks." He was in good spirits. At the roadside, indicating Fernando and his parents and himself, he said, "Beautiful! Three generations of poverty!"

In the car, I remarked that Fernando had seemed sincere about going to New York, and Cesar nodded. Obviously he thought so, too, and had been pleased, but something in their past experience had kept him from communicating his pleasure to his son. For a while as we drove south, he spoke proudly of Fernando. "We'll make a good organizer out of him yet!" he concluded, delighted, then caught himself and laughed. "I know," he said. "This time I'll let him come on his own decision, with no pressure. That will be best."

(Late the next day, after work, I found Cesar puttering in the empty offices, running his farm workers union by himself. We sat around for a little while, and in this time he got a call from Sylvia, who is called Mia. Cesar listened to her request, then said gently, "No, Mia, I'm going to deny you permission, because you tried to work it through a third party instead of coming to me directly. This isn't for punishment, you know, but just for education, okay?" His tone was soft and humorous, with no edge, and at the same time urgent and attentive, never careless; he may be absent a good deal, but when he is present he gives the children the true courtesy of complete attention. He was smiling at her response, and his eyes said to me, If only you could *hear* this. "I'll give you a kiss when I get home," he said. "When? I don't know. If I'm not home in a little while, Mia, then save something for me, okay?" He hung up, grinning. "In one ear and out the other! She didn't complain at all! They're great, you know, just great!")

From San Jose, we continued south on U.S. 101—"the Royal Way," El Camino Real, long since buried under concrete, which once connected the old Franciscan missions of California. By this time it was clear we would never make the Friday evening meeting, and although Cesar officially regretted this, he did not let it spoil a plan to visit one of the most beautiful of all the missions, which was only a few miles off our route. "Our time is our own for the rest of the evening," he said. "We can spend it as we like."

On the railroad track which parallels the highway were big overflowing freight cars of coarse sugar beets; Cesar said they were probably bound for a sugar refinery in Salinas. On both sides of the road were pretty orchards, but he took no pleasure in them. Belted in, shrunk down in his seat, he peered out at them through the corner of his window. "Oh, I picked a lot of prune, a *lot*. I hated it." Farther on, the orchards gave way to the soft-flowing golden hills of the small Santa Clara Mountains, and here and there, like islets in the stream of golden grass, stood old dark sturdy oak trees. The oaks made him sit up again, and he pointed out the more beautiful trees. *Los robles* are Cesar's favorite trees, but he has no plans to plant an oak at the Forty Acres; they are very slow-growing and would need a century to mature. Disgusted, he pointed out a place where giant oaks had been hacked down to make way for a big raw metal cistern.

Coyote, Madrone, Morgan Hill, San Martin, Gilroy: here, in 1903, California's first farm workers association, the Fruit Workers Union, demanded $1.50 for a ten-hour day, with overtime at 20 cents an hour. It was late in the summer day at Gilroy, though the light was still warm on the round crests of the low hills. On one of these hills, down to the south, the mission of San Juan Bautista was built in 1797. Its hill overlooks a small fat valley and is in turn overlooked by higher hills, which rose out of the twilight valley into the deepening sky.

The mission is white stucco roofed with tiles of fine old reds, and the mission portico forms one side of a Spanish plaza fronted on the other three sides by high frame buildings of the nineteenth-century West—the "Golden West," to judge from the nugget color of their paint. The columns of the portico are three feet thick; they reminded Cesar of the walls of the adobe farmhouse in the North Gila Valley. He laid his small brown hand on the old surface. "You can always tell when adobe walls are thick," he said, "even from head-on and far away. It's almost magical."

We walked the length of the empty portico. Dark was coming, and the mission was still. Cesar pointed out the old floor of the portico, which was a broken, weathered mix of stone, adobe, ancient brick and concrete—anything that had come to hand over the years. He longed to have such a floor in the buildings at the Forty Acres, but the members would never tolerate it. "They're real Americans," he said affectionately. "They want everything to look slick and expensive, to show the world that their union is a success." He laughed. "Well, we're going to design a wall around the Forty Acres, to make it a kind of cloister like this mission, and the beautiful side will be facing *in* so that the people who built it can enjoy it. If outsiders wish to come in and look, they'll be very welcome."

Our shoes whispered on old stones. Slowly we walked around the mission in the gathering dusk, and Cesar talked quietly about the spirit of these places, and how it had seeped into him long ago. He liked to think that his adobe buildings at the Forty Acres would weather as well as the old missions, but the state had demanded steel reinforcements; he said this as if steel, lacking the right spirit, might prove to be the weakest link.

"I can't remember where my interest started; it must have been very deep. When I got married, Helen didn't know too much about missions, so on our honeymoon we visited just about all of them, from San Diego north to Sonoma. What appeals to me is their ability to withstand the ages. Some are two hundred years old, you know. And this is for me a sort of symbol of what happens to people with the right attitudes. Everywhere else, they slaughtered the hell out of the Indians, all across the country, but in the missions it was different. Everywhere else the Indians were exploited; whatever religion they had was taken away from them and they were made Christians. Of course the missions used them too, but the whole spirit was different. The Mexican government perceived this, and that's why they destroyed the missions. Oh, they were animals, some of those Mexican governors! They were *animals!* You see, in what was really a dark age in terms of human life, the missions gave sanctuary to the Indians, and it was a whole new approach to human beings. The Franciscans came and they said, 'These are human beings.' And the missions reflect this spirit—not just the architecture, but the way they have lasted." A little awed, he added, "And they're beautiful. They are peaceful. And I think that comes from a kind of crusading spirit, completely opposed to what was happening in the country, before and afterward. There were few Indian uprisings here, very few. The big fight was between the Franciscans and the governments, first Spain and then Mexico, to keep the soldiers from rape and looting. Those Spanish soldiers were terrible. Hopeless. They were always at odds with the Franciscans, because the priests wouldn't give in on moral grounds: 'You can't abuse Indians, you can't abuse women.' The Franciscans made the soldiers respect the Indians. There were abuses on their side too, but in general the moral force was great. Their history was long and most of the records have been lost, so the abuses by Franciscans have been exaggerated. Most people don't realize what these priests did for the Indians, in South America and Mexico as well as here, and at great cost. They neutralized the governments. If the Church had been active in the United States at the time the Negroes were coming in, and had used the same kind of moral force, the present mess would never have developed. And it wouldn't have happened with the Indians—the mass slaughters, wiping them out." He sighed. "Bartolomeo de las Casas. He was a great Franciscan, and he fought the Crown, and finally he made them understand.

"Today the Franciscans only own about four of the old missions; the rest belong to the state. There's one that's been fully restored by the government, La Purisima, near Lompoc, on the coast. They made the tiles exactly the way the tiles were made by the Indians, and it's beautiful, but it's empty. It's cold. When the Church is not there, the people—it loses its life, it dies.

"Anyway, these things attract me to the missions. They could have done here what they did to the Indians in the Dakotas and all over the country. But the Spanish began to marry the Indians, and I think this was the Church influence: they couldn't destroy them, so instead of wiping out a race, they made a new one."

The sky turned from blue to black, but the light was so clear that different reds could still be made out on old tiles of different ages. The mission was a jumble of roofs made harmonious by broken corners; all was softened by ancient evergreens and crusting lichens. In places the stucco was chipped or fallen from old stones, and a cactus grew up in a forgotten doorway. We peered over the walls into the garden, so different from that rigid "garden" at the airport motel in Bakersfield; here nature had been allowed to stray.

From under the mission eaves, violet-green swallows flitted and returned, and from quiet trees, the evening song of a hidden bird descended as lightly as a leaf. Already, in August, the swallows were gathering to start south.

On the north side of the mission, in an unpublic and unused area shaded by trees, a beautiful wooden door was inset in an arch in the stone walls. This door led nowhere any more, and we looked at it for a long time.

It was dark when we returned to the front of the mission and stood in the cool shadows by the door. Cesar pointed out the stone baptismal fonts and the beams of *palo colorado,* that huge cypress which must have so astonished the first red and white men who came down out of the forests to the north or through the passes of the Sierra or by sea, into this once most magnificent of all kingdoms of North America.

Low, hazy shreds of cloud were still visible along the hills, but the red roofs had turned black, and the first stars were just beginning to appear. We got some supper in the old mission parish house, now a sedate restaurant with a Valley prospect.

At dinner Cesar talked about writing and the few novels he had ever found time to read; he had liked Steinbeck's early books, *The Red Pony* and *The Long Valley,* in particular, and he was stirred especially by Dostoevsky. "*The Idiot*"! he said. "It was so *different!* Different from anything!" From *The Idiot,* the conversation progressed to the Grand Inquisitor, and from there to the uses of power —specifically, the concept of Black Power, how right it was in theory and how unfortunately, in the main, its ideas have been interpreted. "There's more fight about words than anything else," Cesar said. "A leader doesn't have to say so many things. Just *do* them. You keep it simple and you do things, and you let those actions be interpreted."

Cesar talked for a little while about Malcolm X, whose autobiography had moved him enormously. In its very intensity, his admiration for Malcolm can be taken as a negative comment on the rest of the black leadership; certainly he feels that the Black Muslims are the only group with any kind of lasting organization, without which a militant group must inevitably fall back on violence. "Without organization," he said, "you have plenty of leaders but no followers." As an organizer, Che Guevara had also been a professional: "He did his homework, but in Bolivia he tried to repeat Cuba, and the problems were not the same."

The discussion turned again to race and violence, and Cesar rubbed his closed eyes with his fingers. All the talk he had been hearing from what passed for leadership was just that, he said, but talk could get the quiet people killed. Avoiding the use of names, he described an evening he had spent with two celebrated militants who did nothing but declaim loud vows of violence. Reliving the episode, he lifted a stricken face out of his hand and gazed at me as he must have gazed at them. "I'm not violent," he said quietly, reverting to the voice he had used that evening, "but if I *had* to be violent, I think I'd have more guts than people like you who talk so much about it."

At San Juan Bautista, still one hundred and eighty miles from Delano, we left the Camino Real and headed eastward, up over the Pacheco Pass and down into the San Joaquin Valley at Los Banos, once a wild grassland of lost lakes, today a reservoir. Soon we crossed what was once the San Joaquin River, now dammed and doled out in concrete canals to the farm factories of the south. Even at night the heat of the valley was awesome; we rolled up the windows and began to breathe the conditioned air fed to us by machine. The desert night moved past, and after a while we talked no more.

Toward midnight, north of Fresno, we came off the long black desert roads onto U.S. Highway 99, which rolls like one joyless carnival of lights down the whole length of the Central Valley; by the time I left Cesar at his door, it was after one. Once he had looked up, startled, gazing with dread into the Valley darkness beyond the silence of the window glass. "I'll see you when I send myself over to New York," he said, sinking back into the innocence of sleep. As he dozed, I thought of something he had said at supper: "One day when I was thirty-five, I woke up in the morning a little tired, so I went back to sleep again. When I woke, I was still a little tired, and I've been a little tired ever since." The year he got tired, I realized now, was 1962, the year he had started the farm workers association.

12

TWO weeks later, when Chavez sent himself to New York, we went to the Jewish Hospital in Brooklyn to see Dolores, who had flown to New York on August 11 and collapsed two days later in exhaustion; we sat for a while on the edge of her bed and talked and laughed and ate a bag of Fritos. Dolores asked after her daughter Alicia. Alicia Huerta had been living with the Chavezes since the day her mother left for New York; Cesar himself was in Delano for at least five days after Alicia began living at his house. Yet when Dolores referred to Alicia's presence there, he expressed surprise, then deep embarrassment, and Dolores just looked at me and laughed, not altogether happily; he had not really been aware that the child was there.

From the hospital we went to a conference of Puerto Rican activists in the Bronx, stopping off first at a Chinese restaurant near the Hunt's Point Market. Manuel was already at the meeting. "You've gotten too fat to breathe," Cesar said in a worried voice to Manuel, who merely grunted. Moments later, finding Cesar's picture in a news account, Manuel said, "Who's this fat guy? Do we know him?"

Cesar introduced *"mi hermano Manuel"* to the gathering, and his choice of Spanish over English was intensely cheered, although most of the Puerto Ricans spoke English. Afterward the two cousins bashed away for minutes at a recalcitrant candy dispenser, not because they were anxious to have the peanut bar but because they were anxious to show me how much smaller the true bar would be than the fat fake bar in the machine's façade.

Early next morning Cesar held a strategy meeting for the strikers in the pleasant office at Twenty-first Street and Fourth Avenue in Brooklyn, loaned to the United Farm Workers by the Seafarers' International Union of the AFL-CIO. Richard Chavez said the strikers were spreading their efforts too thin: "We can't be like butterflies, just touching, just meeting people." Manuel Chavez, who worked in Harlem, said that they had to work with the local leadership to get at the grass roots. "There won't be grapes here in February," he concluded. "We'll all be in jail or insane, maybe, but no grapes." Mark Silverman, who is working on the Lower East Side, reported that his picket captain was a niece of Chiang Kai-shek, "a twenty-one-year old Maoist."

Calling them to order, Chavez discussed organizing difficulties (black communities would no longer accept white organizers; Puerto Ricans preferred organizers who spoke Spanish) and deplored the lack of progress; he suggested stiff competition between the strikers. "I'm going to compete with *him*," Manuel said fiercely, pointing at Richard. "No!" Richard said. "I want *real* competition!" Chavez did not smile. He pointed at a map on which green pins indicated the stores that carried grapes. "It's all clearly marked," he said in a hard voice. "Don't anybody come back with any bullshit about what you did do or what you did not do. Just do it." He left the meeting.

By the time he reached the sidewalk, he was grinning. "I just want to give them time to let that settle," he said. "I'm trying to break their patterns, get them started fresh, because we're losing ground—that's why I'm here." He had just come from a Boston Grape Party at which grapes were hurled into Boston Harbor, and that night he was off to Philadelphia. We walked slowly through depressed low streets in a shimmering heat. At the bottom of the concrete hills of Brooklyn rose the masts of a freighter on the waterfront. Chavez spoke of the poverty programs—all the committees and paper work and lack of action, and also the emphasis on money and the helplessness without it; he much preferred Black Power's hope of self-sufficiency. "If you do things right, the money comes by itself," he said.

Chavez had brought news of Gilbert Rubio from California. There had always been trouble between Rubio and Manuel Rivera, the spirited striker who was crippled on the picket line; both parties, in fact, had complained to the police about harassment by the other. On August 14 Rubio had sideswiped Rivera's automobile outside his house; Rivera, who was in the car, took off in pursuit, and the two vehicles came screeching past the Union offices at Asti and Albany, where both drivers were glimpsed by Chavez, Mack Lyons and Leroy Chatfield. Some minutes later Mack and Leroy decided that they had better investigate. A few miles south, on the road to McFarland, they came upon a group of cars: a young boy clutching a lead pipe came running out to see who they were, then gave the alarm. Rivera's attackers took off; Rivera himself, half conscious and mouth choked with mud, was taken to the hospital, where he claimed that he had been struck with the lead pipe.

When the Delano police refused to arrest Rubio, the Union picketed the police station. "We should have done it years ago," Chavez said. At one point the police were picketed by twelve hundred marchers, including people hostile to the Union who wished to express their resentment of the police. A few days later the police arrested Manuel Rivera, on assault charges filed by Gilbert Rubio. Meanwhile the Union had filed countercharges, and a warrant was finally obtained for Rubio's arrest; immediately afterward he was bailed out by the Giumarras.

An hour later, at the Rockefeller Foundation in New York, Chavez sat in a soft, windowless modern space decorated by modern woodcuts of languid grape pickers —a coincidence, presumably—and spent most of the afternoon fending off money. "The danger is that if foundation money is offered for our nonviolence center, we would put together a program whether we were ready or not, a synthetic program, just because that money was there. And people's expectations are raised—the foundation's expectations, too—because you pump up a lot of activity with all this money, and when it's gone you don't just descend back to where you started, you go one step further down."

To judge from their reactions, the three young funders had not had much experience with this attitude. One explained that specific proposals in terms of costs, personnel, materials, would be required for a presentation to the trustees. "I didn't come here to beg for money, you know." Chavez smiled. "Well, not today. If there's some interest in what we hope to do, that's all I care about. It's going to take time to put a good program together. But I think the non-violence center is an exciting idea, very, very exciting."

. . .

As a Kennedy delegate, Chavez saw no point in committing the Union to another candidate, despite AFL-CIO pressure to endorse Humphrey; he returned to California before the 1968 Democratic National Convention on August 27. Dolores went to Chicago in his place. Describing it, she was close to tears; she had not dared walk outside for fear of breaking her vows of nonviolence. Inside, she accused the Louisiana delegates of racism, which so intrigued them that they bought her food and smuggled her HUELGA banners past the guards, who had instructions to keep anything out of the Democratic convention that was not pro-Humphrey. A young plain-clothes man assigned to her made a remark that stuck in Dolores' brain, and sticks in mine. Like the Louisiana people, the cop was intrigued by her frankness and followed her everywhere. He was a Chicago Irishman who had never heard of the Molly Maguires; he had to *talk*, he said. He said, "How can I like niggers and P.R.'s when I already hate wops and Polacks? I hate them, but I don't know *why* I hate them, and I gotta find *out*."

In September and October I spent some time in New York City with Manuel and Richard and Dolores, who took me along to meetings and picket lines all over town. In the poor districts, where a natural sympathy for the farm workers existed and where the militants were strong, the boycott was complete; elsewhere it was not doing well. In mid-October five A & P stores were fire-bombed; the fire department said that there was no evidence linking the bombings to the United Farm Workers, but pointed out that all five stores had been picketed unsuccessfully by the grape strikers. The strikers themselves acknowledged that the bombings were probably the work of sympathizers whom they could not control, and I recalled a conversation that Manuel and I had had in September with a Puerto Rican leader of the Black and Latin League, an unofficial organization of militants who try to find areas where blacks and Puerto Ricans can work together. Like most militants, he endorsed Chavez but merely tolerated his nonviolence. "SNCC and Black Panthers, they're like jackknives," he said admiringly. "They don't argue, man. They go up to the guy and say, 'Don't sell.' It's unfair, it's undemocratic, but it works. Like any fight, your first shot has to be your best. If the Panthers bomb a store, so what? All you people have to do is say, 'They didn't bomb because of *grapes,* whitey! The Panthers are *your* problem.'"

The BALL man agreed with Chavez on the need of the poor to participate if reforms were to mean anything. "Your street cat wants action—you can explain it to him later. Education doesn't precipitate action, not in street people— it's the reverse. The poor man can't see beyond his plate, can't see the issues; he's got to be a participant, not a recipient. Otherwise the System is perpetuated. Not that the System is inherently bad; it's just gotten locked in the wrong hands. We're trying to unlock it. The first job of a welfare worker is to eliminate his own job, right? It's like the school thing, decentralization; the street people are sick of having mistakes made for them. They want the right to make their own mistakes, even if the first mistake is reverse racism."

One morning Richard and Dolores visited a Bronx Shop-Rite store where the red Tokay and green Thompsons on the stands were selling for 19 cents a pound; at some stores the price was even lower, and it was obvious that the growers were dumping grapes just to break the boycott.

In the basement of the store, a summit meeting between strikers and store officials had been arranged; the Union representatives sat across a table from three negotiators named Leon, Bernie and Rudy. Leon, a cold-faced man dressed nattily in flat gangster style, was the spokesman ("Don't *help* me, Bernie," he kept saying) and he declared that Shop-Rite had conducted itself with honor, keeping "the grape" off the stands longer than anybody—why pick on a friend? But if the Union *had* to picket Shop-Rite, then Shop-Rite would turn the other cheek, and "*co-operate* to keep everything nice—set up tables on the sidewalk, maybe serve you people coffee—"

"We don't want coffee," Richard said in his soft voice. "We want the grapes off."

"Leon means no cherry bombs," Bernie said.

"Don't *help* me, Bernie," Leon said. Rudy looked nervously at Bernie.

"We don't want a *sitting* picket line," Dolores said. "We want a walking, talking, singing, *shouting* picket line!"

Bernie cleared his throat.

"Bernie," Leon said. He laid both hands palms up on the table in a plea for reason. "You people want to listen to me? We kept the grape off for four weeks after our competition." He gazed at Richard and Dolores sadly, shaking his head. "Four weeks." He was trying to smile, but the smile didn't look well. "We didn't sacrifice enough?"

"You're talking about four weeks' sacrifice of a small profit," Dolores said as she stood up. "We're talking about years of sacrifice of people's lives."

. . .

In California, Chavez had been disabled by his bad back, and spent most of September at O'Connor Hospital in San Jose. While there, he received a basket of grapes with a sarcastic note from the man who took the photographs for the John Birch publication *The Grapes: Communist Wrath in Delano*. Then, late one night, a stranger called who claimed to be Dr. So-and-so; he was to visit Cesar early in the morning at the request of Dr. Lackner, he said, and wished to know which room Mr. Chavez was in. The receptionist gave him the room number, then thought better of it and called Dr. Lackner, who came to the hospital and had Cesar transferred to the maternity ward. The San Jose police were notified, and a guard posted.

What made these episodes so sinister was that the choice of hospital had been kept secret; only a few people in the Union knew that Cesar was in San Jose. In the past months there had been several ominous events, such as the invasion of the law office by an armed stranger. Cesar himself was shaken, and the people close to him were extremely upset. He disliked the idea of being guarded; he felt that doubters, in the Union and out, might regard the crisis as a publicity stunt, and he refused to take responsibility for an expense that would be devoted entirely to himself. But the farm workers had no intention of risking the man who had brought them hope. In an emergency meeting, the Union officers and membership voted that Cesar should be accompanied everywhere—in Richard's words, "whether he liked it or not." (As Whitney Young commented, after another such crisis the following spring, the Union board had to ignore Cesar in this matter. "He must be made to understand that it's the cause that is being protected, not just himself; he is a symbol. The cause has gone too far, and it's

: *311*

too important; his board just has to take this matter out of Cesar's hands." It was this that, until recently, it had failed to do.)

Meanwhile, on September 18 in Fresno, Governor Reagan delighted the growers by calling the grape strikers who picketed him "barbarians." On this occasion he was accompanied by Richard M. Nixon, who declared his intention to eat California grapes "whenever I can." Two weeks earlier, in San Francisco, Mr. Nixon had termed the grape boycott "illegal": the boycott should be put down "with the same firmness we condemn illegal strikes, illegal lockout, or any other form of lawbreaking . . . We have laws on the books to protect workers who wish to organize, a National Labor Relations Board to impartially supervise the election of collective-bargaining agents, and to safeguard the rights of the organizers."

"One might believe from this statement," Democratic Congressman James O'Hara of Michigan told the House of Representatives, "that Mr. Nixon does not really understand the status of agricultural employees under federal labor law. But this explanation must be dismissed. Mr. Nixon was a member of the Committee on Education and Labor which reported the Taft-Hartley Bill. His own statement refers to his knowledge of labor matters gained by his 'experience' in the 1959 steel strike. He therefore certainly knows that farm workers have been forced to resort to the boycott precisely because they have been excluded from the coverage of the 'laws on the books.' . . . It is a crude deception to condemn the grape boycott as a 'descent into lawlessness,' while referring to laws which someone of Mr. Nixon's background knows full well do not apply to farm workers. It appears to me that Mr. Nixon's statement on the grape boycott is just one more dreary example of the tactics of misrepresentation which have been associated with earlier Nixon campaigns, and which have surfaced again this year."

It also transpired that Massachusetts Senator Edward W. Brooke, who had traveled on the Nixon campaign plane to San Francisco, had warned the Nixon people that the proposed boycott statement was inaccurate, but that Nixon went ahead and made it anyway. "I think," O'Hara concluded, "the American voters can legitimately question the good faith of a candidate for President who, with knowledge of a statement's inaccuracy concerning our laws, still issues that statement."

In Fresno, Mr. Nixon did not withdraw the charge of "illegality," but he did not repeat it, either. This time he claimed that the average income of migratory farm workers was "around the poverty level" (it is less than half of the present poverty level of $3,000). He granted that the workers' living conditions were "shockingly inadequate," but did not feel that a higher wage was the solution; it was not the farm workers but the growers, Mr. Nixon said, who should be given "economic incentives" so that they might invest in better housing.

"Laughingly," as the saying goes, the two friends consumed grapes for the cameras, but the implications of this well-fed fun were very serious for the farm workers. Under a Nixon Administration, the very survival of the boycott is threatened, and there is little hope that they will receive the long-sought protection of the National Labor Relations Board without also becoming subject to the Taft-Hartley and Landrum-Griffin amendments. These would serve to negate the boycott, which is the only weapon the farm workers have left; if it is suppressed, the strikers will find themselves without recourse of any kind after their long struggle. In this case, violence seems inevitable, because the workers will not return peaceably into the past. "We *can't* go back," as Manuel once said. "We got nothing to go back to."

In October, Cesar was brought back to Delano, where he tried to run the Union from an old hospital bed. The atmosphere was tense; in San Francisco, Lupe Murguia had been beaten by a Mayfair store manager, and Fred Ross, Jr., had a shot fired over his head by a security guard. Both had been picketing. Meanwhile, Kathy Murguia was harassing the shippers at the docks, where tons of boycotted grapes were being rerouted for Vietnam. The growers, badly hurt, were spending thousands of dollars on propaganda, but on October 11 their arguments were denounced point by point in a Senate speech by Senator Harrison Williams, who accused the growers of "misleading and untruthful statements."*

Meanwhile, the saga of Gilbert Rubio continued. After the Rivera episode, his backers decided that Gilbert was no asset to their cause. They allowed AWFWA to perish, and sent Joe Mendoza on a tour around the country as a farm spokesman. Gilbert, left out in the cold, formed a gang of young boys, furnishing beer and transportation to win and keep their allegiance; the aim of his new group was never quite clear, since its first formal activity was broken up by the police, who alleged that on October 11 Gilbert's band

* See Appendix.

had created a night disturbance in Delano. One boy was seized, and when Gilbert protested he received an elbow in the mouth; now that the growers had abandoned him, he was just another Mex. The police arrested him for the third time in a year, and handled his whole group so roughly that one of the boys suffered a broken wrist.

When he heard that Rubio was in jail, Chavez's first reaction was a protective one: a Mexican had been roughed up by the police. A second reaction was more practical; he got hold of Jerry Cohen, who visited Gilbert in jail, whereupon the police notified John Giumarra, Jr., counsel for the Giumarras, that Cohen had visited Rubio, and immediately Gilbert was bailed out, with the warning that he must not talk to Union people. But Rubio, injured and bitter, had already talked, and he has been talking ever since. In tears, he told Cohen that he had run away from the Rivera beating because he was afraid of violence. He also admitted that AWFWA had been an illegal, company-dominated union, and that the company most involved had been Giumarra. Since then the Union has acquired an affidavit from another defected Mendoza aide to the same effect, and is bringing suit against Giumarra.

The farm workers picketed Nixon wherever they could (NIXON IS A GRAPIST), and meanwhile, Humphrey's people pursued Chavez for an endorsement, and so did the New Left. Chavez is the only leader in the nation who has gained the fierce allegiance of the New Left without appeasing it. The students and black militants are not drawn to Chavez the Revolutionary or Iconoclast or Political Innovator or even Radical Intellectual—he is none of these. In an ever more polluted and dehumanized world, they are drawn to him, apparently, because he is a true leader, not a politician: because his speech is free of the flatulent rhetoric and cant on which younger voters have gagged: because in a time starved for simplicity he is, simply, a man. Martin Luther King was scorned by militants for his nonviolence; Chavez is not. He is honest and tough, and at the same time he embodies the love that most leaders just talk about. (A difference is that Dr. King was not really a "man of the people." He clung to the old order, the old rhetorics, the ringing statements that had lost all resonance, in his mouth or any other, and was therefore unfairly regarded as the System's man, a house nigger, who only won the support of the New Left when he became useful to it as a martyr.)

Unlike King, Chavez never risked his cause by linking it to the cause of peace, yet he has had support of the New Left from the start. As a figure to rally behind—he says he will never be a politician, and he means it—he would claim support from a new populism of labor, independents and a spirited new middle class, and an alliance of minorities, white, black and brown; in June of 1969 the Black Panthers themselves would call for such a "People's Party," a reverse in policy that must be credited, at least in part, to the healing influence of Cesar Chavez.

In return for its endorsement, the Union wanted Humphrey to bring pressure on John Kovacevich and other growers to negotiate. Because Humphrey could not or would not deliver, an endorsement was withheld until the last few days: at that point, when it actually seemed possible that Nixon could be beaten, the Union declared its support.

Chavez expected a Nixon victory, but the reality was depressing: so was Republican control of both houses of the California Legislature, and the ten thousand angry people of Kern County who voted for the America of George Wallace. At this grim time his back continued to bother him, partly because he refused to take proper care of himself. But he now understood that he must prepare for a long and bitter fight that the Union might not survive, and shortly after the election he went to Santa Barbara for daily therapy in the hot-water pool at the hospital.

13

JUST after Thanksgiving I went to visit Chavez in Santa Barbara, and on the way through Los Angeles, I arranged to talk to Fred Ross and the Reverend Chris Hartmire. On the afternoon that my plane arrived, I met Hartmire at an Alpha-Beta supermarket which he was picketing in West Los Angeles. He gave me a chest board saying DON'T BUY GRAPES, and we got acquainted through and around the windows of shoppers' cars, which we tried to slow down at the entrance to the shopping plaza and inseminate with grape-strike propaganda. The drivers and their passengers had various reactions. Some were frightened, rolling up their windows and staring straight ahead, some were disagreeable and a few were obscene, but most were pleasant, and only one, a store employee, made us jump out of the way.

Between cars Hartmire, a cheerful man with a monkish haircut, talked about the early days of the strike and the prospects for the future. The account of his arrest with Chavez at Di Giorgio's Borrego Springs Ranch was especially interesting.

"There were dogs and guns all over the place, and the ten workers were afraid to go back for their pay," he said.

"Having gotten them to walk off the job, Cesar knew he had a moral responsibility to go with them. But he also knew we would probably be arrested, so he asked me and Father Salandini to go along, to make the most of it. His instinct in these things is fantastic; it's hard to separate his strategic sense from his morality. And of course it worked out even better than he hoped. We got arrested right away, and when they finally got us to jail, they stripped us. The news account made it seem like they stripped us and then chained us, like a line of slaves, but actually we got dressed again before they linked us in threes for the trip to jail in San Diego. We were angry about the stripping and chaining, but the poor workers were really upset. Most of them were newcomers, just up from Mexico. They had been brave and they hadn't done anything wrong—they were released without charges the next day—and they felt humiliated and ashamed. Also, they were horrified that the the police would strip and chain a priest—he was in his collar and everything—but Salandini said he wished to be treated just as his people were, and of course he was right."

East Los Angeles, where Fred Ross works at the Los Angeles boycott headquarters, is a Mexican *barrio* that accumulates jobless farm workers in wintertime. Poor as it is, it lacks the utter desolation of the black ghetto, the famished buildings and mean streets where hope is dead; here the houses, small and made of wood, are full of life. There is a sense of continuity here, and therefore community, which is missing in the hard-edged public housing to which blacks are so often condemned. "Even the poorest Mexicans," Chavez says, "try to get a little paint, a little

: 3 1 9

color; they always have a few flowers and some animals, maybe rabbits or roosters." But the American Civil Liberties Union, in 1968, received well over one hundred complaints of police brutality from the *chicanos* of East Los Angeles, and in early May of 1969, when Senator Javits of New York visited this community as acting chairman of the Senate Committee on Nutrition and Human Needs, he was bitterly attacked; the people told the senator that he *knew* their nutrition was inadequate and that the least of their needs was still another fact-finding committee.

Ross is a bony man with an air of tired but indomitable honesty; he looks like a tall cowhand with new glasses. A native Californian, and a graduate of the University of Southern California, he has been an organizer for most of his adult life ("In the Depression, you were on one side of the desk or the other"). From 1937 until 1942 he worked for the Farm Security Administration; at one time he was head of the federal Weed Patch camp near Arvin which was the last hope of the desperate Okies of *The Grapes of Wrath*. Subsequently he helped the displaced Japanese of World War II, and after the war was hired by Saul Alinsky for the CSO. In the early fifties he retired from the CSO to begin writing a book about organizing; he joined the United Farm Workers in 1966, after the *peregrinación* to Sacramento. He and his wife had come down from San Francisco for the end of the march, and Chavez, catching sight of him, embraced and complimented him in public, then pestered him with so many questions that Ross finally agreed to help out for a short time in Delano. "He organized me," said the man who became the Union's director of organizing. Two years later, in the spring of 1968, Ross retired to finish his book, but in September, with the leadership emergency caused by Cesar's disablement, he came out of retirement again to take over the boycott effort in Los Angeles. His book is still unfinished.

Unlike Chavez's Mexican-American associates, Ross was struck by his qualities of leadership from the beginning. "I went home that night and wrote something in my journal about him—something like 'I've met the man among men.'" Chavez was "wary and watchful, but I was impressed by his absorption with his work, his attention to details, and his good sense about people, and still more by the intensity of his loyalty to the Mexican poor—that was *really* something." Ross shook his head, impressed all over again at the memory.

Remembering previous discussions about leadership succession in the Union, I asked Ross who could replace Chavez, and he fixed me with a bleak stare through his pale-rimmed glasses. "Nobody," he said. Despite his insistence on the word "we," and his refusal of personal awards, Chavez has become identical with *la causa,* not because of any personality cult but because of his rare qualities. Yet unless many people, including Cesar himself, are wrong, the farm workers have been given a new spirit, a new identity and dignity, that no calamity is going to kill. "There is something going on here that people never understand, that has nothing to do with me," Cesar says, exasperated by the focus on himself. And this is true: he is the head of a large and vigorous new family that has become self-sustaining. One sees what he means most clearly, not in the Delano offices nor even among the strikers, but in the ranch committees on the Union farms; these men, chosen by the workers, are the spine of the Union and its future leaders, and in their faces is the same wide-eyed, eager *need* that brightens the face of Cesar himself.

On the subject of the "flawless" Spanish that had so impressed Cesar at their first meeting, Ross said, "My Spanish was awful then. I had to use an interpreter." We agreed that Cesar's optimism about the past is characteristic. Later, when Cesar was reminded of Fred's interpreter, he gave his craftiest sweet smile. "Well," he sighed, putting his hands behind his head, "it's true that Fred didn't know many Spanish words, but the ones he *did* know, he pronounced them—"

"Flawlessly?"

"*Flaw*-lessly!" Cesar drew the word out as long as possible to convey the incredible perfection of Fred's Spanish.

That afternoon I had gone up the coast to Santa Barbara, by way of Oxnard and Carpinteria, arriving at twilight at the Santa Barbara Mission. Chavez was a guest of the priests at St. Anthony's Franciscan Seminary, which had been criticized by the Catholic Establishment for giving him sanctuary. The old mission is a soft, sun-weathered place on the face of a pine foothill of the Coast Range: its chapel and long portico overlook the Channel Islands and the sea. The seminary stands in the gardens behind, and near it is a low modest building resembling a stable, half-hidden by vines and flowering trees; it looks like what it used to be, the home of mission gardeners. White cell-like rooms open onto a simple sunny patio with a stone floor. Helen Chavez and his nurse, Peggy McGivern, had the rooms next to him; two other rooms were occupied by strikers Flaco Rodriguez and Joe Reeves.

Cesar was flat on his back in bed. In crisp white pajamas, he looked smaller than usual. He greeted me cheerfully but made no effort to sit up when he took my hand; his drawn face was gray-patched with months of nagging pain. Over his head, three rosaries hung from an extended bar, and with them a Jewish mezuzah on a silver chain that he puts on under his shirt when he goes out. On the wall, as in his office in Delano, was a Mexican straw crucifix. A washstand, two stiff chairs and a small bureau filled the rest of the tiny room; on the bureau was a borrowed tape recorder, with tapes of flamenco music by Mananitas de la Plata, and songs of Joan Baez. There was also a framed photograph of Gandhi and two books.

Cesar felt cut off from the world and from his work, and was starved for talk. Unfortunately, the first thing we talked about was the one thing we do not agree on—the population crisis. As a Catholic, Cesar is formally against contraception, but apparently contraception is less important to him than the fact that the poor are the first target of all birth control programs. As he told a cheering audience in Watts, the System was penalizing the poor for the failures of society; in limiting the numbers of their children, it was depriving them of one of their few blessings as well as weakening the advantage of superior numbers. The governments could take care of the population increase if resources were devoted to humanity instead of to such luxuries of power as wars and the moon. This was certainly true, for the moment, at least, but I wondered aloud if so many children were really a blessing for poor women or only another burden; the more children there were, the less hope for each. Looking cross, Cesar said that the poor tend to reduce the size of their families as decent salaries and educations are acquired: this was true, too, but time had run out. I felt that everything we were saying was beside the point: the crisis had gone far beyond religious interpretations, women's rights, and even the objects of birth control programs. Once the environment was damaged, these questions had small relevance or none.

Our exasperation had begun to show, and Cesar made me crank him up in bed, the better to defend his views. Plainly, my doomsday statistics and demographical projections did not interest him. How about all those miles and miles of unused land that he had seen from the air on his journeys across the country? If those in power were not so selfish, there would be room enough for all.

"As one looks at the millions of acres in this country that have been taken out of agricultural production," he has said, "and at the millions of additional acres that have never been cultivated; and at the millions of people who have moved off the farm to rot and decay in ghettos of our big cities; and at all the millions of hungry people at home and abroad—does it not seem that all these people and things were somehow made to come together and serve one another? If we could bring them together, we could stem the mass exodus of rural poor to the big-city ghettos and start it going back the other way, teach them how to operate new farm equipment and put them to work on those now-uncultivated acres to raise food for the hungry. If a way could be found to do this, there would be enough employment, wages, profits, food and fiber for everybody. If we have any time left over after doing our basic union job, we would like to devote it to such purposes as these."

. . .

Every morning at eight, and again at two o'clock, Cesar exercised under the direction of a therapist in the heated pool at the hospital. The early sun, pouring through the windows of the pool, gave his face an eerie greenish cast; the mezuzah was a small silver glitter on the dark skin of his chest. When his exercises were over, he would float on his back, arms wide, hair drifting, staring blindly at the ceiling. After dressing, he would return to the seminary, where he rested a little, then attended the students' mass. Prayers were asked of the congregation, and at one mass Cesar spoke up quietly for the farm workers, and then for those who had suffered in Vietnam.

Every day in Santa Barbara the weather was warm and clear, and after mass Chavez would walk slowly through the gardens. Even in December, all the gardens were in flower, and white-crowned sparrows sang that wistful song that seeps from the mist and headlands and coastal evergreens of the Pacific Coast. Behind the mission, to the east, its hill is separated by a valley from higher foothills of the Coast Range; below, to the west, the town climbs all the lesser hills, overflowing down the ridges and climbing once again. Beyond, huge offshore drilling rigs march the length of the glittering Santa Barbara Channel, breaking the mysterious distances between the mainland and the islands to wrench the tax-free oil deposits from the ocean bed.

That first morning, we had hardly started out when Cesar told me as he walked along that before coming to Santa Barbara, he had been raising earthworms, with the idea of improving the soil at the Forty Acres. He had an earthworm population crisis, he said; did I think that the overcrowding that must have occurred since his departure would turn his worms psychotic? We both laughed.

In his walks Cesar was always followed patiently by Joe Reeves. When we got back to his room, he took off his outer clothing and climbed into his high bed, where he hung his mezuzah among the dangling rosaries. "I'm sure Christ wore a mezuzah," he said. "He certainly didn't wear a cross." Sitting upright against the white bedsheets, he gazed at me. When I had closed the door he said, "If I had a hundred brothers out there, it wouldn't stop anybody who meant business."

During his long fast Cesar had made good progress in his fight against the fear of his own death ("If I hadn't, I'd have died a thousand deaths"), but at times he was still seized by apprehension. Also, he was discouraged sometimes by private lapses in his dedication to nonviolence, and by impure motivations in his actions. Earlier, on the subject of Gilbert Rubio, he had spoken of the Israelis' mistake in executing Eichmann: "So rarely do you get a chance for real forgiveness," he said. What emotions had come first on the night he heard that Rubio had been beaten and jailed: pity or the instinct that helping Rubio might be the good move that it turned out to be? Once again, Chavez anticipated the question. "I hope I wasn't a hypocrite about Gilbert," he said. His instincts are so bound up with what is good for the Union that to sort them out is probably impossible.

Daily, after lunch, Cesar paid a second visit to the hospital, and then rested. In the warm Pacific sunlight outside his room, I talked with Helen for a while. She told me that when the fast began, Cesar had concealed it from her for three days; he would pretend that he had already eaten or that he wasn't hungry. Then one day Manuel said to her, "Is he still fasting?" After that, she offered Cesar everything he liked, and still he neither said nor ate a thing. Finally she confronted him in his office, and when he admitted he was fasting, she became upset: she was sure he would harm himself. "The kids were already worried," Helen said. "And when I told them, they said, 'Dad looks awful—will he be okay?' But after another day or so, we got used to the idea and went along with him."

In talking about their early days together, Helen said that her family had not been so much *against* Cesar and his union as convinced that he was doomed to fail. She spoke fondly of Fernando, whose nickname is "Polly"; the boy was still drifting. In talking about her life, she speaks with impressive candor, softening nothing for her own sake or her listener's, neither disappointed nor defensive, merely concerned. Here in Santa Barbara she looked pretty and relaxed; she was seeing more of Cesar than she had in years.

Unlike her husband, Helen takes pleasure in stories about Manuel's hot temper; she described a day when Manuel stood up to both of the Dispotos during the 1967 picketing at Giumarra. Bruno Dispoto had come along in his pickup and started to abuse a group of women strikers, Helen among them, calling them whores and worse. Manuel, nearby, yelled contemptuously at Dispoto; the Dispotos were famous for insulting women and beating up cripples, he said, but he, Manuel, was not afraid of them, and he would take on Bruno and Charlie together. Both, to the delight of the pickets, declined. From then on, Helen said, the strikers yelled, "Look out, we'll call Manuel!" every time the Dispotos came by.

Manuel himself came to Santa Barbara two days later, and was reminded of this story. "Those guys are *big*," he said. "I think either one could take me with one hand."

Obviously he didn't believe this, and neither did Chavez, who was shaking his head on the white pillow. "Manuel would have kicked the shit out of them," he said quietly, with a hard satisfaction he made no attempt to hide.

On Tuesday, December 3, there was bad news from Delano. Mack Lyons had found two groups of non-Union pruners working in Di Giorgio's Arvin vineyards; questioned, the pruners said that this 1,100-acre tract had been sold to a rancher named A. Caratan. Without bothering to notify the Union, Di Giorgio was selling off the whole Arvin operation, and since the Union had failed to obtain a successor clause in the arbitration of the original contract, the new owners—whom Di Giorgio refused to identify—were not obliged to hire Union workers. Since this huge ranch gave work to a large fraction of the Union membership in the Delano area, this was a serious blow, and Chavez called an emergency meeting, to be held in Santa Barbara as soon as possible.

The lieutenants arrived at suppertime on Tuesday evening. Manuel Chavez came up from East Los Angeles; Jerry Cohen and Dave Averbuck came down from San Francisco; Jim Drake, Tony Orendain and Philip Vera Cruz came from Delano; and Mack Lyons came from Lamont, as did Fermin Moreno, who had been in charge of the 1967 Giumarra strike. They squashed into the tiny room, sitting on chairs and tabletops; Mack lay across the foot of Cesar's bed.

For two days Cesar had been cheerful, and the new emergency did not appear to dampen him at all. Mack Lyons gave his account of the crisis; he had sent a wire to the Di Giorgio office in San Francisco, demanding that the new owners be identified. Since the Union had not been notified of change of ownership, its position was that non-Union people were on the ranch illegally; names of the new owners were needed as the basis for a legal suit. The rumor was that the major new owner was W. H. Camp, a friend of the right-wing Texas billionaire H. L. Hunt, who had recently paid Camp a visit, and that the main purpose of the deal, which Di Giorgio might be helping to finance, was an anti-Union plot on the part of national agricultural interests, which know that the farm workers' plight is not confined to grapes or to California.

Chavez talked quietly about possible maneuvers, arriving finally at the necessity of a confrontation. A committee of Union workers would march into the fields and harangue the pruners, on the grounds that this was Union territory; to have them arrested for trespassing, the new owners would have to reveal their identity. An arrest would be foolish, but the growers had done foolish things before, and possibly the committee would have to spend a few days in jail. Sometimes jailing is desirable, in a test case or to win public support; unwanted arrests usually happen to people who are untrained. "Under pressure," Chavez says, "some people fall back from the offensive to the defensive, and one of two things happens: they blame their companions or they make the fight *personal* and get put in jail. In trying to prove something, they lose sight of the cause."

Somebody pointed out that the membership might be disillusioned if the Union failed to bail out people who had gone to jail for it, but this was a risk that had to be taken. "I'm just throwing this idea out," Chavez said with his usual deference. "It's just an idea." But nobody seriously ques-

: 3 2 9

tioned it, not even Tony Orendain, who tends to question. As Union treasurer, Orendain would lead the confrontation group. "We aren't going to *try* to be jailed," Cesar warned him. "We just have to be ready for it." Orendain had got himself jailed in Texas, where bail for Union members has been very expensive; he nodded and said nothing, and Chavez turned to Mack.

"You got any white guys on your ranch committee?"

"Yah. Two."

"They got any guts?"

"One of 'em do. But he's out of town, man. I ain't so sure about the other."

"We want an integrated committee. You got any black guys that have guts?"

"Mm-hm."

"Well, you tell your men that it's time somebody else made sacrifices, not just a few of you." Cesar grinned. "Tell 'em we'll get some women instead if they haven't got guts enough to go to jail."

Mack Lyons laughed. Their relationship is laconic and close; they respect each other. During Cesar's fast Mack came up from Lamont to say, "I dig what you're doing, man, I really do."

It was late when the strategy meeting ended. The men had a three-hour drive back to Delano and had to rise again at dawn, but Cesar, excited and intense, did not stop talking. He spoke of the lean Nixon years ahead, and the new pressure on the Union that the Di Giorgio sale was going to bring; it was important that everybody show a new spirit and solidarity. For example, when somebody came into the credit union he should be welcomed, not just serviced; it should be made clear to all members that this was *their* union. And in Filipino Hall the brothers should mingle and share things—no more Mexicans on the left and Filipinos on the right. When he got back to Delano, he intended to go to the hall each day for the noon meal, and he hoped everyone else would do the same. ("We got to make them damn Mexicans eat Filipino food, and the Filipinos eat Mexican food," Manuel said.) "It shouldn't be just a noon meal," Cesar said, "it should be a happy occasion, kind of a revival: we'll greet each other, we'll acknowledge individuals, what they've done, we'll sing the way we used to do, we'll teach a few people to play the guitar." ("You do *that*," Manuel said, "and they'll leave the Farm Workers and join the musicians' union.") "Maybe we'll have to learn all over again how to organize. You could learn a lot from Goebbels; that's why I wanted some of you to read him." He grinned at Jerry Cohen, who has refused to do this. "That's one thing Goebbels really under-stood—how to bring people together." Manuel winked at Cohen, at the same time jerking his head toward his cousin, but catching Cesar's eye, restrained his joke.

In a little while the men were gone, all but Manuel, who decided to stay over until morning. Slowly Cesar got out of bed and went down along the empty portico to the wash-room at the end of the building. It was past midnight. While he was gone, Manuel said that he had been jailed the night before in East Los Angeles; he had kicked a cop who falsely accused him of intoxication, then shoved him around. Another cop had held his arms while the first slugged him in the belly. Manuel laughed. "They're not so tough," he said. Helen, who had just come in, glanced toward the washroom. Knowing how Cesar worries about

: 331

Manuel, she said in a whisper, "Did you tell him?" Manuel said no. But when Cesar came back and got into bed, Manuel immediately revealed all. It was his way of teasing Cesar about nonviolence, but in the telling, he was like a boy confessing a bad deed of which he is secretly proud.

Surprisingly, Cesar did not get angry at Manuel. "Did they hurt you?" he asked in a stricken voice. He made Manuel come to the bed and hoist his shirt up and display his bruises, which were not serious. "Do you need a pain-killer? Maybe you should have an x-ray!" Manuel slapped himself on the belly and dropped his shirt. Cesar was serious, but he was also teasing Manuel by taking the account so seriously.

Cesar forgives Manuel what he will not forgive in any-body else; he loves him, but he also depends on him. In Union work Manuel stays in the background, where he is often most useful. "He is very generous," Cesar says, "and doesn't care if other people get the credit. And for sniffing things out, there's nobody like him"—he spread out his arms—"Manuel has a nose this long."

After mass the next morning Manuel drove Cesar over to Summerland, near Carpinteria. "We used to camp here every summer, on the way south to the Imperial Valley," Manuel said. Cesar exclaimed over the eucalyptus wood above the sea cliffs; his parents had lived in a tent in the wood, and the children were in a tent out in the open. The old coast road was buried under a four-lane boulevard of asphalt; otherwise, little had changed. "There were eighty or ninety tents right on that little hill," Manuel said, "and they put a water tank up at the top for us. We came to pick tomatoes, on the way from Delano to Brawley; we used to migrate into Summerland every year."

Cesar had gotten out of the car and was gazing out at the swaying kelp and pewter sea. "We used to like it here," he said. "After work, when we were hot, we could wash in the ocean." He turned to Manuel. "Remember those beers we got and buried on the beach? And Uncle Marin stole them? And we put laxative in his food? We were minors," he explained to me, "but we liked beer."

"You were very bad," Manuel said. "You were always getting me into trouble. We were in the same grade, but I guess you were five years older than me, right? Maybe ten."

From Santa Barbara I drove to Delano, stopping first at the simple Santa Ynez Mission, in the Santa Ynez Valley, then continuing north and east over the mountains of the Los Padres National Forest, winding down out of the clear skies of the Coast Range to the murky Valley floor at Maricopa; there was a police car on the lonely road west of town, and for want of anything better to do, it followed me through Maricopa and out a little ways on the far side.

In December, the Valley mists had darkened. At Maricopa there were no cover crops, no green, only a flat brown world without horizons. In the autumn dusk the skeletal black mantis-headed pumps were still rocking up and down, probing the water table; here and there, the mantis figures were as many as twelve to the square mile, herding like great Cretaceous creatures in the cold mist. To the east, a full moon loomed in the brown night that shrouded the far Sierra, but I could see no sky. On U.S. 99 I took my place in the angry chain of lights that was whining its way northward. From northeast to southeast, for 100 degrees across the cold bare land, there were no houses or tree silhouettes, no landmarks, nothing, only the huge brown-silver moon in the upper left quadrant of the void, and weak car lights far away on Sandrini Road, probing the murk like the eyes of a night animal.

By morning the murk had thickened, a rank heavy gloom that penetrated to the skin. Cars bumped through the streets of Delano like blind bugs under a log. I groped my way to Albany Street, then followed the ghostly cotton fields to the farm workers' offices at the edge of town. The cotton fields were a grim reminder of the urgency of the farm workers' plight: the automation of the cotton industry destroyed the jobs of thousands of unskilled workers who were unprotected by a union.

My errand done, I planned to continue north to San Francisco, but the fog made it impossible; I would have to turn back to Los Angeles. I stopped for a fine Mexican lunch at Leroy and Bonnie Chatfield's house in the rose fields of McFarland, then went on south. (Not long before, a shot had been fired at this house from a passing car, and shortly after my visit, Leroy and Bonnie were evicted because of their association with the Union; they now live in Delano.)

A winter sun spun through the mist, but all the highway lights were lit, and other lights shone from the railway sidings, tanks, and anonymous towers of light industry, on the far side of metal fences that run down both sides of U.S. 99. Below McFarland the highway crosses the Friant-Kern Canal, a steep-sided concrete trench perhaps fifty feet across that bores across the Valley like a giant gutter; in the canal the water was low and in the old Kern River bed, just north of Bakersfield, there was no water at all.

The fog thinned and high billboards became visible, looming over the sunken trenches of the freeway. Where the freeway was at ground level, the signs were smaller: Auto Supply and The Best Cement Pipe Co. and a sign for car wreckers, off the road to Oildale (2 mi.). On either side of the highway, utility wires wandered in the mist; the low winter sun took shape and then withdrew. Stalled by the fog, strange yellow machines squatted on their mounds of heaped raw earth, and the few weed trees that straggled skyward did less to offset than to set off the desolation. Otherwise, all lines were straight: the six lanes and their center lines, the concrete island down the highway spine, the steel barriers flanking the concrete, the railroad tracks and ties, the vine rows in the rectangles of the uniform flat fields. Here and there a strip of planting had been jammed into the concrete of the "median divider"—a last rigid line in the pattern of progress laid down like an iron grid upon the land.

At the south end of the Valley the road climbed quickly to the sky. Northward the mist lay banked, like a brown cloud on the Valley floor. To the south, closing off the whole horizon, was the great gray-yellow contamination that hangs over the spreading megalopolis.

14

FOR Cesar Chavez and his people, the dank winter in Delano has always been a time of low morale, and the winter of 1968–69 was darkened further by the Di Giorgio sale and by Chavez's physical inability to provide active leadership. When he came home from Santa Barbara in December, Cesar was still half crippled by pain, and finally the Union acquired another house next to its present headquarters, so that he could try to administer from bed. In mid-January he delivered an impassioned speech at Filipino Hall, asking the members for renewed sacrifice and dedication. There were plans to extend the Service Center to other cities in California, Texas and Arizona, and to establish a retirement farm for the Filipino members. In Delano, Leroy Chatfield and Marion Moses were revitalizing the Union's health and welfare program, which now includes a medical insurance plan to which all Union ranches contribute. With the expansion of the clinic had come a need for a full-time doctor as well as a program of preventive medicine; too many of the clinic's patients were half dead by the time they came in for help. At a meeting of two hundred farm workers it was discovered that nine out of ten had never been to a dentist, and that only three had ever had X-rays of the chest. Most of the farm workers' complaints were based directly on deprivation, but the most serious illnesses were caused by exposure to agricultural chemicals. In early January, in a letter to the growers' organizations calling for negotiations to avoid a third year of boycott, Chavez said that the Union wished to negotiate this problem of "economic poisons . . . even if the other labor relations problems have to wait."

The growers did not answer his letter, and on January 25, at a general meeting in Delano, plans were set up for an intensified boycott, as well as an effort to draw public attention to the irresponsible use of agricultural chemicals.

Four days after this meeting in Delano, court hearings began in Bakersfield in response to a UFWOC suit demanding access to public records on the use of pesticides kept by the Kern County Agricultural Commission. In August 1968, because of numerous worker injuries in the Coachella and San Joaquin valleys, Jerry Cohen had gone to the commission and asked to see the records. "I went there at eleven in the morning. I was told to come back the next day. At one thirty-three the same day a temporary restraining order was issued preventing me from seeing the reports of the spray. That's one of the fastest injunctions ever issued in the Valley."

The county agricultural commissioner testified that "no farm workers have been injured by the application of economic poisons in Kern County to my knowledge," and his counsel supported this astonishing statement by fighting introduction of evidence to the contrary from the records of the state Department of Public Health. The assistant state director of agriculture, a recognized authority on pesticides, also refuted the commissioner: he referred repeatedly to poisoning cases in Kern County, including an episode in Delano in which sixteen out of twenty-four workers who entered a field more than a month after it had been sprayed were hospitalized for parathion poisoning.

For want of a better defense, the growers had called on the crop-dusting companies to fight public identification of the "economic poisons" on the grounds that the poisons were "trade secrets." But one crop duster testified that four of the five men who mixed his chemicals had been too sick to work at one time or another during the past year, and another acknowledged that his company abandoned the use of TEPP (tetraethyl pyrophosphate) after he himself had become very ill from exposure to it. The hearings were recessed after one week at the request of the crop dusters' attorney. A few days later at hearings of the state Department of Agriculture at Tulare, a department expert, noting that California used more pesticides than any other state, admitted that his department made no tests on these products, preferring to accept the word of the chemical companies. This policy was vigorously attacked by a Los Angeles physician, Dr. Bravo, who owns a ranch in the Imperial Valley and is a member of the state Board of Agriculture: in his opinion, the word of the chemical companies isn't nearly good enough. Accusing them of fraud in labeling their fertilizer and pesticide products, he declared that their prices were exorbitant—one common pesticide, he said, sells at a 3,000 percent profit—and that the labels were misleading in regard to the dangers of the products; research on the immediate and long-term effects had been totally inadequate. "Seven or eight hundred persons per year," he understood, "are injured from these chemicals. The mortality rate is high." It was also brought out that much pesticide use was inspired by unscrupulous advertising campaigns rather than a real need. Since the chemical companies had failed to regulate their own ethics, the doctor called for legislation of the kind that had been imposed on the drug companies, which like so many other American industries had failed miserably in its responsibilities to the people who made it prosperous.

On March 14 (in the *Medical World News*), there appeared a preliminary report on a five-year study by the National Cancer Institute which declared that many common pesticides act as carcinogens; the institute felt obliged to deny that it was under pressure from the chemical industry when, at the last minute, the five-year study was withdrawn as inconclusive. Meanwhile, at the hearings in Bakersfield, a Public Health Department report was cited to the effect that among ninety-four agricultural workers reported injured by pesticides in Kern County in 1968, fifty-four were farm laborers, and Judge George Browne of the Kern County Superior Court, in a decision handed down on March 27, acknowledged that "many commonly used pesticides—particularly the organic phosphate and chlorinated hydrocarbons—are highly toxic and can constitute a hazard to human health and welfare, including death, if not properly regulated and used." Nevertheless, Judge Browne prohibited disclosure of the public records on pesticide use, basing his decision on the pesticide industry's economic importance to the state and on the growers' contention, which he dutifully accepted, that UFWOC's "efforts to organize agricultural workers, and the grape strike and the boycott having been unsuccessful, the intervenor's [i.e., Jerry Cohen and UFWOC] motive and purpose are not in fact as herein above stated, but are to use the information acquired to keep alive controversy with the growers, to assist in selling unionization to workers, and to invoke public sympathy and support and to force unionization not only through publicity but by using the information to commence and prosecute groundless lawsuits for alleged pesticide injuries against growers and owners."

Though it called the Superior Court decision "appalling," the Union had won a propaganda victory. To keep the issue alive, it appealed the decision, and in April filed a series of suits with the declared intention of forbidding further use of DDT in California, where over 1,300,000 pounds of this long-lived poison are still used annually in the San Joaquin Valley alone. In Washington, Senator Gaylord Nelson of Wisconsin was calling for a national ban on DDT ("The accumulation of DDT in our environment . . . is reaching catastrophic proportions"), citing the recent confiscation by the FDA of ten tons of contaminated salmon from Lake Michigan, and the Department of Health, Education, and Welfare announced that the average American diet contains 10 percent more DDT than the limits set down by the World Health Organization. California's leading newspapers, the conservative Los Angeles *Times* and San Francisco *Chronicle*, were also clamoring for regulation of the pesticides which had grossly polluted California's rivers and were threatening the fisheries. Under the circumstances, the California Farm Bureau Federation thought it best to join the hue and cry against DDT, which it did officially on May 25.

The growers' troubles were just beginning. Under the Landrum-Griffin Act of 1959, all new labor groups must file a report on their organization with the U.S. Department of Labor, and on February 22—eight months late—the report of the Agricultural Workers Freedom to Work Association was finally filed by its president, Gilbert Rubio, and Shirley Fetalvero, its secretary-treasurer. The report declared that AWFWA was and had been from the beginning an organization set up by the growers, with the support of the John Birch Society, to fight the effect of Chavez's union by disrupting UFWOC efforts to organize and boycott, to seek worker support for AWFWA (propaganda, free picnics, no dues), to obtain information on UFWOC sympathizers, activities, and future plans, and so forth. The AWFWA staff was paid through a front outfit that called itself "Mexican-Americans for Democratic Action," and was furnished office space and typewriters at the Edison Highway headquarters of the Giumarra corporations in Bakersfield; use of mimeograph machines, office supplies, and the like, were furnished by the Di Giorgio ranch at Arvin, despite a clause in Di Giorgio's contract with UFWOC that prohibits activities tending to undermine the Union.

The report also stated that AWFWA was set up originally at a lunch meeting in Sambo's Restaurant in Bakersfield, in May 1968. At this meeting it was decided that Gilbert Rubio and Joe Mendoza would be hired at $120 a week to oppose Chavez, and that a number of growers not present at the meeting would be solicited for support. "Several meetings involving many persons were held but only John Giumarra, Jr., Robert Sabovich and Jack Pandol gave orders to Mendoza and AWFWA."

In early March, UFWOC announced that court action would be filed in Bakersfield against the John Birch Society, the National Freedom to Work Committee and a group of growers on grounds of conspiracy to form an illegal employer-dominated union; a separate suit would be filed against the Di Giorgio Fruit Corporation for intentional subversion of its Union contract. Meanwhile Mendoza, claiming that AWFWA no longer existed, had been sent on an anti-boycott lecture tour of the Eastern cities by the National Right to Work Committee, and appeared at a committee banquet in Washington, D.C., where he was presented with an award by Senator Everett Dirksen for his efforts on behalf of American farm workers.

On March 7, two weeks after he had filed the AWFWA report, Gilbert Rubio was haled into the Delano court for his part in the October disturbance for which his gang had been arrested. Although his probation report had recommended a maximum of thirty days, he was given a sentence of three months. (After a week the Union got him freed on a technicality, but the jail term is still pending. Since then, the luckless Gilbert had been hospitalized with head injuries suffered in a fall, and has been arrested once again, charged with drunken driving.)

If its own report is true, AWFWA was nothing more than an inept right-wing conspiracy whose founders undertook to destroy a legitimate organization and smear the reputation of its leader, Cesar Chavez. The usual cheap Americanism was invoked, and the law of the land purposely broken, for no worthier cause than their own wallets. In the list of sponsors of this enterprise, most of the names are predictable enough: I was sorry to see "John J. Kovacevich" among them.

.   .   .

During the winter the Union had maintained the boycott pressure. Except for the Gristede chain, New York
City was reported "clean" of grapes by January, and in
Chicago the wholesalers acknowledged that the warehouses held fifty thousand boxes, still unsold. In California,
storage grapes were sold off for wine at the disastrous price
of $26 a ton. The boycott had even taken hold in the big
cities of the South; in Atlanta the campaign was led by Dr.
Martin Luther King, Sr., in recognition of the esteem in
which Chavez had been held by his late son. In London,
on February 12, British stevedores refused to unload a
grape shipment of seventy thousand pounds, and their protest spread to other ports in England, Sweden, Norway
and Finland. The following day, February 13, Jack Pandol
and Martin Zaninovich declared at a public meeting of the
state Board of Agriculture in Tulare that no strike existed
and that the boycott had had no effect.

This was too much for Lionel Steinberg, the Coachella
grower who is thought of as the "liberal" on the Board;
most of Steinberg's workers had gone out on strike in June
1968, after his refusal to hold elections or negotiate with
the Union, and another Coachella grower, Harry Carrian,
had declared bankruptcy. Steinberg said it was "short-
sighted" of the Board to pretend that no strike existed.
He was also annoyed that the rice farmers, dairymen and
others on the Board, in the hope of deferring their own
confrontation with the Union, were crying fiercely for a
"fight to the death" against Chavez; it was the grape
growers, after all, who were doing all the fighting, and it
was the grape growers who were faced with death in 1969.
The harvest season in Coachella was only a few months

away, and markets all over the country were pleading with the growers to resolve the boycott crisis before the start of the new season.

Of all the supermarkets, the most intransigent was Safeway, which has well over two thousand stores and is the largest buyer of table grapes in the West. The interlocking business interests of Safeway's board of directors give a vivid idea of what is meant by "agribusiness." One director, J. G. Boswell, is also president of J. G. Boswell, Inc., one of the largest cotton growers in California—it owns 135,000 acres in California alone—and the largest grape grower in Arizona: in 1968, for *not* growing cotton, Boswell received over four million of the taxpayers' dollars in subsidies from the U.S. government. Another director is Ernest Arbuckle, who is also a director of the Kern County Land Company; KCL received $838,000 in cotton subsidies. Other board members own, direct or have large financial holdings in sugar plantations, the Southern Pacific Railroad, Del Monte canned foods, the 168,000-acre Tejon Ranch, and other huge components of California agribusiness. (Compared with agribusinessmen like these, the Giumarras are small farmers, having received but $278,-000 in cotton subsidies in 1968.)

Nevertheless, Safeway styled itself "neutral" in the grape dispute, stating its intention to protect the consumer by offering grapes as it has always done. Robert Magowan, the company's chairman of the board, declared that "there has been flagrant injustice for the Mexican migrant worker . . . but we are not a party to the dispute. That is between the growers and the Union." The chairman is a director of the J. G. Boswell farm empire as well as of such huge agribusiness corporations as Del Monte, Southern Pacific and Caterpillar Tractor: his recognition of "flagrant injustice" and his simultaneous refusal to act on it call to mind the signs that appeared this winter in East Los Angeles, after one of the street kids was killed by a policeman: GRINGO JUSTICE IS SPELLED M-O-N-E-Y.

In early March, Chavez was visited by Dr. Janet Travell, whose treatment had worked so well for President Kennedy. Dr. Travell discovered that Chavez's "disc trouble" was actually a painful muscle spasm: his right leg is shorter than his left, one side of his pelvis is smaller, and he has what is known as a "transitional vertebra"; in consequence, the muscles on his right side were doing all the work. As he grew older and less resilient, these muscles could no longer compensate, and spasms developed which gradually became constant. "She is really phenomenal," Marion Moses wrote me on March 20. "By a few simple mechanical adjustments, using books, scissors, paste and felt, she got him where he was comfortable. Then she uses a spray technique with a surface anesthesia which relaxes the muscle so it can be stretched to relieve the spasm. Today for the first time in years Cesar said that he woke up without pain. He looks much better, most of the pain lines are gone from his face most of the time—and most importantly of all, he is following the treatment very faithfully. He really is very anxious to get well and start organizing again." In fact, he was anxious to go to the Coachella Valley, but Manuel Chavez and many others were dead set against it: the strong possibility of victory should not be endangered by the increased tension that Cesar's presence there would bring.

·   ·   ·

The growers, expecting sympathy from a Nixon Administration, were lobbying for new farm labor legislation, and on April 16 Dolores Huerta, Jerry Cohen and Robert Mc-Millen, the Union's legislative representative in Washington, appeared before the Subcommittee on Labor of the Senate Committee on Labor and Public Welfare, which was holding hearings on a new bill to include farm workers under the National Labor Relations Act. Other farm workers, from Wisconsin, Texas, Florida and Colorado, also testified. Mrs. Huerta read a general statement by Chavez, who could not be present; he was concerned about the illusory protection that the NLRA would give to farm workers unless the new union was at least temporarily exempted from the Taft-Hartley and Landrum-Griffin amendments, which would deprive it of the only weapons at its disposal, and thus legislate it out of existence. "Under the complex and time-consuming procedures of the National Labor Relations Board, growers can litigate us to death; forced at last by court order to bargain with us in good faith, they can bargain in good faith—around the calendar if need be–unless we are allowed to apply sufficient economic power to make it worth their while to sign.

"We want to be recognized, yes, but not with a glowing epitaph on our tombstone."

Unfortunately, the Union had not publicized its position on the NLRA before the hearings, and Chavez's resistance was misunderstood and resented, even by some segments of the press that had been sympathetic. Inevitably, the growers and their spokesmen ridiculed his fear that the "protection" of the NLRA might legislate his union out of existence. "By opposing various measures newly introduced in Congress to improve the bargaining position of farm workers, the head of UFWOC has shown up his cause for what it is: neither peace-loving nor compassionate, but a ruthless grab for power," cried an editorial in *Barron's* on June 2; in this same issue, three months after AWFWA had been exposed as a disreputable fake, *Barron's* was still taking it seriously. Meanwhile the growers were spending hundreds of thousands of dollars on anti-Chavez propaganda prepared by expensive advertising firms, including an attack by the president of the California Grape and Tree Fruit League which blamed UFWOC for "the terror tactics visited upon the grocery outlets of this nation"; he referred to the fire bombings at A&P stores in New York City in October 1968 which the Union long ago admitted were probably the work of misguided sympathizers. Out of context, *Barron's* quoted from Chavez's "Marxist" response to the League's attack: " 'While we do not belittle or underestimate our adversaries, for they are the rich and the powerful and possess the land, we are not afraid or cringe from the confrontation. We welcome it! We have planned for it. We know that our cause is just, that history is a story of social revolution, and that the poor shall inherit the land.' " The word "revolution" is the key to *Barron's* uneasiness, but the truth is that the United Farm Workers have never asked for land reforms, nor considered revolt against the American Way of Life; they ask only for a share in it.

An example of what *Barron's* means by legislation "newly introduced in Congress to improve the bargaining position of farm workers" is the "Food Profits Protection Act," sponsored by a legislator who has called the farm workers' strike "dishonest."

WASHINGTON, Apr. 30 [1969] (AP)—Senator George Murphy (Rep., Cal.) Tuesday unveiled a plan that he said would protect customers and agriculture from persons he called "of narrow interest, limited vision," such as organizers of the California grape boycott . . .

Murphy said his bill would safeguard production and marketing of food products from labor disputes and provide "an orderly system within which agricultural workers may organize and bargain collectively."

He would prohibit secondary boycotts, efforts to persuade a farmer to join a union or employer organization or to recognize or bargain with an uncertified union, picketing at retail stores, and inducements to employees not to handle or work on an agricultural commodity after it leaves the farm.

"Strikes at farms are not permitted if the strike may reasonably be expected to result in permanent loss or damage to the crop," Murphy said.

He said that he expects to get President Nixon's endorsement of his plan but has not solicited it . . .

President Nixon endorsed instead a plan attributed to his Secretary of Labor, Mr. Schultz, under the terms of which farm workers would remain excluded from the jurisdiction and protection of the NLRB but would be subject to the strike-killing provisions of the Taft-Hartley amendment that forbid secondary boycotts and organizational picketing; a special "Farm Labor Relations Board" could delay any strike at harvest time (in farm labor disputes, a strike at any other time is a waste of effort) with a thirty-day period of grace that could be invoked at the discretion of the grower. After thirty days, when the harvest in any given field would be largely completed, the workers could strike to their heart's content.

The Nixon plan was strongly criticized by Senator Walter Mondale of Minnesota, who had taken over from

Senator Harrison Williams as head of the Subcommittee on Migratory Labor, and by Senator Edward Kennedy, who had inherited a vested interest in *la causa* from his brothers. Mondale and Kennedy led the dignitaries who assembled, on May 18, to greet a company of strikers who had trudged one hundred miles in a 100-degree heat from Coachella to Calexico, to dramatize their protest against the unrestrained importation of poor Mexicans to swamp their own efforts to better their lot. Cesar Chavez addressed the rally in Calexico, and so did Senator Kennedy: a country that could spend $30 billion every year on a senseless war, send men to the moon and present rich farmers with millions of dollars in subsidies for crops they do not grow, Kennedy said, could afford to raise the standard of living of the poor who fed the nation. Both Kennedy and Mondale pledged themselves to a fight for new green-card legislation.

The strike in Coachella began ten days later, on May 28. Over one hundred local workers manned the picket lines, and though the harvest had scarcely started, another two hundred walked out in the first two days. Many signed affidavits of the sort required to certify a strike, and thereby make illegal the importation of scab labor into that field, but this year the two observers from Mr. Schultz's Department of Labor refused to interview striking workers or inspect their affidavits. When David Averbuck, the Union attorney, protested to the department's regional director, he was told that "orders from Washington" forbade the Labor officials to investigate or certify strikes: unless the strikes are decreed official, there is no legal recourse against the wholesale importation of Mexican strikebreakers. Since an estimated fifty thousand workers are available in this border region, with only three thousand needed to harvest the grapes, the strikers would be giving up their jobs for nothing.

Averbuck was also told that the federal men would make no investigations whatever but would base all decisions on the reports of inspectors sent by Governor Reagan. One of the latter declared frankly that the state men would not interview the strikers either. They were willing to accept signed affidavits, which would then be made available to the growers; if the growers used the affidavits to compose a blacklist, that was no concern of theirs.

Averbuck, a cynical young man not easily surprised by perfidy, was stunned. "It's a Nixon-Reagan conspiracy to screw the farm workers and to help the growers recruit workers illegally," he said. "It's so blatant it's unbelievable."

In any case, the Coachella strike got off to a slow start, and the growers, emboldened by open federal and state support, were making the same old arguments. "If my workers wanted me to sit down at the negotiating table, I would," said a Coachella grower interviewed by a *New York Times* reporter in early June. "But my workers don't want Union recognition. If they did, they would have walked out and joined the strike."

But one of his workers, interviewed in the same report, refuted him. "I belong to the Union but I'm working here because I have bills to pay. The Union can't pay them and I can't work anywhere else. A lot of people like me are forced to do this. How can you stand on a picket line when your family is hungry! It's hard for me to work here when the Union is out there picketing, but I can't help it."

　　　　・　　　・　　　・

By the time I returned to Delano in late July 1969, the strikers were back from the Coachella Valley and were preparing for the harvest in Lamont. Dave Averbuck was convinced that the campaign in Coachella had been a great success, whereas Jim Drake, while acknowledging progress on all fronts (including fair treatment from the Riverside County police, who did much to prevent the violence of the previous year's campaign), was sorry to come back without a contract. Everyone agreed, however, that most or all of the Coachella Valley would be under Union contract before a single grape was harvested in 1970, and although much the same thing was said last year, the evidence for this year's confidence is much better. Grape sales were off 15 percent, and even those chain stores that were still selling grapes have used the boycott as an excuse for paying the growers so little that many grapes were left unharvested. As a group, the Coachella growers were admitting that they had been badly hurt, though a few still refused to be led from the burning barn. "The Union's boycott has failed," Mike "Bozo" Bozick declared manfully on July 11, the day after the local agricultural commissioner estimated that 750,000 boxes of Coachella grapes had been left in the fields to rot, and one week after eighty-one of his fellow grape growers filed suit against UFWOC, claiming boycott damages of $25 million.

A turning point, not only in the Coachella campaign but in the four-year strike, was a sit-in, in early June, by Filipino strikers at Bozick's Bagdasarian Grape Company's labor camp Number 2 that led to a wave of sit-ins at other ranches. By the time Bozick had the last holdouts evicted and arrested a few days later, the Union had won its most significant victory since the Schenley capitulation in 1966, and Dolores Huerta gave much credit for this to the Filipinos of Bagdasarian. "Their courage, their actions, may have been the final straw that scared the growers into opening discussions," she said.

On Friday the thirteenth of June, ten growers, who claimed to represent 15 percent of the state's table-grape production, held a press conference at Indio at which they declared willingness to negotiate with the Union. Their spokesman was Lionel Steinberg, whose Douglas Freedman Ranch is the biggest in Coachella. Steinberg, acknowledging publicly that the boycott had been costly, said, "If we have a conference and discussions with the Union and we see that there is a give-and-take attitude on their part, there is no question that we are prepared to recognize UFWOC as the collective-bargaining agent."

Five of the growers were from Arvin-Lamont, the next area to be harvested, and the spokesman for the Arvin group was John J. Kovacevich, who had been holding private talks with Jerry Cohen ever since March. Publicly Kovacevich was still fulminating about the "illegal and immoral boycott," but this did not spare him the damnation of the Delano growers, led by Martin Zaninovich and Jack Pandol, who said that the 93 percent of the table-grape industry that they spoke for would fight Chavez to the end rather than sell out the consumer. The actions of the ten, according to Pandol, were "un-American and un-Christian," an opinion apparently shared by the Christians unknown who attempted to gouge out the eye of one of the ten, William Mosesian, in a night attack outside his house, and burned a stack of wooden grape boxes belonging to another, Milton Karahadian, in the Coachella Valley. Grower Howard Marguleas was warned not to set foot in Delano, John Kovacevich was snubbed by friends in Top's Coffee Shop in Lamont, and Lionel Steinberg, after years of membership, resigned from the California Grape and Tree Fruit League due to the viciousness of the League's attempts to defame the ten growers and sabotage the negotiations.

The Union, of course, had welcomed the meetings, which began on June 20 in the Federal Building in Los Angeles; the negotiations were supervised by three officials of the Federal Mediation and Conciliation Service of the Department of Labor, whose job it was to keep them from breaking down. Most of the ten growers were present at most of the meetings, which continued until July 3; the Union was represented by Jerry Cohen, Dolores Huerta, Larry Itliong and Philip Vera Cruz, and by Irwin de Shettler, an observer for the AFL-CIO. At the last conference, on July 3, the ten were joined by Bruno Dispoto of Delano. Dispoto had been hurt that spring in Arizona, but many Union people felt that he had been sent in by other Delano growers to find out what was going on. Bruno, introduced to Dolores before the meeting, said, "I haven't seen you since the old days on the picket line."

The talks were recessed for the Fourth of July and have not been resumed. There had been inevitable differences (wage scales, Union hiring halls, jurisdiction of workers, safety clauses, and other matters), but the one that derailed the talks was the matter of pesticides. The growers agreed to abide by the lax state and federal laws regarding the use of dangerous chemicals so long as the Union did "not embark on any program which will in any way harm the industry to which the employer is a member." This clause, which also gave immunity to the non-negotiating growers, would stifle all campaigns by the Union against pesticide abuses, including the matter of chemical residues on grapes; it was presented in the form of an ultimatum by the growers' negotiator, a fruit wholesaler named Al Kaplan, and was promptly rejected by the Union. The growers retired to think things over. At a press conference a week later, they denounced the Union for its bad faith and demanded a new "fact-finding commission," to be appointed by President Nixon. (The growers' charges were excited, but it is true that the Union was not overly accommodating: except on very favorable terms, a settlement with a small part of the industry was simply not worth the inevitable weakening of the boycott.)

The bad news was received in the Union offices with a certain levity—"We were very upset," Cesar says, "but what could we do? We just made jokes." The growers' demand seemed to bear out certain people in the Union who suspected that the breakdown of negotiations had been planned from the start as an excuse to go to the Nixon Administration for help. But Dolores Huerta was convinced that most of the ten growers were serious, and so was Jerry Cohen. "One night, you know, like it was maybe two in the morning, and everybody was worn out, and Kaplan was still abusing us with all this bullshit, and there was this popcorn on the table, so I started to eat popcorn. And finally the things he was saying got so stupid that I started to crunch the popcorn, and the stupider he got, the louder I crunched, you know, just to bug him. Well, our side was trying like hell not to laugh, especially Dolores, and Kaplan was beginning to get sore, and finally this grower named

Howard Marguleas couldn't stand it any more—he flipped. He said, 'How can you be so rude! Here we are trying to settle something which is very serious, and you sit there eating popcorn that way, and all you Union people smirking!' So there was this silence for a minute, I was sitting there like I had lockjaw, and then I said, 'Can I swallow, Howard?' Well, this just about broke Dolores up, and the meeting too, but anyway, Howard is usually a pretty calm guy, and the incident told me a lot about the strain they were under and about how serious they were about finding a solution."

In mid-July, as the negotiations broke down, Senator Mondale's subcommittee was advised in Washington that the Department of Defense, by its own estimate, would ship eight times as many grapes to Vietnam in 1969 as in any previous year. Like the chain stores, the Defense Department was getting a bargain on the grapes, but in the opinion of the Union, this was no more the reason for the incredible jump in grape consumption than the dehumanized excuse of "increased troop acceptance" that issued like a machine chit from the Pentagon. Claiming the usual collusion within the military-industrial establishment, the Union filed suit against the Defense Department for taking sides in a labor dispute in contravention of its own stated policies: in effect, using public funds to offer a "market of last resort" to a special-interest group.

The Mondale hearings, which continued until August 1, later heard testimony from Jerry Cohen that the growers were using dangerous chemicals in dangerous ways and in dangerous amounts, among them Thiodan, which caused the recent fish kill in the Rhine, and Amino Triazole, residues of which, ten years before in New Jersey, caused the confiscation of wholesale lots of cranberries. By common estimate, it had taken the cranberry industry nine years to recover from the public scare, and the Union did not introduce this evidence without having given the growers a chance to regulate their own practices and come to some satisfactory arrangement about pesticides without being committed to a Union contract. But the growers had not bothered to respond to this offer from Chavez in January, and when, after negotiations had fallen apart on the pesticide issue, Cohen called John Kovacevich to advise him of his intention to bring up the use of Amino Triazole at the Senate hearings, Kovacevich thanked him for the warning but could not bring the growers to act on it. As Averbuck says, "Sometimes they seem to want us to do exactly what we don't want to do, which is to put them out of business."

Cohen told the senators about reports from Micronesia of decreased cannibal acceptance of American missionaries; the poisonous residues in American bodies had become so great, he said, pointing a finger at Senator Henry Bellmon of Oklahoma, that "you are no longer fit for human consumption." Subsequently, an official of the FDA testified that Mr. Cohen's remarks were accurate enough, but that his agency was ready and able to protect the public against grapes with chemical residues that exceeded the federal tolerance level. Asked by Senator Mondale for the tolerance level on the pesticide known as aldrin, he said, "One tenth of a part per million." The senator then submitted a laboratory report obtained by the Union on two batches of grapes purchased the day before at a Safeway store in Washington, D.C. One batch, carrying the label of Bozo Bozick's Bagdasarian Fruit Company, contained aldrin residues of 1.4 parts per million, or fourteen times the permissible amount; another batch from Bianco Fruit Company carried eighteen parts, or one hundred and eighty times the federal tolerance level.

"They won't understand that we will not compromise on the pesticide issue, that we will give up wage increases first," Chavez said. "They're just not ready yet to negotiate seriously; they need more pressure, and they're going to get it. But I think some of them were serious. Jerry and John Kovacevich were able to talk like human beings, right from the start; if Kovacevich had done their negotiating for them, we might have hammered out a contract in two days."

Like all his people, Chavez was upset by the damage that the growers' recalcitrance is doing to the industry. "The longer the boycott continues, the more damage will be done. We *still* hear of people boycotting Schenley, you know, even after they are told that the Schenley boycott has been over for two and a half years."

As of early August, Union people agree that a meaningful settlement of the California grape strike is unlikely in 1969, since contracts could not be written in time to help the growers; even the ones most likely to sign would probably prefer to hold out until the spring of 1970, in the hope of legislative help from the Nixon Administration. If that help is not forthcoming, however, the Coachella growers will probably give in, and once Coachella falls, the Arvin-Lamont area will fall too. The Delano growers have a longer season and are better equipped with cold-storage sheds, but it seems doubtful, even so, that they could compete indefinitely with Union competitors who are not harassed by the boycott (although how the boycott will be made selective without losing its impact remains a problem). And if Delano falls, so will all the ranches to the north, because Delano is the heart of the resistance to its own foremost citizen, Cesar Chavez.

Even if the present talks remain suspended, their implications are momentous for the Union. The precedent for negotiation is a gaping crack in the monolithic wall that the growers have shored up for four years, and that crack can only erode faster and faster. *Hay más tiempo que vida,* as Chavez says, and time is on his side.

Cesar, though still based in bed, was sitting in a chair most of the day. He looked much better than he had eight months before; the pain lines and grayness were gone from his face, and the gaiety had returned to it, and he had taken up photography again. His therapy of massage and exercises was working; also, he was using a shoe correction and a pillow under his hip to adjust the imbalance of his weight. He hoped to be fully active by the end of the year. Meanwhile he was working twelve hours a day, talking to aides and visitors, directing strategies, discussing plans; he ate the regular meals that Helen prepared for him in the bungalow kitchen, but he did not stop talking or listening. By his side was a young German shepherd named Boycott, who was very uneasy when more than a few feet from Cesar and already extremely protective of him. There was another dog outside. "That one is *mean*," Cesar said. "He can't seem to learn who are my friends. But Boycott is really very nice." He paused a moment to scratch the ears and neck of the first dog he has ever owned. "The one thing that really bothers him is a stranger coming in with something in his hand—you know, a swinging purse or something—he doesn't like that. It's instinct, I think. And even when he sleeps, he wakes right up when something changes in the room; when I'm in my chair, he lies against it, so that he will wake up if I move."

Cesar was out of bed almost all the next day, running a series of meetings with his board. When the meetings were finished, he sat still for a liver-extract shot from Marion Moses, who was now his nurse. As Marion finished, I looked up from an article that concluded ". . . the involvement of Soviet agents (and their dupes) in the Chavez operation deserves our attention—before they succeed, not after," and said, "I didn't realize how dangerous you were." Cesar, arms extended, had begun a slow painful kneebend, his pajama bottoms poking out from beneath his trousers and Boycott's leash draped around his neck. "Ex-*treme*-ly dangerous," he said, scowling dangerously. Watching the man, I could appreciate the feelings that Marion has when she administers to him: "How often I've thought," she says, "that this whole thing is held together by this small piece of skin and these few bones." Yet this small man is very, very tough.

Cesar's son Babo came in to play with Boycott, and soon after that, Fernando, or "Polly." In the past year Polly's face had matured and so had his whole manner. This spring, after refusing induction into the Army, he had gone with Manuel to Arizona and worked there as an organizer. "One morning," Cesar said, "he just announced, 'I don't think I'll go,' and he meant it." Father Mark Day, who accompanied Polly to the induction office in Fresno, said that the boy had given the matter a lot of thought before he decided that he was a conscientious objector. He had been influenced by his father's fast, and said that any kind of violence made him sick. A mass for nonviolence, given by Father Day outside the induction office, was duly photographed by FBI agents attracted to this subversive event by a newspaper report on Chavez's son's decision. "I got some awful letters," Cesar said, "even from some of the membership. But I believed in him, and I couldn't forsake him out of expedience. Finally, I held a meeting about it. 'When we started this union,' I said, 'I told you you were welcome to everything I had, even my life. Well, now I am going to take something back. You are welcome to my life, but not to my principles.'"

When he said this, Cesar was at home in bed after a workday that had ended at ten in the evening. His children came and took his shoes off, and he lay back in the hot summer night behind drawn shades, his mezuzah glistening on his chest. Outside, in the living room, the girls fiddled with one another's hair, and Boycott lay at the foot of the bed, watching the door.

I was just back from Africa, and Cesar asked me about the death of Tom Mboya, and about Julius Nyerere of Tanzania; he was pleased to hear a high opinion of Nyerere, whose picture has joined the gallery in his office. We discussed sharks and his earthworm population (the worms were prospering on a diet of oatmeal), and many other things. The subjects didn't matter; Cesar is so intensely *present* that talking to him is like going to a source, a mountain spring; one comes away refreshed. At one point we spoke of the oil damage at Santa Barbara—"I thought of you the minute it happened!" Cesar grinned, referring to my impassioned speeches on environmental pollution of the autumn before—and I recalled a speech made on April 6, 1969, at Stanford University by Professor Richard Falk of

Princeton, who is working on a research project "devoted to world order in the 1990's." Professor Falk recommended making people "angry at what is happening to their environment, and the prospect for themselves and their children as a consequence of allowing so much public policy to be determined by the selfish interests of individuals, corporations, nations, and even regions of the world. I think the kind of community reaction that occurred in Santa Barbara recently, as a consequence of the oil slick, is the sort of thing that is going to happen more frequently and more dramatically in the years ahead. When it is understood that these occurrences are not isolated disorders but threads in the pattern of disaster, then a more coherent response will begin to emerge . . . A movement toward a new system of world order will be a serious part of the political life of the community when people are willing to go to jail on its behalf and are put there by those who fear the challenge. The outcome of this confrontation will shape the future of planetary history—in fact, determine whether the planet is to have a future in history."

In the past year, the interior of Cesar's house had changed a little. Helen had an enormous collection of strike, peace and political buttons mounted on a burlap sheet on which was painted in plump psychedelic lettering, WOW LOVE WOW!, and Cesar showed me a big cartoon of an astronaut aghast at finding a striker on the moon. The striker, strolling past the lunar vehicle, was carrying a sign that read BOYCOTT GRAPES. "Look at him!" Cesar laughed, delighted. "He doesn't even need a space suit!"

Outside, the house had not changed at all. A year later,

the old Volvo was still there, and the leaky hose, gleaming in the summer moonlight, and the faded old stickers on the windows. But as I left, a little after midnight, a man rose from a chair in the house shadows and watched me go. Chavez had become a national figure, and his door was no longer open to any stranger. It was not Chavez who had changed but the limited nature of his struggle, which had taken on a significance far beyond the confines of the Valley. That autumn, when he left California for the first time since his fast, in 1968, he had recognized that *la causa* was no longer separable from the new American revolution. On September 28, in a speech at the Washington Cathedral to a dedicated gathering of twenty-five hundred, he enlisted his *campesinos* in the great strike for peace-in-Vietnam to be held on October 15, and the following morning, in testimony at hearings of the Senate Subcommittee on Migratory Labor, he attacked irresponsible use of farm poisons as a threat not only to human beings but to the despoiled American environment. Under the hard lights of national television, the small clear-voiced, wide-eyed man in a green sweater contrasted strangely with Senator Murphy of California, who sat stiff as a puppet on the high rostrum, coached from behind by an attorney for the growers: the senator, wearing silver hair and enormous dark glasses, was insinuating in sepulchral tones that farm worker Manuel Vasquez, seated beside Cesar on the witness stand, might have tampered with the aldrin-tainted grape samples from Safeway (even though Safeway, after running its own tests, had suspended further grape shipments from Bianco Fruit Company). Later I asked Manuel, the one-time co-captain of the Sacramento march, if he had felt nervous as a witness, and Manuel, whose spirit is typical of these strikers, who have been away from home for a year or more without complaint, laughed at the question. "Why be nervous? All I had to do was say the truth!"

Senators Mondale, Kennedy and Cranston were sympathetic to Chavez, and Mondale attacked as partial and unfair the testimony of the FDA that questioned the laboratory reports of aldrin residues on the Safeway grapes. But that testimony stood: the government agencies, as Chavez had claimed the night before at the cathedral, were siding with the growers.

"This is the last time I'll ever testify," Cesar said. In pain after three hours on the witness stand, he was resting in the camper-truck that would carry him on a six-week fund-raising circuit of the Eastern cities, and he took no pleasure in the white citadels of American law and justice that glistened in the blue September sky on Capitol Hill. "I'm tired of all the promises and all the words. I've never known anything in Washington but anger and frustration and disappointment." From here, he would go eventually to New York, where Mayor John Lindsay was anxious to present him with a key to the city. The resultant publicity would be useful to them both, but the emptiness of such a ceremony made him shake his head. "I remember once they gave us the key to somewhere else. We thought it looked beautiful, shining in its box, but you know, it was only tinfoil. By evening, it had already fallen to pieces." He laughed, and his face cleared again. "Maybe this one will be made of wood," he said, as if refusing to give up hope for a new America.

15

IN early October Chavez returned to New York City to address a rally that climaxed a march on the Federal Building; there, from a car top, he attacked the Pentagon attempt to break the strike by buying up boycotted grapes. Chris Hartmire, who had come east with Cesar, was organizing his time with great efficiency, and resting him where he could, for Cesar often looked haggard with pain; for once, a little leisure time in New York City had been provided for. We went to the Museum of Modern Art, where Cesar admired Picasso's *Guernica* and the work of Joan Miró, and later attended the Pearl Bailey performance of *Hello, Dolly!*, the first Broadway show that he had ever seen.

One evening a meeting was arranged with Danilo Dolci, the great organizer of the desperate Sicilian peasantry. Like Chavez, Dolci has learned that "by loving people they become lovable," and in their defense, he has taken on the Sicilian equivalent of the System, an unholy collusion of Mafia, church and state. Unlike Chavez, Dolci received a formal education, and he had an assured future as an engineer when he "suddenly realized that I was about to become fossilized. I was about to bury myself in a materialistic society . . . Better to be penniless and in shirtsleeves and a nobody, than merely alive in the midst of life."

Dolci was escorted by Dorothy Day, head of the *Catholic Worker* and guiding spirit of the radical Catholic movement. Dolci looks like a big, vague, pale official who has wandered out without his tie, but there is nothing vague about his manner. "He never repeats himself," Miss Day remarked, "and he's always saying something even when he's asking questions." Dolci meets everyone with complete attention; hearing your name, he says, "Oh!" with pleased surprise, even if he has never heard of you, and taking your hand, there is a distinct recognition, as if he were confronting another aspect of himself.

Through an interpreter, Dolci and Chavez went immediately to the business of organizing, which both men regard not as some spiritual vocation, but as plain hard work. As Chavez has said, organizing people "becomes difficult only at the point where you begin to see other things that are easier. If you are willing to give the time and make the sacrifice, it's not that difficult to organize." (Interview) To Dolci he said, "You have no problem with minority groups, whereas we are a small nation within a large one"; otherwise, they agreed, their problems were much the same.

As Chavez nodded, Dolci emphasized that the people must first *agree* to organize, and that whatever program was set up must be made to work; as he has commented elsewhere, "We cannot afford the luxury of losing." At meetings it was crucial that people learn to speak one at a time, and that they understand the position and feelings of the opposition. The great difficulty was getting people to act who were resigned to the idea that any resistance to the way things were was hopeless. "There are a few who will work all day, every day, for change," Dolci sighed, "and there are a few who will really dig their heels in to resist it: the people stand by and watch who will hold out the longest."

On a subsequent visit to Delano, Dolci was much offended by the many photographs of Robert Kennedy that decorate the offices; in his mind the Kennedys were equated with capitalism and the System. This attitude seemed intellectual to Chavez, whose goal is the advancement of the farm workers and who is not particular about where help comes from so long as his own freedom of action is not compromised. Chavez found Dolci very intelligent and admired his ideas, but he wondered if the intellectual in Dolci did not keep him at a distance from the people.

In early 1970 I had supper at Cesar's house on Kensington Street in Delano before going on to a meeting at the Forty Acres. Cesar had become a strict vegetarian, but not being able to exercise on account of his bad back, he had put on weight, and now he said, patting his stomach, "I have decided to give up emulating Gandhi and try to be more like the Buddha."

We discussed the great white shark with Babo and Birdie, but soon Cesar's conversation turned to the murder a few weeks before of the United Mine Workers' Joseph Yablonski. Helen Chavez, who was making supper, had been listening with only half an ear, but now she turned, fork in hand, to stare at her husband. "What—?" she began, then stopped speaking as Cesar gazed at her. "We're talking about the assassination of that union leader," he admitted softly after a moment. "Oh!" Helen said abruptly, turning her head away as if she had been slapped. Her gesture reminded me of one that her husband had made, at another supper on the night he talked with Dolci. A child had suddenly burst out, "Hey, Cesar! Hey, Cesar!" When Chavez turned, the child, eyes wild, pointed a finger. "*Bam, bam, bam!*" he yelled. "I've come to assassinate you!" Cesar turned his head away much as Helen had just done, while the room suffocated in bad silence.

In the cold poisoned smog of January, Delano was as gloomy as ever, all the more so because everyone knew that the grape strike would be won this year or never. Cesar himself was very serious, and in his frustration had swung farther to the left; he was open now in his impatience with liberals, whose words were so much more eloquent than their acts. Lately he has been speaking a lot on campuses and in prisons, making the point that students and prisoners had become repressed minority groups and must organize to protect themselves. Nevertheless, he was still committed to nonviolence; "Nonviolence by itself is impotent," he told me, "but as a vehicle for action it is potent: it fails when it is not applied to concrete goals." He was unconcerned that he had been referred to as a "fanatic," since against the power now arrayed against him, only a fanatic could effect a change; as Saul Alinsky has said, fanaticism and a sense of humor are the two crucial qualities of a great organizer.

Once again the farm workers were preparing for a hard fight in Coachella, and the past year's surplus grape crop together with the economic recession of 1970 were working in their favor. On March 31—Cesar's forty-third birthday—even before picketing was under way, Lionel Steinberg, representing the David Freedman Company, became the first grower of table grapes to sign a contract with the Union. The growers were dumping their cold-storage grapes at 29 cents a pound, yet nobody was buying; in fact, anti-grape sentiment was so pervasive that months later, when the first Union grapes from Coachella reached the market, the customers were openly hostile and suspicious. More Coachella growers had already approached the Union when on May 21, in Fresno, concluding negotiations mediated by the Church, contracts were signed by the Bianco and Dispoto fruit companies. "I am firmly convinced that Cesar Chavez and his union are here to stay," Bruno declared, while Anthony "Cookie" Bianco told the press, "It was time we stopped thinking with our hearts and started thinking with our heads. Unionization is . . . just the American way of life."

These positive thoughts were not shared in Coachella, where the militant Brown Berets turned out in support of the strikers, and where the growers, resurrecting the specter of Communism, persuaded high-school students to pick their rotting melons as a patriotic duty. But in spite of judicial efforts to cripple the strike by outlawing marches, picketing, the use of bull horns, and even the display of the black Aztec eagle—known to the growers as "the Bird"—more and more workers left the fields. In Coachella, there is always harvest tension—a few weeks of June may determine the success of a whole year—and at the cold-storage sheds known as "Fort Marguleas," other growers watched Lionel Steinberg's grapes vanishing rapidly while their own, priced at a dollar and a half less per box, climbed remorselessly toward the shed roof. When the Mayfair chain stores announced its decision to stop buying non-Union grapes, one grower called Union negotiators to a meeting in a motel, where they found him stretched out like a rape victim on the bed. "Okay," he sighed, "just tell me what I gotta do to get the Bird." Another, asked if he wanted a lawyer to advise him on the contract, cried out, "Look, I don't need no legal asshole to tell me what I need—I *know* what I need! I need to get that goddamn Bird on my goddamn boxes and get'm *outa* here!"

One by one the Coachella growers were capitulating ("They all died," Marshall Ganz says without gloating, "in varying degrees of ignominy"), and in Arvin-Lamont, toward the end of June, contracts were signed by S. A. Camp and Tenneco, which together controlled 11,500 acres and had been regarded as among the most recalcitrant of the right-wing corporations. In this same period the Armenian growers of Arvin, led by William Mosesian, also came around, but John J. Kovacevich, who had been negotiating fitfully with Jerry Cohen for more than a year, could not bring himself to sign; with his close ties to the "Delano Bunch," mostly Slavic in origin, he did not want to be the "first Slav" to give in. But by early July he realized he had no choice, and he was followed a few days later by Mike "Bozo" Bozick, one of the last holdouts in Coachella. "John broke the ice for me," Bozick admitted. Even Giumarra, the last important holdout in Arvin, was caving in; a Giumarra truck that had been picketed as it left Arvin on a Wednesday was greeted by forty more picketers when it arrived in Kenosha, Wisconsin, on Saturday morning. "Jesus!" he cried, "I just can't shake you people!" The grapes were finally dumped at a severe loss in Montana.

Delano local feeling ran so high that an ugly riot between cops and Chicano students spoiled the June 12 graduation ceremonies at Delano High School. To the south, the grape industry had capitulated, and the Delano Bunch set up a negotiating committee led by the very people—the Giumarras, Martin Zaninovich, Jack Pandol, Louis Lucas—who were formerly most bitter in their opposition. A few days earlier the huge Hollis Roberts ranch, with headquarters at MacFarland, had signed a contract. (Later Roberts had the courage to say, "I learned to like Chavez and found that a lot of things we had been told about these people were not true. I had been told they were Communists, and I had been advised never to talk to them in person . . . I don't think we could have been any more wrong . . . It will be good for the country if agriculture is organized.")

On July 26 Chavez was speaking in San Rafael, in northern California, when he got a call from Jerry Cohen, who had just heard from John Giumarra, Jr. The Giumarras were threatening a mysterious move—still a mystery to this day—that might have "drastic consequences" for the industry. "They want to talk," Cohen told Chavez. "Right now. Tonight." Knowing he would not get back to Delano before one in the morning, and exhausted by the pain in his back, Chavez told Cohen to set up a meeting for 1 P.M. the next day. He knew that the growers were beaten and was undismayed by Giumarra's last-ditch threat. "They're very insistent," Jerry said. "They want to meet as soon as you get back; they'll come at five in the morning if you say so."

Relating this, Chavez paused briefly and gave me the flat baleful stare that reminds one of his deadliness of purpose. "No, I told him. They kept us waiting for five years: they can wait another five hours." Nevertheless, on his arrival in Delano that night, he was persuaded to meet with the Giumarras, and with Cohen, Larry Itliong and Dolores Huerta he went to the Stardust Motel. When John Giumarra, senior and junior, arrived at 2 A.M., Chavez apologized for not getting off the bed. John senior sympathized; he too had suffered from back trouble, and the two discussed this problem for ten minutes, breaking the ice.

Giumarra is proud of having started out as an immigrant pushing a fruit cart in Toronto. "You got to admit," he said, "that this little Sicilian gave you a helluva fight."

"The Mexicans did all right, too," Cesar reminded him. And Larry Itliong said, "Don't forget about the Filipinos." Subsequently they got down to business, and a little after daylight a rough agreement had been hammered out.

At one point during this meeting Giumarra grew almost rhapsodic about the excitement of the grape strike; it had been so much fun, he said, that he kind of hated to see it over. "We'd move here," he said, with swift motions of his hands, "and *bam*—you'd stop us! We get through here, we get around you there, but over here you nail us . . ."

But at a contract meeting with all the Delano growers held later in the day in a classroom at the Catholic High School (the Union people held the lectern, while the growers lined up like scholars in the seats), the Giumarras and others protested the conditions for signing laid down by Chavez, who demanded among other things that the hostile local press report favorably on the proceedings, and that the signing be repeated for the benefit of the media on Union territory at the Forty Acres. Having no choice, the growers gave in. Though he remained silent at the back of the room, Jack Pandol was especially unhappy; "He looked kind of hurt," Marshall Ganz told me, "and very, very bitter."

On July 29, 1970, the grape strike officially ended where it had begun five years before when twenty-six major growers of Delano signed contracts with the United Farm Workers that guaranteed $1.75 per hour plus 20 cents a box, as well as hiring halls, seniority, and strict pesticide controls, including the prohibition of DDT. Inevitably, Governor Reagan bewailed the workers' "tragic lack of choice" in the new contracts, but the growers themselves called the signing a "mutual victory." John Giumarra, Jr., as their spokesman, hailed a "new era" and "an experiment in social justice," and added, "We are happy, perhaps over-joyed, that peace has come to the Valley." The workers present, who before the signing had sung "Nosotros venceremos" ("Deep in my heart, I do believe, we shall overcome one day . . ."), were less equivocal about their joy, and greeted Giumarra's enthusiasm with not a few cynical mutters. (A few months later, on a Thanksgiving visit to New York, Cesar told me that the Giumarras were already chiseling on their contract by selling grapes from the last few holdout companies under their Union label.) As the Giumarras made victory signs for the TV cameras,

Chavez merely grinned his slyest grin. "From now on," he said, "all grapes will be sweet."

Because it had been inevitable for months, Cesar described the great victory as anticlimactic, all the more so because only forty-five minutes after the signing, he was on his way to Salinas to deal with a new crisis. In mid-July, with victory imminent in the vineyards, Chavez had sent a wire to the lettuce growers in Salinas, urging them to permit elections among their workers to determine the union of their choice. On July 23 these growers announced that they had signed contracts with the Teamsters, who once again had violated the spirit of their understanding with Chavez that UFWOC had jurisdiction over workers in the fields. The Teamster contracts guaranteed no job security, seniority, hiring hall or protection against pesticides, despite the fact that the state of California, unable to avoid the mounting evidence of human sickness, including the injury of sixteen citrus workers in a single episode that June in Tulare County, had only recently increased from seven to thirty days the minimum interval between spraying and the entry of the workers into the fields.

Earlier in the month, in an effort to build a case against this ruling, the Niagra and Chemagro chemical companies had actually paid desperate farm workers, including women and children, to serve as human laboratory rats in experiments with organic phosphates in Tulare County. According to investigators for Ralph Nader's Project on Corporate Responsibility, at least forty-nine of these people suffered serious medical effects. A spokesman for the chemical companies protested that the conditions of the test were "not unlike normal worker conditions," and a spokesman for Monsanto, a leading manufacturer of parathion, commented in the *Wall Street Journal:* "I wouldn't want to say illness reports are phony, but I suspect some of the reported illness is psychological." Monsanto, which once launched a smear campaign against Rachel Carson instead of cleaning up the abuses pointed out in her book *Silent Spring,* is apparently unconcerned about corporate responsibility to the public that made it fat.

The grape-strike victory party, planned for years, never took place at all. "We hardly had time for a beer," says Marshall Ganz, "before Vivian Levine called up from San Francisco with the first news of the Teamster contracts." Nevertheless, the crisis served to continue the momentum of *La Causa* at a time when victory might have slowed it to a halt. "Those growers in Salinas did us a favor," someone said. "Now we're the underdogs again."

In Salinas on August 10 Chavez began a six-day fast of protest against the Teamster "stab in the back," and this act dramatized the organizing that was already under way. In nightly rallies the importance of a strike was carried to the workers, who were instructed to spread the word, to elect five-man ranch committees to represent them and to prepare for hardship. As for his own people, Chavez says, they felt "invincible," and on August 24 the workers were called out of the fields. The response was overwhelming, far beyond anything recorded in the five-year history of the grape strike. The massive walk-out in the face of high harvest wages was the final blow to the growers' contention that the "real worker" wanted no part of Cesar Chavez.

According to Marion Moses, who ran the strike clinic in Salinas, so many flags were being made that no red or black cloth was available anywhere. She laughed. "You couldn't buy American flags, either. Then we decided that the right wing didn't own the American flag—we felt patriotic, too—so both sides flew them."

In a matter of days, the Salinas strike became the largest farm-labor strike in U.S. history. By the estimate of both sides, over five thousand workers had walked off the job to join the picket lines, and red flags were flying for miles up and down the roads. "It wasn't a matter of organizing the workers," Ganz describes it, "but of keeping up with them. It was the most exciting thing I ever saw."

As usual, the growers had obtained a temporary injunction against the strike, this time on the grounds that it was a jurisdictional dispute between two unions in which the growers were innocent victims. But in Santa Maria, in late August, the injunction was revoked; in the judge's opinion, there was insufficient evidence that the Teamsters had any real support from farm workers. The Teamsters had already expressed willingness to cede their new contracts to UFWOC, thereby betraying the two hundred or more growers who had signed with them; enraged, the latter swore to hold them to their contracts.

Hostility to "agrarian reformers" has been rampant in Salinas since the notorious reign of the Associated Farmers in 1936. Vigilante groups (Citizens for Justice) and inflammatory signs (REDS LETTUCE ALONE!) sprouted up all over town, and Teamster goons—known to the workers as *los gorillas*—joined cheerfully in the terrorism. A Modesto Teamster, one Ted "Speedy" Gonsalves, rode around offering his services in a Cadillac limousine bulging with weapons, including machine guns and grenades bought with Teamster funds, and a farm worker named Cleofas Guzman was shot in the foot in a wild fusillade intended to intimidate the strikers.

In sympathy with UFWOC, the Packinghouse Workers of the AFL-CIO had struck the coolers where lettuce is dehydrated and chilled for shipping, and the AFL-CIO's Bill Kircher narrowly escaped a working-over by some Teamsters who had him trapped in a motel. On August 25 Jerry Cohen went to investigate a report that *los gorillas* had been sent into a broccoli field to beat up workers who, forbidden to strike by the temporary injunction, had sat down on the job in order to get fired. Later these workers came marching out, whipping red flags from beneath the yellow rubber suits they used in spraying water on the broccoli, but Cohen himself was beaten brutally by a mixed gang of goons and growers, and sent to the hospital for a week with concussion injuries and damaged sight.

The disorder and ugly publicity persuaded two of the largest produce companies—Interharvest, a subsidiary of United Fruit, and Freshpict, a subsidiary of Purex—to sign contracts with the Union; like the wine companies before them, the parent companies were vulnerable to a nationwide boycott. As a man at Interharvest said, "The Teamsters have our contract, but UFWOC has our workers." For signing they were picketed anew, this time by the wrathful farm community. Later the D'Arrigo Company also signed, but the rest decided to hold fast, and on September 14 they were granted a permanent injunction against all strike activity in the area. The obliging judge was Anthony Brazil, who as a lawman thirty-five years before had deputized the entire white male population of Salinas in the classic confrontation between right and wrong on which Steinbeck had based "In Dubious Battle" ("A Communist, mister, is any sonofabitch who wants 35 cents an hour when I'm paying a quarter").

The Union expressed contempt for the decree, a contempt perhaps shared by the judge's daughter, Helen, who had written such fair appraisals of the strike for the Salinas *Californian* that she was taken off the job. Nonetheless, the strike came to an end. Officially, Chavez called it off because of the threat of violence, but the court decree, in combination with lack of money in the strike fund and thousands of strikers to take care of, were the practical considerations.

Three days later Chavez announced a nationwide lettuce boycott, directed primarily against the gigantic Bud Antle Company ("Bud" brand lettuce) which controlled 50,000 acres. The Antle Company had signed its first sweetheart contract with the Teamsters as early as 1961 (the union had given the company a $1 million loan) in a successful move to subvert a strike led by Larry Itliong's AWOC, the Filipino-dominated group with which Chavez was later to join forces. As it turned out, Antle was in partnership with Dow Chemical, the company known best for Saran-Wrap and napalm, which owned 15 percent or more of Antle and had one of its officers on Antle's board. Dow had bought 17,000 acres of Antle land, then leased 7,000 back to the company, and supplied pesticides and packaging material for the huge operation, including the 2,4-d defoliant used in the Pentagon experiments on the ruined landscapes of Vietnam. But like United Fruit (also sensitive to publicity due to the slaughter of inconvenient peasants on its Guatemala holdings by government militia that had been trained and paid for by the CIA and Pentagon), Dow dreaded more evil repute, and promptly disclaimed any responsibility for the Antle operation. Dow's position was that it had been dragged into the mess only because it had manufactured napalm, a regrettable episode in terms of public relations, and even worse, economically unsound. On the other hand, UFWOC contracts with their strong restrictions on the use of pesticides would not be popular among those stockholders with stomachs strong enough to stay with Dow, quite apart from the unwelcome attention they would certainly attract to 2,4-d, and in consequence Dow has made no discernible attempt to modify the thought processes of Bud Antle, who identifies the "real trouble" with the fact that "Chavez thinks he is king of the Mexicans."

In early October, the Antle company solicited the Monterey County Court for an injunction against the lettuce boycott, and were duly favored with a ruling of the sort issued earlier by Judge Brazil. In sincere contempt of court, the Union ignored this ruling (later suspended by the California Supreme Court), and Chavez was ordered to appear at a court hearing on December 4, to show cause why he should not go to jail. In the meantime he sought support for the new boycott. At Thanksgiving, 1970, in New York, making the usual rounds of AFL-CIO rallies, church meetings, foundation offices and City Hall, he seemed worried that Union strikers and sympathizers, jaded by the long struggle with the grape strike, would not respond to a boycott of lettuce, which was a staple, not a luxury; it was hard to make clear that the only lettuce under boycott was the plastic "head" or "iceberg" variety without weakening the impact of the whole campaign. The press had virtually ignored the lettuce boycott, which was faltering, and most of Chavez's visit was spent casting about for a means of bringing it back into the news. In terms of publicity if nothing else, the best turn of events would be the jailing of America's apostle of nonviolence; when I suggested this, Cesar shook his head. "They wouldn't be that stupid," he said. But as Joseph Kennedy once observed, the brain of the American business man is the most overrated commodity in the country, and on December 4 Chavez was jailed until such time as he obeyed the court decree. "Boycott the hell out of them!" he yelled joyfully from the front pages. From prison, he reported, "I'm in good spirits, and they're being very kind to me . . . I am prepared to pay the price for civil disobedience . . . and I'm not bitter at all." As an observer said, "Jail was the one credential he didn't have; now he has that, too."

Chavez spent three weeks in prison, and was ordered released on Christmas Eve by the California Supreme Court. In early January of 1971 he returned to New York, where the Union was filing suit against Secretary Melvin Laird and the Department of Defense, which had now discovered "increased troop acceptance" of lettuce and was paying more than the market price for the boycotted "Bud" brand while cutting down its purchases of Interharvest produce. United Fruit-Interharvest made no protest, since millions of dollars had been used by the Pentagon to shore up its holdings in Guatemala, and its turn at the trough would come around again. "Our supporters," Chavez told one rally, "know that it's not a case of here today and gone tomorrow. When we take on a fight, we take it on to the end."

But the fight has a long way to go. The grape strike has been won, the first successful agricultural strike in U.S. history, and the strike is expanding into other crops, in other states. But the vast majority of the nation's farm workers are as badly off as ever, and their hopes are not improved by the regressive policies of the Nixon Administration, displayed as early as the inaugural, at which Vice-President Agnew faithfully devoured scab grapes. Under the Nixon Administration, an American renaissance has been deferred. But Chavez's cause has become a holding action for change that is inevitable, a clash of citizens versus conformism and fear. And sooner or later the new citizens will win, for the same reason that other new Americans won, two centuries ago, because time and history are on their side, and passion.

"But you know what I—what I really think? You know what I really think? I really think that one day the world will be great. I really believe the world gonna be great one day."

The man who said that was a migrant farm worker, and a black man. Cesar Chavez shares this astonishing hope of an evolution in human values, and I do too; it is the only hope we have.

I think often of the visit to the archdiocese on that summer day in San Francisco, and the way Cesar vanished into the cold modern house of God, so unlike the simple missions he prefers. An elevator must have rushed him to the top, because moments later there came a rapping from on high, and Cesar appeared in silhouette behind the panes, waving and beckoning from the silences of sun and glass like a man trapped against his will in Heaven. His dance of woe was a pantomime of man's fate, and this transcendental clowning, this impossible gaiety, which illuminates even his most desperate moments, is his most moving trait. Months later I would still see that human figure in the glittering high windows of the twentieth century. The hands, the dance, cried to the world: Wait! Have faith! Look, look! Let's go! Good-bye! Hello! I love you!

Appendix

Senate

A FACTUAL REBUTTAL TO
THE FARMERS AND GROWERS ATTACK
ON OUR NATION'S FARMWORKERS

Mr. WILLIAMS of New Jersey. Mr. President, in September the United Farm Workers Organizing Committee, AFL-CIO—UFWOC —began the third year of their strike and boycott against California growers of fresh table grapes. They are solemnly dedicated to non-violent, direct action as a tactic to obtain human dignity, and to guarantee by contract improved living and working conditions through collective bargaining with their employers.

The recent impact of the boycott is indicative not of worker desperation, but of increasing worker commitment to their cause, which heretofore has been frustrated by grower intransigence. Employer importation and use of strikebreakers, presence of Mexican alien greencarders, and court injunctions severely limiting the union's right to picket, left no recourse for the workers but to seek public support through a consumer boycott of grapes.

It is not meaningful to characterize the consumer boycott of California table grapes as successful or unsuccessful, for any such measure is ambiguous. A boycott is costly—workers do not like to strike or boycott; the grower suffers economic hardship; and, our entire agriculture economy is affected.

The reports from the Department of Agriculture indicate a slowdown in the transporting, wholesaling, and distribution of grapes; the prices are lower than in previous years; and, the number of sales on consignment have increased. The response from the industry to the boycott, rather than an expression of purposes to mediate with the union, has been a resort to an extensive newspaper, radio, and television campaign allegedly to inform the public of the industry's position.

The zeal of the growers in resisting progress has been accompanied by the raising of the strawmen as issues; reliance on misleading and untruthful statements; and, the imposition of unacceptable conclusions on the public.

The growers say that the workers do not want a union. This conclusion is based on pure speculation. The best way to resolve the issue of fact of whether the employees want a union is to have a fair, secret ballot election in the best of democratic traditions. It is just this type of election proceeding that is provided by the National Labor Relations Act—NLRA. But the agriculture industry is specifically excluded from NLRA, and Congress has again this year failed to enact my bill to extend this law.

Furthermore, if it is so obvious that the workers oppose a union, why do not growers agree to elections to prove their point. Prior to every strike and boycott, UFWOC offers to join with the grower involved to set up fair elections to determine the will of the workers. In every case the grower has refused even to discuss such an election. After having closed the door on the only democratic method available to convince the public that their workers are content, the growers then ask the American public to accept their word about the feelings of their workers.

Whenever an election has been held, the fieldworkers have voted overwhelmingly to be represented by the union. And the labor situation has been peacefully stabilized to the equal satisfaction of both farmer and employee. These elections are the only hard evidence we have as to the will of the workers.

Growers say that workers are happy and don't want a union, as proven by workers now in the fields. When the strikes were first called, workers left the fields to join the strikes. The companies then proceeded to recruit strikebreakers. As strikebreakers come in, the union is able to get some of them to join the strike, but the companies then recruit more strikebreakers to take their place. This cycle continues.

Many of these strikebreakers are greencard immigrants who live in Mexico and commute seasonally to California to cash in on the harvest season. Others cross the border illegally, and the few who are caught, several hundred a month, are returned to Mexico. They do not support their families on the U.S. cost of living index. Their major objective is to make as much as they can, as fast as they can, so they can return to Mexico and invest it in their homes, businesses, and families there. They are, in this latter respect, perfect strike-breakers. Although the cost of labor for the harvest is increased tremendously by extensive recruiting and other costs, the growers are apparently willing to pay the cost in order to fight the union. Many of the grape strikers meanwhile are forced to take other jobs, or go back into the fields, by economic necessity.

The growers say that 90 percent of their workers are local people, not migrants, and that they have year-round work in table grapes. The figures of the Farm Labor Service say something, else. There are three major work periods in table grapes; in Kern County, Calif., in 1967–68, for example:

Pruning and tieing peak: December 18–January 27, 6 weeks, 3,200 workers needed at peak.

Thinning and girdling peak: May 13–June 1, 3 weeks, 3,500 workers needed at peak.

Harvest peak: August 7–September 2, 4 weeks, 6,000 workers needed at peak.

There are migrants at work in each of these seasons. At the peak of the harvest approximately 50 percent of the fieldworkers are migrants. At other times of the year there is less work; for example, October 28, 1967: 3,000 workers; December 2, 1967: 200 workers; February 24, 1968: 200 workers; March 30, 1968: 0 workers; July 13, 1968: 800 workers. In the United States, there are well over 1 million migratory seasonal workers. In California, there are over 200,000—about one-third migrants and two-thirds local seasonals.

Recent full-page advertisements have asserted that farmworkers have said publicly that the real workers do not want a union. This is not true and there is no evidence to substantiate it. The only public evidence that we have—elections and card checks—proves the opposite: that fieldworkers want the protections of a contract negotiated by UFWOC. From the beginning of the strike the growers have supported and made use of labor contractors, local business people, and a small number of farmworkers in their efforts to oppose unionization. The first group was the Kern-Tulare Independent Farm Workers, exposed by the late Senator Robert Kennedy in hearings of my subcommittee as a "company union" with no actual farmworker leadership.

Subsequently there has been the Facts From Delano group, Mothers Against Chavez, Men Against Chavez and now the Agricultural Workers Freedom to Work Association—AWFWA. The AWFWA has been sued by UFWOC as an employee organization financed and controlled by employers in violation of the California code. This case is pending. It calls UFWOC a Communist conspiracy, and is alined with the National Right to Work Committee and other antiunion forces of the State and Nation. This organization appears to be only another pitiful example of man's willingness to sell out the rightful aspirations of his brothers for the sake of personal gain.

Opponents of the union say that California grape workers make $2.50 per hour and more. It is true that some workers earn more than $2 per hour during certain parts of the harvest season. Of course, the work is backbreaking. But the harvest season is short and families should live in decency year-around. Through the whole year, day in and day out, hourly wages in California agriculture average $1.62. Even this low wage level has been reached as a result of union pressure for higher wages, and the recent termination of the *bracero* importation program. Add to these low wages the seasonal nature of farm labor and it is then easy to understand why annual income for male farmworkers in California is just under $2,000 and family income is between $2,500 and $3,000 per year.

Average hourly wage for all farmworkers—including year-around hired hands—in 1967 was $1.33 for the entire Nation, and $1.62 for California.

In 1965, average hourly earnings of farmworkers in the United States and California was one-half that of factory workers.

Average annual earnings for migrant workers in the Nation in 1967 was $1,307.

The average migrant only finds 82 days of farmwork a year and supplements his meager income with other low-paid work. Very few workers get any free food, transportation, or housing. Even for those who do, the value does not come close to the paid insurance, vacations, and other fringe benefits common in America.

Growers say that the smaller landowners, the marginal table grape growers, will be destroyed by the boycott. A boycott is costly to all involved, and the workers do not like to strike or boycott. They have given assurances that they will call off their economic warfare activities any time their employers agree to bargaining.

Meanwhile, the union has offered to use the boycott machinery to market the grapes of any grower who will sit down with his organized workers. Some chain stores which have stopped selling grapes would unquestionably prefer to sell union-harvested grapes.

However, neither large or small farmers can justify their own survival in business if it is purchased at the cost of suffering for farmworkers and their children.

Furthermore, the union fully realizes that small farmers are often exploited at the marketplace. Both small family farmers and field-workers are at a competitive disadvantage vis-à-vis the huge agribusiness concerns in selling their labor and their products. In California, for example, 10 percent of the farms employ 80 percent of the farmworkers. 6.0 percent of California's farms own 75 percent of the land, and 5.2 percent of California's farms pay 60.2 percent of the farm labor wages.

The unionization of these gigantic farming operations will help the small farmer by making his own labor worth more. In fact, the National Farmers Union and the National Farmers Organization have raised their voices in support of UFWOC's demands for union recognition and the inclusion of farmworkers under the NLRA. Farmers need to get together to change injustices caused by agribusiness just as their workers are getting together to change longstanding injustice in the fields.

By extending the NLRA, an equalization of bargaining power would be accomplished, and both employer and union would be subject to provisions of the act forbidding ruthless power that intimidates and threatens other parties and individuals covered by the act.

The growers say they favor unionization, but that UFWOC and Cesar Chavez are untrustworthy. Some agricultural organizations have consistently opposed the extension of the NLRA to agriculture. The Council of California Growers, the California Farm Bureau Federation and the American Farm Bureau Federation are among the major opponents of present efforts to extend the NLRA. The big-business segments of the agricultural industry have given lip service to the rights of their workers to organize but in every specific instance they have bitterly opposed unionization. Cesar Chavez is proving to the world his dedication to the aspirations of his own people, and indeed to the needs of all men. He is a leader in nonviolence, known and supported by the major religious bodies in this country, and the Nation's labor movement is firmly supporting his efforts.

Cesar Chavez and the workers with him have no desire to destroy anyone, least of all their own employers. The agricultural industry may someday recognize with gratitude that they can choose to bargain with humane and reasonable men.

What are some of the provisions of the existing UFWOC contracts? There are now nine contracts negotiated between organized workers and their employers. These contracts provide for better wages, establish grievance and arbitration procedures, and make provision for job security, overtime pay, rest periods, a jointly administered health benefit plan, certain holidays and vacations with pay, health and safety protections on the job, and other benefits. The contracts include "no-strike" clauses for the life of the contract with stringent immediate binding mediation and court action in the event of a violation of this clause.

Growers say that collective bargaining is not possible or feasible in the agricultural industry, because of the perishable nature of fruits and vegetables. These nine contracts between the UFWOC workers and their employers, each including a "no-strike" clause, serve as adequate evidence that collective bargaining can and does work. Furthermore, other industries with perishable products that have a seasonal need for a large number of temporary employees are covered by the NLRA, and have successful collective bargaining relationships. An example of such industries, related to agriculture, are fruit and vegetable packing, canning and freezing, sugar processing, and fishing. In Hawaii, there is a long history of collective bargaining for sugar and pineapple industry field employees. And in many foreign countries, agricultural employees have long been permitted to form and join labor organizations for the purpose of collective bargaining.

The growers say that the union has not offered to bargain. This is false. UFWOC has corresponded directly with all California table grape growers and their representatives, offering to discuss union representation elections and other matters of concern to growers and workers. To date there have been no responses to those offers. Further, UFWOC has repeatedly offered to join growers in establishing fair procedures through various third parties for secret ballot elections which would determine whether the workers want to be represented by UFWOC. The growers have rejected all efforts to mediate the dispute.

Collective bargaining threatens to destroy the grower and farmer. Contracts with workers that provide humane wages and just working conditions do cost money. No one has ever denied they cost money. One company, Di Giorgio, that does bargain with a union, has recently sold table grape acreage, but this was in accordance with a Government agreement that in return for publicly subsidized irrigation water for 160 acres of its land, that Di Giorgio would sell its excess acreage.

Growers say that the migrant is surviving and working. Death rates of migrant farmworkers as a percent of the national rates in 1967 are shocking:

Infant mortality: 125 percent higher than the national rate.

Maternal mortality: 125 percent higher than the national rate.

Influenza and pneumonia: 200 percent higher than the national rate.

Tuberculosis and other infectious diseases: 260 percent higher than the national rate.

Accidents: 300 percent higher than the national rate.

Life expectancy for migrants is 49 years, as opposed to 70 for all others.

Wages paid farmworkers are only a small part of food costs; for example:

Retail price in 1965	Cents
Lettuce (per head)	21
Lemons (per pound)	24
Field labor cost in 1965	
Lettuce (per head)	1.2
Lemons (apiece)	0.8

Farmworkers are specifically excluded from unemployment insurance and collective bargaining laws. They are discriminated against in minimum wage coverage—$1.15 for farmworkers, $1.60 for others—and social security laws. Children working in agriculture are excluded from child labor and school attendance laws. Without contracts, farmworkers do not have protections that other workers take for granted; for example, job security, overtime pay, holidays and vacations with pay, sanitary toilets and drinking water, health insurance, grievance procedure, rest periods, and so forth.

Many public figures say the boycott is illegal. Contrary to the statements of some misinformed persons, it is perfectly legal to engage in a primary boycott, variously called a primary, or product, or consumer boycott, calling on consumers to stop purchasing a product directly involved in a labor dispute—for example, California table grapes. It is also legal under Federal law for farmworkers to engage in a secondary boycott, since the NLRA, which prohibits a secondary boycott, specifically excludes agriculture from its protections and benefits. When four unions in New York that are actually covered by the NLRA were charged with participation in a secondary boycott, the unions stipulated that they would not participate in the future in such activity surrounding the grape dispute. This action has nothing to do with the legality of the consumer boycott.

Why do farmworkers not use the legal machinery that is available to get elections and settle the strike, as some politicians have suggested? Farmworkers are specifically excluded from the National Labor Relations Act—NLRA. They have no rights under the law to seek elections that might lead to collective bargaining. If growers refuse elections—as the table grape growers have—workers have only one recourse: to apply economic pressure until they have gained union recognition and collective bargaining.

The union has attempted to gain private agreements with growers and farmers to have impartial parties conduct elections and supervise collective bargaining. This method of private settlement had proved successful in the wine grape industry, but the table grape growers' unwillingness to accept similar mediation now is a primary cause of the present boycott.

The growers say that Cesar Chavez and other union leaders are power- and money-hungry labor agitators. Cesar Chavez was a migrant farmworker and came from a family of migrants. He was a community organizer for the Community Service Organization—CSO—from 1952 to 1962. Because of his deep feelings about the suffering of farmworkers and his conviction that

: 392

farmworkers had to protect themselves and improve their conditions through their own organization, he left his job at CSO in 1962; and his wife, Helen, and their eight children moved to Delano, Calif. They lived on farmwork and began organizing the National Farm Workers Association. Before the strike, Chavez's union salary was less than $75 per week. Since the strike began he has been supported by the union; food comes from the strike store or kitchen; and only $5 per week is paid to him, as all adults who work in the strike. The food and money come from unions, churches, individuals, et cetera. Without these contributions, there would be no strike.

What do the farmworkers intend to accomplish by their boycott of grapes? The primary goal is to obtain union recognition and assurance of good faith collective bargaining from their grower and farmer employers.

The best way to achieve this goal would be to include the agricultural industry under the protective provisions of the National Labor Relations Act.

With the elementary rights of union recognition and collective bargaining, in addition to all the other protections of the NLRA, the farmworkers and farmers and growers would have access to the same legal protections and forum that has been so very successful in the past 30 years for all other industry, so that they can work together with their employers toward:

A living wage, so that their children do not have to quit grammar school to help earn food;

Sanitary facilities placed in the field to protect themselves, and the consumer, from disease;

The right to work and live with dignity;

Recognition of the worker's basic humanity and dignity as a free moral agent who may exercise his right to help form his own destiny and to responsibly better his own conditions;

Securing collective bargaining agreements, similar to the nine already signed, that provide for higher wages, grievance procedures, overtime pay, job security, rest periods, health insurance, holidays and vacations with pay, and other benefits;

Strong and strict enforcement of laws already on the books that are intended to regulate farm labor contractors and crew leaders, transportation, sanitation, child labor and school attendance, discrimination in employment, workmen's compensation insurance, minimum wage, wage payment and collection, State labor relations acts, unemployment insurance, temporary disability insurance, health and welfare benefits, and social security laws.

The grape strikers do not ask for pity or charity, only their rights. They are not rejoicing in the boycott. It is tragic that the grape industry will not talk with representatives of their employees. It is tragic that the boycott toll will be measured not only in present sales and price decline, but measured by a taint on grapes not easily removed in the future. Wholesalers, for example, who will not handle grapes now, will no doubt be disinclined to re-enter the market and re-establish lost customers. The half-life of the spirit and purpose of the boycott will likely continue as an economic scar on the industry for years.

But the farmworkers solemnly feel they are resorting to nonviolent action as the only way to obtain their liberation from decades of poverty and exclusion as the forgotten Americans.

They want to expose to the American public the continued resistance by the farmers and growers to the union's demands for recognition and the right of collective bargaining. They want to explain that they have a just cause, and that the continued resistance to their demands constitutes a denial of social justice and provides the basis for continued exploitation, discrimination, and other anti-social behavior on the part of the producers of food products. They want growers to recognize their worth and dignity, and bargain with them as men.

The consumer's interest in the boycott shows that the American public will not remain indifferently silent or inactive when our fellow human beings are deprived and ignored. Citizens of this Nation will help those on the lower rungs of the ladder. The greatness of our country lies in the sympathy and support each of us renders to our fellow citizens. We must put forth every effort to secure justice and righteousness as the foundation of our civilization.

Passage of legislation to include the agriculture industry under the protective provisions of the National Labor Relations Act will be the first step in that direction.

About the Author

PETER MATTHIESSEN leads two lives, as a naturalist-explorer and as a novelist; he has published four works of nonfiction and four novels, the last of which, *At Play in the Fields of the Lord,* was nominated for the National Book Award.

Southern Methodist Univ.
331.67C512ZM1973
Sal si puedes: br

3   2177   00900   6634

DATE DUE

MAY 1 2 2009	

DEMCO, INC. 38-2931